Communications
in Computer and Information Science 1288

More information about this series at http://www.springer.com/series/7899

Anna Kalenkova · Jose A. Lozano ·
Rostislav Yavorskiy (Eds.)

Tools and Methods of Program Analysis

5th International Conference, TMPA 2019
Tbilisi, Georgia, November 7–9, 2019
Revised Selected Papers

 Springer

Editors
Anna Kalenkova ⓘ
University of Melbourne
Melbourne, VIC, Australia

Jose A. Lozano
Intelligent Systems Group, UPV/EHU
Donostia, Spain

Rostislav Yavorskiy ⓘ
Tomsk Polytechnic University
Tomsk, Russia

ISSN 1865-0929   ISSN 1865-0937   (electronic)
Communications in Computer and Information Science
ISBN 978-3-030-71471-0   ISBN 978-3-030-71472-7   (eBook)
https://doi.org/10.1007/978-3-030-71472-7

This Springer imprint is published by the registered company Springer Nature Switzerland AG
The registered company address is: Gewerbestrasse 11, 6330 Cham, Switzerland

Preface

This volume contains the proceedings of the Fifth International Conference on Software Testing, Machine Learning and Complex Process Analysis, TMPA-2019[1], which was held on 7–9 November 2019 at Ivane Javakhishvili Tbilisi State University.

The conference attracted a significant number of students, researchers, academics, and engineers working on different aspects of quality of software and different methods and tools for program analysis. The broad scope of TMPA makes it an event where researchers from different yet related domains such as static program analysis, software testing, and process mining meet and exchange ideas. The conference allows specialists from different fields to meet each other, present their work, and discuss both theoretical and practical aspects of their research. Another important aim of the conference is to stimulate scientists and people from industry to benefit from the knowledge exchange and identify possible grounds for fruitful collaboration.

The program committee of the conference included 35 experts from leading institutions of Australia, Estonia, France, Germany, Italy, Japan, Russia, South Korea, Spain, Sweden, the Netherlands, UK, and USA.

Out of 41 submissions only 16 papers were accepted for regular oral presentations. Thus, the acceptance rate of this volume is around 39%. 18 papers that passed the quality threshold were presented as posters, and the other submissions were rejected completely. By default, each submission was single-blind reviewed by three reviewers, experts in their fields, in order to supply detailed and helpful comments. The authors of the accepted regular presentations had 4 additional months after the conference to update and improve their papers and incorporate comments and suggestions they got during the event.

The conference featured a tutorial on *Petri Nets and Their Extensions* by Irina Lomazova and three invited talks:

- *Applications of Computational Topology to Artificial Intelligence* by Alexander Gamkrelidze,
- *Passive Testing Techniques in Practice* by Ana Rosa Cavalli,
- *Partial Specifications of Libraries: Applications in Software Engineering* by Vladimir Itsykson.

Besides, a panel discussion was organized to talk over AI in Software Testing, Testing of AI Systems, Research Challenges in Complex Process Analysis, and other topics of current interest for the community.

We would like to thank the authors for submitting their papers and the members of the Program Committee for their efforts in providing exhaustive reviews. We would also like to express special gratitude to all the invited speakers and industry representatives.

---

[1] https://tmpaconf.org/events/tmpa-2019/.

We are very grateful to the partners and sponsors of the conference: Ivane Javakhishvili Tbilisi State University and Exactpro Systems. We are deeply thankful to all the organisers and volunteers, whose endless energy was indispensable at all stages of the conference project.

November 2020   Anna Kalenkova
                                                          Jose Lozano
                                                    Rostislav Yavorskiy

Organization

Program Committee Chairs

Anna Kalenkova   University of Melbourne, Australia
Jose A. Lozano   UPV/EHU, Spain
Rostislav Yavorskiy   Higher School of Economics, Russia

Program Committee

Marat Akhin   Saint Petersburg Polytechnic University, Russia
Mikhail Belyaev   Saint Petersburg State Polytechnical University, Russia
Nikolaj Bjørner   Microsoft, USA
Dmitry Boulytchev   Saint-Petersburg State University, Russia
Franck Cassez   Macquarie University, Australia
Adnan Causevic   Mälardalen University, Sweden
Goran Frehse   ENSTA Paris, France
Carsten Fuhs   Birkbeck, University of London, UK
Roberto Giacobazzi   University of Verona, Italy
Peter Habermehl   LIAFA University Paris Diderot (Paris 7), France
Iosif Itkin   Exactpro LLC, UK
Alexander Kamkin   Institute for System Programming RAS, Russia
Max Kanovich   University College London, UK
Victor Kuliamin   Institute for System Programming RAS, Russia
Alexei Lisitsa   University of Liverpool, UK
Irina Lomazova   Higher School of Economics, Russia
Panagiotis Manolios   Northeastern University, USA
Roland Meyer   TU Braunschweig, Germany
Claude Michel   Université Côte d'Azur, CNRS I3S, France
Mikhail Moiseev   Intel, Russia
Uwe Nestmann   TU Berlin, Germany
Nikolay Pakulin   Pax Datatech PTE, South Korea
Silvio Ranise   FBK-Irst, Italy
Paweł Sobociński   Tallinn University of Technology, Estonia
Tachio Terauchi   Waseda University, Japan
Dmitry Tsitelov   Devexperts LLC, USA
Tim Willemse   Eindhoven University of Technology, The Netherlands
Victor Zakharov   Institute of Informatics Problems RAS, Russia
Vladimir Zakharov   Lomonosov Moscow State University, Russia
Santiago Zanella-Béguelin   Microsoft, UK

Organizing Committee

Anna-Maria Lukina	Exactpro LLC, Russia
Elena Vasina	Exactpro Systems LLC, Russia
Gia Sirbiladze	Tbilisi State University, Georgia
Natia Sirbiladze	Exactpro Systems LLC, Georgia
Zaza Tsiramua	Georgian Technical University, Georgia
Zhanna Zabolotnaya	Exactpro LLC, Russia

Contents

Short Papers

Keynote

Partial Specifications of Libraries: Applications in Software Engineering

Vladimir Itsykson[1,2]([⊠]) ⓘ

[1] Peter the Great St. Petersburg Polytechnic University, Polytechnicheskaya str., 29,
195201 Saint Petersburg, Russia
vlad@icc.spbstu.ru
[2] JetBrains Research, Saint Petersburg, Russia

Abstract. The article presents a comprehensive approach to solving a number of problems that arise during the design, development, debugging and maintenance of multicomponent applications. The approach is based on a created formalism that allows specifying the structure and visible behavior of the component external to the application. At the same time, the mathematical approach used in the formalism is based on the system of extended finite state machine, which allows analyzing specifications in an acceptable time. For a programmer to set formal descriptions of the components, the LibSL specification language is developed. It allows the programmer to describe the specification of a component or a library in the form that is understandable to the programmer, without going into the mathematical basics of formalism. In this case, the interface of the library and its behavior, which is visible from the outside, are set. The implementation details are not included in the specification.

The presented formalism and language are used to solve a group of topical software engineering problems: automated application porting, cross-language integration of applications and libraries, detection of software errors in multicomponent projects, detection of integration errors, automated testing of multi-component applications, etc.

The paper demonstrates the use of formalism and language to solve these problems, as well as shows other areas in which the approach can be effectively applied.

Keywords: Partial specification of libraries · Library Specification Language · Software integration · Analysis of program

1 Introduction

The software design process has changed rapidly in recent years. Most modern software applications are designed not as independent software products but as multi-component systems that include their modules as well as third-party modules and libraries [1, 2].

This research work was supported by the Academic Excellence Project 5–100 proposed by Peter the Great St. Petersburg Polytechnic University.

© Springer Nature Switzerland AG 2021
A. Kalenkova et al. (Eds.): TMPA 2019, CCIS 1288, pp. 3–25, 2021.
https://doi.org/10.1007/978-3-030-71472-7_1

An increasing number of required functions are already implemented in a library and, consequently, there is less need to develop custom modules to achieve the project goals. This shift in focus in software design affects the requirements for software design and building tools: tools that allow integration of components, conduct integration testing, detect integration errors, etc. become more popular.

This paper provides an overview of the approach developed under the author's guidance, in which the above-mentioned and other problems are solved on the basis of a designed formalism based on the system of interacting extended finite state machines. The formalism that allows specifying interfaces of multicomponent systems and their behavior is briefly described. Individual components of the system are described using the developed domain specific language LibSL. Such descriptions are translated into the internal formal representation of the tool. In the future, formalized representations of components are used to solve one of the following software engineering tasks:

- porting an application from one library environment to another;
- approximation of libraries' functions when performing the static analysis of programs;
- cross-language component integration;
- detection of application and component integration errors;
- specification extraction from software repositories;
- etc.

Every above-listed task is related to the design, development, analysis, reengineering, or verification of multicomponent systems. This article describes the way to apply the approach to all of the above-listed tasks.

The rest of the article is organized as follows. The second section discusses problems that arise when designing, developing, and debugging multicomponent applications. The third section describes the approach proposed by the author that allows solving problems of designing multicomponent systems. The fourth section is devoted to a brief description of the formalism for the external libraries specification. The fifth section provides a brief description of the LibSL specification language. The sixth section focuses on applications of the proposed approach in five different areas of software engineering. Finally, the seventh section summarizes the results and out-lines the areas for further research.

2 Problems with External Libraries

The current experience of distributing software libraries, unfortunately, does not help streamline the interaction between parts of multicomponent software systems. The following library distribution options are most common:

- distribution of the library "as is" without any relevant documentation;
- distribution of the library with some brief informal documentation. In this case, instead of exhaustive detailed documentation describing all aspects of the library functioning, the way of interacting with it, restrictions on input and returned data, the authors provide only a brief informal description of the library key functions, without any details about using API;

– distribution of the library with a brief description of API functions and data types used;
– distribution of the library with several examples of its use.

All these options have common disadvantages – they do not allow getting a de-tailed idea of the library functioning and the way of interaction with it.

To fully work with the library, it is necessary to know the following information:

– description of all data types used;
– description of data item values if specific values have a specific meaning;
– description of all API calls;
– description of the conditions under which specific library functions can be called;
– description of the library impact on the environment, that is, a list of application objects that can be modified by the library;
– description of the library scenarios that include valid sequences of API function calls;
– etc.

For building highly reliable applications, it would also be useful to have a formal description of the library properties listed above provided by the author to be able to automatically check the integration correctness.

The result of this practice is the appearance of many program errors that occur, when an external library is included in the application, and are related to the lack of the library description and the absence of its formal description. These errors include:

– calling library API functions with incorrectly prepared input data;
– incorrect interpretation of data returned by library functions;
– incorrect sequence of library API function calls in the program;
– incorrect work with objects which state is affected by the library;
– using non-optimal methods for obtaining results due to the lack of suitable scenarios;
– etc.

In addition to direct errors resulting from incomplete documentation, some tasks are impossible or difficult to perform due to the lack of a strict formal library description. These tasks include:

– automatic creation of software interfaces to libraries for the possibility of using libraries written in one programming language from programs in another program-ming language;
– migrating applications from one to another library environment with the same or similar functionality;
– adding library semantics to the application development tools (IDE) to implement the functions of intelligent assistants that prompt the programmer with parameter types, valid API calls, etc.

All these errors and limitations indicate the need for new approaches to documenting, formalizing, and distributing libraries.

3 Approach

We offer a comprehensive approach to solving the problems of software integration, based on the specifications formalization of external components. The approach is based on the formalism for specifying the structure and behavior of an external component or library. The main idea is that the formalism describes the library interface and the behavior of library objects in detail and, at the same time, the behavior of the library API functions is specified in an enlarged way, without describing implementation details and only the externally visible behavior of functions is set.

For the programmer a more user-friendly mechanism is offered that is the domain specific language LibSL, which allows setting library specifications using a more familiar tool – the program in a specialized language. At the same time, the proposed language is independent of the library implementation language, which allows applying the approach to a wide range of programming languages.

The proposed formalism and specification language offer several options for using formal specifications in solving problems of program engineering:

- comparison of specifications with each other to determine the compatibility of libraries;
- joint analysis of two specifications for the synthesis of the program conversion algorithm;
- forming an approximation of the behavior of the library function based on specifications;
- automatic generation of tests based on specifications;
- synthesis, which is based on the specifications, of the wrappers and stubs to access the library from other programming languages;
- using specifications as a reference oracles to analyze the behavior of the application;
- etc.

The following sections describe in more detail the formalism, the language of modifications, and the application of the approach to solving various problems.

4 Formal Specifications of Libraries

When creating a new formalism for describing software components, there are several aspects to consider. Firstly, a formalism should be powerful enough to be able to describe most existing software libraries. Secondly, it should be simple enough to perform automated analysis of library descriptions.

The full library specifications exhaustively describe the structure of library and the behavior of its functions. Full specifications are extremely complex and cannot be used in practice for specific applications. The proposed approach specifies not the full behavior of a library, but the observable from the outside. However, implementation details and other minor aspects remain outside the specification. Thus, the proposed approach defines partial specifications of libraries.

Partial specifications should describe the static and dynamic semantics of the library, which in turn define the structure and behavior of a library. The elements of the static semantics are:

- data types used in the library;
- library variables and objects;
- interface of the functions available in the public API.

The dynamic semantics includes:

- API function semantics (function behavior, function contracts, and function side effects);
- behavior of the library itself (including its usage rules).

Libraries are described as a composition of automata, each of them being an extended finite state machine [3]. Each automaton describes the behavior of a single library object. The automaton states correspond to the object states, transitions correspond to API function calls, and creating a new automaton is a side effect of calling API functions. Each API function is characterized by a signature, a contract [4], high-level behavior, and actions to perform (semantic descriptions).

Formally, the L library specification is defined as a tuple:

$$L = <F, B> \tag{1}$$

- F – set of library functions
- B – behavioral description of library

A set of F functions defines the library public API:

$$F = \{F_i\} \tag{2}$$

- F_i – concrete API function

Each specific F_i function is defined as a tuple:

$$F_i = <Name, Args, Res, Pre, Post, A, CondA, D, CondD> \tag{3}$$

- Name – name of the function
- Args – set of the formal arguments of the function
- Res – result of the function
- Pre – preconditions of function
- Post – postconditions of function
- A – set of semantic actions performed by the function
- CondA – set of conditions for semantic actions
- D – set of launched child automata
- CondD – set of launch conditions for child automata

The B library behavior is defined by a set of automata:

$$B = \{M, S_1(q, P), \ldots, S_n(q, P)\} \tag{4}$$

- M – main automaton describing the behavior of the entire library
- S_i – i^{th} child automaton launched if certain conditions are fulfilled
- q – initial state of the child automaton
- P – optional parameter of the child automaton
  A specific M or S_i automaton is set by a tuple:

$$S = <Q, Q_0, X, V, C, C^A, C^D, T>$$

- Q – set of automaton states
- Q_0 – set of automaton initial states
- X – set of automaton finish states
- V – set of internal variables
- $C = \{C_i\}$ – set of function calls acting as stimuli, C^i is the call of an ith function; $C_i \in F$
- $C^A = \{C_i^A\}$ – set of semantic actions initiated by the function launch
- $C^D = \{C_i^D\}$ – set of child automata launched by the function
- T – transition relation.

For a more visual representation of specifications their graphical representation can be used. Figure 1 presents a visual representation of the server-side TCP socket library specification. Automaton L describes the behavior of the library itself, automaton P corresponds to a server-side TCP socket intended for receiving connections from TCP clients, and automaton S corresponds to a socket generated when receiving an incoming request from the client and responsible for data exchange. The states of all automata are shown as rectangles, and the final states when the automaton is destroyed are highlighted in red. Transitions between automata states are represented by arcs marked with API functions that activate these transitions. Creating instances of automata while executing API functions is represented by dotted lines.

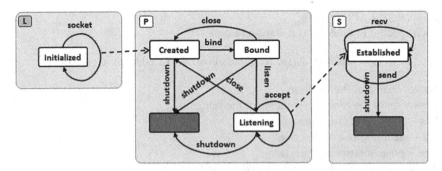

Fig. 1. A visual representation of the TCP server socket specification

For more information about formalism, see [5].

5 LibSL: Library Specification Language

The formalism presented in the previous section can be used to solve a number of problems related to software quality as well as to automate many software engineering tasks. However, the formalism that is convenient for automation cannot be used by practical programmers, since it is over-formalized and operates with mathematic objects rather than software objects.

In such cases, theory and practice use domain specific languages that are on the one hand close to the object domain (in our case, library semantics), and on the other hand are simple enough for practitioners to understand and to use (in our case, for software architects and developers). To bridge the gap between theory and practice, the authors developed the domain specific language LibSL (Library Specification Language), which is briefly described in this section.

5.1 General Specification Structure

The LibSL specification is a declarative description of the structure and behavior of the library, the specification structure is shown in Listing 1.

The specification begins with the keyword *library* (line 01), which specifies the name of the library being described. This is followed by the import section (lines 02–03), which implements the modular principle and provides the ability to create multi-file specifications. Each special external component is specified by the statement *import*. Lines 04–06 contain a section of semantic types starting with the keyword *types*. This section declares all semantic types, which are essentially classic types of programming languages, enriched with additional semantics defined with the help of annotations. The automata specification section (lines 07–11) contains descriptions of all classes of automata available in the library. Each automaton class is defined by the *automaton* construction. The library API is described as the collection of public library functions (lines 12–16). Each function is described by the keyword *fun* and contains the description of the function signature and its behavior. The specification ends with the description section of the description of global objects (lines 17–22), in which global variables are set and instances of automata are created.

```
01 library <LibraryName>; // Name of the library
02 import <FileName>;
03 ...
04 types { // Semantic types
05 ...
06 }
07 automaton <AutomatonClass>: <Type> {
08 // Automaton description
09 ...
10 }
11 ...
12 fun <FunName>(<Params>): <Type> {
13 // API function description
14 ...
15 }
16 ...
17 var <VarName>: <Type> = <Value>;
18 // Global variables declaration
19 ...
20 var main: <Type> = new Main(<InitState>)
21 // Main automaton creation
22 ...
```

Listing 1. Structure of specification

5.2 Semantic Types Descriptions

The semantic types section (Listing 2) provides several mechanisms for specifying semantic types. Lines 02–04 show the definition of alias types according to the programming language used. The types on the right side (int32, unsigned32) are built-in types of the LibSL language, and their aliases on the left side correspond to a specific programming language. Lines 05–08 show how to specify simple semantic types that add semantic annotations to the ordinary types. For example, the *SOCKET* type is an *int* type, enriched with the *SOCKET* annotation meaning that a variable of this type contains a socket descriptor. Lines 09–18 show the assignment of complex semantic types that have separate value annotations in addition to the type annotation. These annotations can be used when porting applications between libraries when different libraries use different encoding of variable values.

```
01 types {
02   int = int32;
03   unsigned = unsigned32;
04   byte = unsigned8;
05   SOCKET (int);          // Socket type
06   BUFFER (*void);        // Socket buffer
07   LENGTH (int);          // Socket length
08   PROTOCOL_TYPE (int);   // Socket protocol ID
09   SOCKET_TYPE (int) {    // Socket type
10     STREAM: 1;           // Stream socket
11     DGRAM: 2;            // Datagram socket
12     RAW: 3;              // Raw Socket
13     SEQPACKET: 5;        // Stream packet socket
14   };
15   SIZE (int) {
16     ERROR: -1;
17   }
18 }
```

Listing 2. Example of semantic types description

5.3 Automata Description

The automata description section (Listing 3) is intended for specifying classes of automata that specify the behavior of libraries. Each automaton class is defined by the name and type of the descriptor (*bsd_socket* and *int*, line 01, respectively). Extended finite state machine used in formalism can contain additional state variables, in the language such states are specified by the *var* construction (line 02). The states of the automaton are set by the *state* and *finishstate* constructions (lines 03–07). The ordinary states of the automaton are described by means of *state*, and *finishstate* describes the final state of the automaton, after which it is destroyed. Automaton transitions are set using *shift* constructions (lines 08–16). The first parameter is the initial state of the transition, and the second is the final one. Two meta-variables are used: *self* means that the final state is the same as the initial state (lines 12, 14, and 16), and *any* means that such a transition exists in all states of the automaton (line 16). The third transition parameter describes the transition activation condition. In libraries, the transition is activated by calling any public API function. For example, in line 10, the socket goes from the *Bound* state to the *Listening* state when the *listen* method is called from the main program.

```
01 automaton BSD_SOCKET: int {
02    var blocked: boolean;
03    state Created;
04    state Bound;
05    state Established;
06    state Listening;
07    finishstate Closed;
08    shift Create->Bound (bind);
09    shift Bound->Create (close);
10    shift Bound->Listening (listen);
11    shift Listening->Bound (close);
12    shift Listening->self (accept);
13    shift Established->Created (close);
14    shift Established->self (recv);
15    shift Established->self (send);
16    shift any->Closed (shutdown);
17 }
```

Listing 3. Example of an automaton description

5.4 API Functions Description

The API functions description section (Listing 4) is intended for specifying the interface and behavior of functions included in the library API. The description of an individual function begins with the *fun* keyword, followed by the function name (lines 01, 05, and 09). The function signature also contains a description of formal parameters and return values (lines 01–02, 05–06, and 09–10). Both regular types and previously entered semantic types can be used as type identifiers. If the function is associated with the instance of an automaton, the automaton variable is annotated with the "@" character (lines 05 and 09). The description of the visible behavior of a function is contained in its body. Here internal variables of the automaton can be changed, new automata can be created (lines 03 and 07), conditions can be checked (line 11), and semantic actions can be performed (lines 12 and 14). The important feature of descriptions is the lack of opportunities for organizing loops and recursions.

```
01 fun socket(domain: DOMAIN, type: SOCKET_TYPE,
02     proto: PROTOCOL_TYPE): SOCKET {
03   result = new BSD_SOCKET(Created);
04 }
05 fun accept(@s: SOCKET, addr: SOCK_ADDR,
06     addrlen: SOCK_LEN): SOCKET {
07   result = new TCP_SOCKET(Established);
08 }
09 fun send(@s: SOCKET, msg: BUFFER, len: LENGTH,
10     FLAGS: int): SIZE {
11   if (len > 0)
12     action SEND(s, msg, len);
13   else
14     action ERROR(Send01, "Parameter error");
14 }
```

Listing 4. Example of API Functions Description

5.5 Global Objects Section

The global objects declaration and initialization section (Listing 5) is intended for declaring, creating, and initializing global objects that are necessary for the library to function. Line 01 shows an example of declaring the global variable *stdout* from the *stdio* library. Lines 02–03 show examples of simultaneous declaration and initialization of variables. Lines 04–05 show simultaneous declaration of the instance of an automaton and its creation. Line 06 shows creating the instance of an automaton and its assigning to a pre-declared automaton variable.

```
01 var stdout: int;
02 var errno: int = 0;
03 var status: int = 1;
04 var stdin: int = new File(Created, mRead);
05 var stderr: int = new File(Created, mError);
06 stdout = new File(Created, mWrite);
```

Listing 5. Example of Global Objects Section

For more detail information about LibSL language see [6].

6 Applications

The formalism and specification descriptions language presented in Sects. 4 and 5 are the basis of a comprehensive approach developed under the author's guidance for solving several complex software engineering problems. The following paragraphs provide brief descriptions of the areas of application of this approach.

6.1 Porting of Software

One of the challenges of software engineering is the software evolution. It is often necessary to make changes to a developed and debugged project related to adding new functionality, expanding the scope of its application, or changing the conditions for its execution [7]. One of these changes may be porting the application to a new environment, in which the functionality of the application itself should not change, while the external environment may differ significantly from the original one. Examples of such situations can be, as follows:

- migration to a new operation system;
- migration to a new hardware platform (e.g. mobile);
- moving from the old version of the library to the new one;
- moving from one library to another with similar functionality;
- translation of the source code to another programming language;
- etc.

In all these cases, the new environment is represented by a set of software libraries that perform similar functions but have a different interface, implementation, behavior, and ways to interact with the application. In this case, the porting task is reduced to modifying the original project from using old libraries to new ones (see Fig. 2).

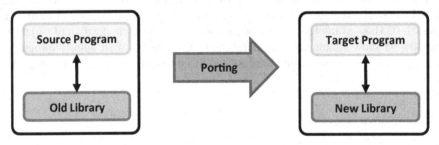

Fig. 2. Porting of software to a new environment

Currently, this type of problems is solved in one of the following ways:

- if a project is moved to a new system environment (for example, another operating system), cross-platform libraries are used;
- an intermediate software layer is developed, which is the interface between the initial project and the environment;
- manual migration to a new environment is performed, and all the source code that interacts with the environment is rewritten.

The main problems of these approaches are related to the need to perform many manual routine operations: each old library API function call should be rewritten, taking into account the syntax and semantics of a new one. However, the resulting application requires all the quality assurance procedures, for example, a full testing cycle. This is due to the fact that the rewritten application is a new software product, and all the results of the previous original application quality assurance procedures cannot be used.

This fact is especially depressing, since the business logic of the main application has not changed, but only the interaction with the environment has changed, so repeating all the procedures for checking the quality of the application is seen as an inefficient repeated waste of effort.

Using a formal approach based on library specifications, allows automating the software migration process and maintaining the quality level of the source application without the need for additional testing of the target application.

The common transfer algorithm in this case is as follows:

– creating the initial library specification (or using a previously created one);
– creating the target library specification (or using a previously created one);
– verifying compatibility of libraries on the basis of the analysis of compatibility between the two specifications;
– in case of compatibility:

  • creating the initial program model;
  • conversion of the model in accordance with the specifications;
  • generating the target application based on the converted model.

Two of the most science-intensive tasks listed are checking the compatibility of specifications and converting models.

The scheme of the application porting process is shown in Fig. 3.

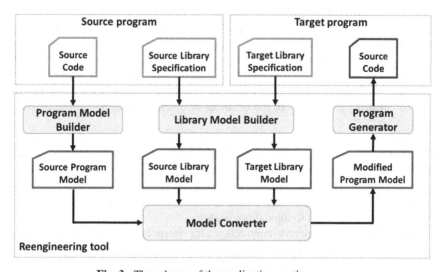

Fig. 3. The scheme of the application porting process

The resulting target application is semantically equivalent to the original application by construction (we assume that the specifications of both libraries are correct). Thus, it does not require additional quality assurance procedures, such as new testing.

According to this scheme, two research porting tools were implemented, one for migrating C programs [8], and the other, more functional, for the Java programming language [9]. Experimental studies were conducted to test the tools. For this purpose, several artificially created projects and several open source code projects taken from open repositories were ported. All projects were automatically converted according to the specified algorithm, and the resulting projects showed their efficiency. The results achieved demonstrate that the specification-based approach to porting is efficient.

6.2 Enhancements of Static Analysis

One of the key methods for ensuring the quality of software systems is the static analysis [10]. Using the static analysis, a wide class of software errors, such as buffer overflow, incorrect operation with pointers, resource leaks, working with uninitialized variables, etc. can be detected. The peculiarity of the static analysis is the ability to detect software errors without running the program under study, while, in some cases, high precision or soundness of detection algorithms can be guaranteed.

A significant limitation of all static analyzers is the complexity of analyzing multi-component programs, which occurs here for two reasons. Firstly, when all the procedures and functions used are included in the analysis, an exponential explosion of the number of program states occurs, which significantly increases the computational complexity of the algorithms. Secondly, the source code of the libraries and components used is often unavailable and, in this case, the analyzer faces significant uncertainty when analyzing function calls, which leads to the sharp decrease in detection precision.

One of the methods for solving these problems is to replace all external functions in the analysis with their simplified analogs – summaries. At the same time, the summaries of the function behavior should be simple enough not to complicate the complexity of the analysis. In addition, the summaries should be able to signal errors that occurred within library functions. The formalism and specification language proposed in this paper can be used to construct summaries of the behavior of external functions during the static analysis.

One of the most promising methods of the static analysis is Bounded Model Checking [11]. On its basis the Borealis [12] static analyzer was developed in the author's research group. Main stages of its functioning are:

- the transformation of the program source code into logical predicates;
- converting checking rules to logical predicates;
- converting function summaries (contracts, Craig interpolants) to logical predicates;
- building a complex predicate from all the simple ones mentioned above;
- solving of a complex predicate using SMT solver (Z3 [13], Boolector [14], etc.);
- interpreting the result obtained by SMT solvers and mapping it to the initial code.

The scheme of applying the approach is shown in Fig. 4. The integration of external function specifications and the program model occurs when the internal model of the

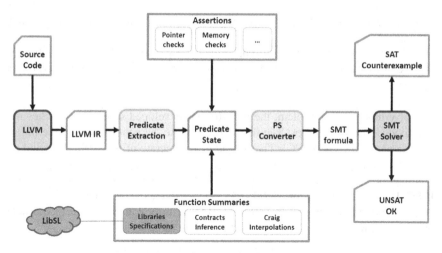

Fig. 4. BMC static analyzer with library specifications

analyzer called PredicateState is formed. The example of the *send* function specification from the *BSD-socket* library is shown in Listing 6. Lines 03–04 describe the valid behavior of the function, and lines 05–06 show the error of parameters detection. In the language, it is described using the semantic action *ERROR*. The predicate corresponding to the detection of this error is integrated into the general complex predicate of the program. If this predicate is resolvable, the error with the Send01 code will be diagnosed, which means that when the program is running, the situation may occur, in which incorrect parameters may be submitted to the *send* function input.

```
01 fun send(@s: SOCKET, msg: BUFFER, len: LENGTH, FLAGS:
02 int): SIZE {
03    if (len > 0)
04       action SEND(s, msg, len);
05    else
06       action ERROR(Send01, "Parameter error");
07 }
```

Listing 6. Example of function specification

6.3 Cross-Language Integration

Often, when developing a multicomponent project, the programmer needs to use a library written in a different programming language. If the author has not provided an interface to the library in the required language, such cross-language integration becomes difficult or, often, impossible. Thus, it is very important to have a mechanism that allows integrating components written in different programming languages without additional effort. The main requirements for such a mechanism are:

- transparency for the user application – no need to modify the application to adapt it to the library;
- minimizing the writing of the additional code linking the application and the library;
- low overhead for linking the application and library, i.e. high performance of the approach.

To solve this type of problem, the industry has developed several approaches that can be divided into two groups. The first is to integrate the application and the library via remote procedure call (RPC). The second is to integrate of the application and the library via the foreign function interface (FFI).

Remote procedure call technologies [15] (for example, gRPC, Thrift, Rabbit-MQRPC, Java RMI, Cap'n'proto, XML-RPC, etc.) provide the mechanism for transmitting of the remote function call parameters and for returning the result via the network environment. However, they all have significant limitations:

- necessity to manually write linking code;
- necessity to adapt software components in some cases (for example, to solve serialization problems);
- low performance.

The foreign function interface mechanism (for example, libffi, JNI, SWIG, etc.) is designed to coordinate semantics and function calling conventions between two programming languages. The main limitations of this mechanism are:

- focus mainly on libraries written in the C programming language; other languages are supported, but additional effort is required;
- need to write additional code and efforts to harmonize different memory management models in different programming languages (for example, manual memory management and garbage collection);
- in some cases need to adapt language runtime environments and virtual machines to work in the same process.

To solve the problem of cross-language integration and to overcome the problems that exist in these approaches, the approach based on formal library specifications was developed. It is focused on the following tasks:

- to allow reusing of existing, well-tested and optimized software components and libraries written for older languages from programs written in new languages.
- to allow adding new features implemented in modern languages to existing projects written in older languages;
- to allow the above tasks to be completed without extensive knowledge of both languages;
- to provide easy adaptation for new languages and libraries.

The main idea of the approach is to automate the generation of matching software code based on formally defined library specifications. In this case, wrappers for remote

API functions are generated in the language of the main application, and the receiving part of the remote library is generated in the language of the library. Library classes are mapped onto automata, constructors and methods are mapped onto transitions. The approach is implemented in the prototype of the LibraryLink cross-language integration tool. The approach scheme is illustrated in Fig. 5.

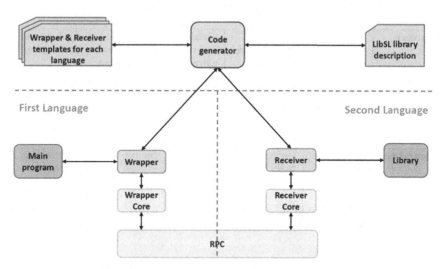

Fig. 5. The approach to cross-language integration

To be able to use the approach for connecting libraries in a specific programming language, the receiver core and receiver template for this language should be manually developed once, the receiver code for a specific library will be generated automatically on the basis of this library specification. To be able to use the approach from a specific programming language, the wrapper core and wrapper template for this language should be manually developed once, the wrapper code itself for accessing a specific library will be generated automatically on the basis of this library specification.

The developed prototype has the following important properties:

– callbacks for libraries and inheritance are supported;
– the need for serialization is minimized by using the handle mechanism;
– semantic information from the specification is used to improve performance (caching and pre-sampling);
– multithreaded applications and various memory management models are supported.

As a result, the approach implemented in the prototype has significant advantages over those currently used. A comparison of the main approaches is presented in Table 1.

Currently, the cross-language integration tool is implemented as a pilot project. Receiver cores and receiver templates have been created for C, Python, and Golang, which provides the support for the libraries written in these languages. Wrapper cores and wrapper templates have been created for Java, Kotlin, and Golang, which allows using the approach from programs written in these languages. The approach has been tested on several popular libraries: Requests (Python), Z3 (C), and Jennifer (Golang). The achieved performance is up to 90,000 function calls per second and up to 270000 in pre-selected mode.

Table 1. Comparison of approaches to cross-language integration

Approach	Wrapper/ receiver creation	Wrapper / receiver core (language support)	Serialization required	Memory management coordination	Caching and prefetching
RPC	Manually	For each language (N)	Yes	Manually	Manually
FFI	Manually	For each pair of languages (~N²)	No	Manually	Manually
LibraryLink	Comparison of approaches to cross-language integration	For each language (N)	No	Built-in	Inferred from a semantic model

6.4 Integration Errors Detection

One of the most common problems when designing multicomponent applications is the incorrect interaction between the application and the used library. The main reasons for this are the lack of clear formal specifications for most libraries, which leads to many software integration errors, which are described in detail in Sect. 2.

These integration errors can also be detected using a formal specification approach. The essence of the proposed method is to use dynamic analysis to detect integration errors. The library specification defines the reference behavior of the library and, in fact, completely defines the protocol for interaction between the main application and the library. To check compliance, the main program is started, and all actions related to the interaction with the library are logged as an execution trace. The resulting trace is checked for compliance with the reference behavior specified in the library specification.

In more detail, the dynamic analysis procedure consists of the following steps:

1. instrumentation of the program under study, controlled by the library specification (specification-driven instrumentation);
2. running an instrumented program and recording the execution route;
3. analysis of the compliance of the trace to the specification.

Items 2 and 3 are performed repeatedly on various test data in order to check as many execution paths as possible.

Instrumentation of the program under study is based on the analysis of the library specification. Only the program elements that are directly involved in communicating with the library are instrumented: library functions calls, modifications of library objects, etc. In this case, not only the fact of the API function call is logged, but also all the parameters being passed, as well as the ID of the library object. This allows separating events related to different objects in the same library in the future. Thus, the collected trace contains all the necessary information for subsequent correctness analysis (postmortem analysis).

Then the instrumented program is run on the test initial data, during its operation a trace containing a detailed protocol for interaction between the application and the library is recorded.

The saved trace is analyzed for compliance with the specification after the program ends. To do this, the trace is filtered: events corresponding to a specific library object are extracted from it. The resulting local trace is played back on the library model:

- pre-conditions are checked before API function calls;
- post-conditions are checked after API function calls;
- it is checked whether the API function call in the state of the library automaton is valid.

If a discrepancy is detected it is added to the error report. This trace is played on the model for all library objects found in the trace. This procedure is repeated many times on different test suites in order to maximize the coverage of the interaction protocol with the library. The scheme of the approach is shown in Fig. 6.

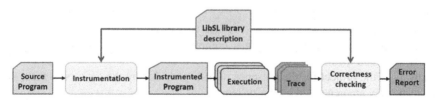

Fig. 6. The dynamic approach to detecting integration errors

Based on the described approach, a pilot tool was implemented that detects integration errors with external libraries in Java programs [16]. To do this, we created specifications for several libraries used in apache/incubator-netbeans repository projects. The tool was tested on several artificially created projects and on more than 400 files from the specified repository.

During the experiments, more than 300 integration errors were detected, most of which were related to non-fulfillment of the library API function prerequisites and resource leaks.

6.5 Specification Mining

The lack of formal specifications for most libraries is a serious problem when applying all approaches based on specifications. As mentioned in Sect. 2, authors usually do not accompany their libraries with formal specifications; at best, they can rely on a partial informal description with usage examples. Programmers using a library can't form a formal specification for it either, because they don't have comprehensive information about its internal structure and functioning. The only way to get information for creating specifications is to use the knowledge accumulated by the programming community.

The global programming community has implemented hundreds of millions of software projects hosted by the authors in free repositories, such as GitHub, BitBucket, etc. If the library that you need to use is not a new product, but has been actively used for several years, then the open repositories can host hundreds of thousands or even millions of projects that use this library. The experience of using the library in each project in the form of a usage scenario demonstrates some knowledge about the functioning of the library [17]. For example, there may be several ways to call library functions. When such knowledge pools are combined with millions of others, a statistically significant sample is obtained, which can be used for generalization in order to build a complete specification of the library or part of it. It is natural that some projects may use the library incorrectly, but such exceptions can be offset by a huge number of examples of incorrect use of the library.

Our approach is currently limited to the Java programming language and projects hosted in the GitHub repository. The essence of the approach for extracting specifications from the open repositories is as follows:

- finding all projects located in GitHub repositories written in the Java programming language and using the target library;
- uploading the found projects into the local storage.

  For each uploaded project:

- project instrumentation for creating a complete trace of interaction between the application and the library;
- analysis of the project for the presence of tests provided by the authors; if there are no tests, they are generated by the system;
- running the project on the native or generated tests;
- collecting execution traces for each test;
- analysis of the received traces and generation of predicates.

Predicates collected from all the uploaded projects are converted into the specification skeleton. The resulting skeleton contains a part of the specification derived from the encountered usage scenarios when analyzing loaded projects. Then the specification can be updated manually by the developer based on the analysis of the library documentation, supplied usage examples, and the developer's own experience.

6.6 Other Applications

The approach considered in this article is not limited to the applications described in Sects. 6.1–6.5. There is also a group of actual software engineering problems that have an effective solution based on formal library specifications.

Static Detection of Integration Errors

In Sect. 6.4, we introduced a method for dynamically detecting application and library integration errors. Dynamic approaches in such problems are characterized by high precision of error detection, but suffer from low soundness. To ensure complete detection, static methods, such as formal verification or static analysis, are required to prove that the application is correctly integrated with the library based on the comparison with the specification.

Automated Specification Building Based on Library Source Code

Section 6.5 describes the approach that allows creating a library specification skeleton based on the open repositories in the absence of the library initial code. If there is an access to the library source code, there may be a solution of the problem of building a library specification or part of it using the static analysis of its source code. If you combine both approaches, the quality of the restored specifications will be significantly higher.

Testing Applications for Environment Stability

One of the important tasks of software quality assurance is testing. In this case, it is necessary not only to check the correct operation of the application on the correct data, but also to test the operation of the application on the arbitrary data in order to assess its stability. Fuzzing is usually used to solve this problem, in which the test data that is fed to the application input is generated randomly. This may not be enough to fully test the application for stability, but it is also necessary to fuzz the entire interaction of the application with the external environment. To solve this problem, formal library specifications can be used in this case, a mock is generated based on the formal library specification, which completely replaces the connected library, executes the library contract, and returns completely random data to the application. Having built the appropriate infrastructure, the application can be placed in an environment where all its interactions with the environment are simulated by the generated mocks, which will allow testing comprehensively the application and detecting errors that lead to the application hanging or falling.

Automatic Creation of Software Documentation

Formal specifications are directly related to the software documentation. The formal specification of the library can be the basis for creating software documentation describing the functioning of the library. Based on the API function specification (function signatures, behavior descriptions), you can automatically generate API function documentation templates. A behavioral description of the entire library can be the basis for creating documentation for library usage scenarios. The created document templates can then be added manually by the developer to get full documentation.

Extensions of Integrated Development Environments Functions

One of the most popular features of modern development environments is smart prompts (auto completion) when typing software text. These suggestions are usually generated by the environment on the fly, using the programming language grammar and structured comments of library functions (for example, Javadoc). The quality of hints can be improved if the smart hint system also uses formal library specifications that contain information about correct function call sequences. Thus, based on the context, it will be possible to offer the programmer only those library functions that make sense to call in accordance with the behavioral description of the library.

7 Conclusion

The article presents the approach to managing software integration based on formal library specifications. The presented formalism is a compromise between fully functional Turing-complete models that are difficult to analyze, and lightweight finite state machines models that have application limitations. The power of the developed formalism is sufficient to describe the majority of existing software libraries. To support formalism, the domain specific language LibSL was developed, which allows setting library specifications in a human-readable form without going into the mathematical aspects of formalism.

The developed formalism and language have been successfully applied or can be applied to solve a wide range of software engineering problems:

– software porting;
– improving the characteristics of static analysis of projects that use external libraries;
– cross-language integration of applications and libraries;
– dynamic detection of integration errors;
– static detection of integration errors;
– directed fuzzing of library calls;
– automated extraction of specifications from projects located in the open repositories;
– automated creation of specifications based on the library initial code;
– automatic creation of software documentation;
– etc.

Experimental studies have shown the effectiveness of the approach for solving specific problems of software engineering.

References

1. Barros-Justo, J.L., Benitti, F.B.V., Matalonga, S.: Trends in software reuse research: a tertiary study. Comput. Stand. Interfaces **66** (2019)
2. Capiluppi, A., Stol, K.J., Boldyreff, C.: Software reuse in open source a case study. In: Koch, S. (ed.) Open Source Software Dynamics, Processes, and Applications, pp. 151–176 (2013). https://doi.org/10.4018/978-1-4666-2937-0.ch008. Accessed 23 Mar 2020
3. Alagar, V.S., Periyasamy, K.: Extended finite state machine. In: Alagar, V.S., Periyasamy, K. (eds.) Specification of Software Systems. Texts in Computer Science, pp. 105–128. Springer, London (2011). https://doi.org/10.1007/978-0-85729-277-3_7
4. Meyer, B.: Design by contract: making object-oriented programs that work. In: Proceedings of the Technology of Object-Oriented Languages and Systems, TOOLS 25 (Cat. No. 97TB100239), Melbourne, Victoria, Australia, pp. 360–361 (1997)

5. Itsykson, V.M.: Formalism and language tools for specification of the semantics of software libraries. Aut. Control Comp. Sci. **51**(7), 531–538 (2017). https://doi.org/10.3103/S01464116 17070100

6. Itsykson, V.: LibSL: a language for software components specification. Softw. Eng. **5**, 209–220 (2018). (in Russian). https://doi.org/10.17587/prin.9.209-220

7. Cossette, B.E., Walker, R.J.: Seeking the ground truth: a retroactive study on the evolution and migration of software libraries. In: Proceedings of the ACM SIGSOFT 20th International Symposium on the Foundations of Software Engineering (FSE 2012), Article 55, pp. 1–11. Association for Computing Machinery, New York (2012). https://doi.org/10.1145/2393596. 2393661

8. Itsykson. V., Zozulya, A.: Automated program transformation for migration to new libraries. In: 2011 7th Central and Eastern European Software Engineering Conference (CEE-SECR), Moscow, Russia, pp. 1–7 (2011). https://doi.org/10.1109/CEE-SECR.2011.6188463

9. Aleksyuk, A.O., Itsykson, V.M.: Semantics-driven migration of java programs: a practical application. Aut. Control Comp. Sci. **52**(7), 581–588 (2018). https://doi.org/10.3103/S01464 11618070027

10. Nielson, F., Nielson, H.R., Hankin, C.: Principles of Program Analysis, 2nd edn, p. 452. Springer, Heidelberg (2005)

11. Biere, A., Cimatti, A., Clarke, E.M., Strichman, O., Zhu, Y.: Bounded Model Checking. Advances in Computers. Academic Press (2003)

12. Akhin, M., Belyaev, M., Itsykson, V.: Borealis bounded model checker: the coming of age story. In: Mazzara, M., Meyer, B. (eds.) Present and Ulterior Software Engineering, pp. 119–137. Springer, Cham (2017). https://doi.org/10.1007/978-3-319-67425-4_8

13. de Moura, L., Bjørner, N.: Z3: an efficient SMT solver. In: Ramakrishnan, C.R., Rehof, J. (eds.) TACAS 2008. LNCS, vol. 4963, pp. 337–340. Springer, Heidelberg (2008). https://doi. org/10.1007/978-3-540-78800-3_24

14. Brummayer, R., Biere, A.: Boolector: an efficient SMT solver for bit-vectors and arrays. In: Kowalewski, S., Philippou, A. (eds.) TACAS 2009. LNCS, vol. 5505, pp. 174–177. Springer, Heidelberg (2009). https://doi.org/10.1007/978-3-642-00768-2_16

15. Nelson, B.J.: Remote Procedure Call. PARC CSL-81-9. Xerox Palo Alto Research Center. Ph.D. thesis (1981)

16. Itsykson, V., Gusev, M.: Automation of library usage correctness detection. In: Proceedings of SEIM Conference, St. Petersburg (2018)

17. Dallmeier, V., Knopp, N., Mallon, C., Fraser, G., Hack, S., Zeller, A.: Automatically generating test cases for specification mining. IEEE Trans. Softw. Eng. (TSE) **38**(2), 243–257 (2012)

Full Papers

Chaotic Time Series Prediction: Run for the Horizon

Vasilii A. Gromov[✉] [iD]

National Research University Higher School of Economics, Pokrovskii boulevard, 11,
109028 Moscow, Russian Federation
stroller@rambler.ru

Abstract. The present article reviews some recent papers concerned with chaotic time series prediction in the context of predictive clustering, and discusses in greater detail some novel techniques designed to avoid 'a curse of exponential growth' – errors grow exponentially depending on the number of steps ahead to be predicted. These techniques are non-successive observations, combined with a prognosis that employs already predicted values, the concept of non-predictable points, and a quality assessment of clusters used. The approach discussed, allows one to separate calculation into two parts: the first part, essentially larger, is performed off-line, the second, immediate prediction routine, is carried out on-line. This makes it possible to design fast and efficient prediction algorithms. A wide-ranging simulation, suggests that the error term associated with the prediction sub-model used, provided that clusters used to predict are chosen correctly, vanishes as the validation set size grows to infinity. Similarly, the error term associated with an incorrect choice of clusters used to predict, decreases when a validation set size increases.

Keywords: Time series prediction · A chaotic time series · Predictive clustering · Cluster prognostic value

1 Introduction

Constant interest in chaotic systems and models expressed by researchers in various fields [2, 8, 23–26, 28], is due to both the fundamental importance of non-linear phenomena for natural and social processes description, and an inherent complexity of their forecasting. The overwhelming majority of information systems are complex and thereby tend to show chaotic behaviour. Mathematically, the problem to forecast such system characteristics is a chaotic time series prediction problem. One should emphasize that regular and chaotic time series, essentially differ, in that the latter features the prediction horizon, which is the maximum number of steps ahead that one can make a prognosis. Quite naturally, this quantity depends on a required maximum prediction error and a time series observation accuracy. Since the prediction horizon is finite for chaotic time series, and infinite for regular, it serves to distinguish the time series of these two types. The prediction horizon is attributed to an exponential divergence of initially close trajectories, due to the Lyapunov instability of chaotic time series [16, 22]. The exponent

© Springer Nature Switzerland AG 2021
A. Kalenkova et al. (Eds.): TMPA 2019, CCIS 1288, pp. 29–43, 2021.
https://doi.org/10.1007/978-3-030-71472-7_2

coefficient is called the highest Lyapunov exponent; for chaotic time series it is positive, and it is readily calculated from a time series [16, 22].

The exponential divergence mentioned above, is also responsible for the exponential error growth for multi-step prediction, and the highest Lyapunov exponent serves here as the exponent coefficient also. This explains the fact that most papers dealing with chaotic time series prediction, discuss results for a single step prediction only, whereas the problem of multi-step prediction for chaotic time series is still unresolved.

It is worthy to stress that the exponential growth of prediction error is intrinsic to a single prediction model for a chaotic time series, whereas, if one predicts using a set of sub-models, the reverse may hold true. As it is very difficult to develop a single model to predict a chaotic time series, it is quite natural to look for prediction methods that are able to combine, either explicitly or implicitly, a set of sub-models corresponding to various dynamic patterns observed in the series [3, 23, 24]. Of the known approaches, predictive clustering [4] stands out as the most robust; here, the sub-models are based upon clustered sequences of time series observations [5, 17, 32].

The present article reviews some recent papers concerned with chaotic time series prediction, in the context of predictive clustering, and discusses in greater detail some novel techniques designed to avoid 'a curse of exponential growth'. These are non-successive observations combined with a prognosis that employs already predicted values, the concept of non-predictable points [7], and quality assessment of clusters used [10]. Actually, any prediction method to a significant number of steps ahead for chaotic series involves prediction based on the values that are predicted themselves. Consequently, it is extremely important to assess whether or not these predicted values are reliable. The aforementioned concepts constitute a set of tools to estimate the reliability – hence they are necessary to make a reliable multi-step prognosis.

The rest of the paper is organised as follows. The next section reviews recent advances in the field. The following Sects. 3 and 4, presents the mathematical statement, the problems under study, and introduce basic concepts and non-successive observations. Section 5 outlines the prediction algorithm. Sections 6, 7 and 8 go on to describe the concepts of non-predictable points and quality assessment. The following sections outline a clustering method, and a method to estimate clusters' prognostic values, and provide the prediction results for the time series which are 1) generated by the Lorenz system, and 2) associated with the Australian energy market. The prediction results are obtained for a single prediction for various quality assessment techniques that makes possible to compare them. The last two sections compare the results to those obtained by other authors, and present conclusions.

2 Related Works

One way to decrease the mean prediction error for predictive clustering algorithms, is to estimate prognostic values of the clusters at hand, with the employment of an additional validation set, distinct from the training (used to generate these clusters) and the testing (used to estimate ultimate prediction error). One may treat these cluster prognostic values as method hyperparameters, as introduced by Goodfellow et al. [11], with the sole difference that, for that case, the number of hyperparameters is equal to the number of clusters, and therefore is large. It is possible to estimate the cluster prognostic value using, say, the mean prediction error (on the validation set) induced by this cluster, or an invariant measure for the phase space region associated with this cluster; the latter alternative allows excluding clusters corresponding to the remote and unfrequented regions.

It is not necessary to present information about clusters prognostic values using scalars, quite the contrary. It is possible to employ, for example, logical rules indicating practicability of utilizing the cluster in question, to predict.

In either case, the prediction error is broken down into two terms. The first is associated with an incorrect choice of a cluster and, consequently, a sub-model to predict. The second is that caused by a discrepancy between predicted and actual values, provided the cluster is chosen correctly, that is, the chosen cluster is associated with the true space phase region where the time series (trajectory) portion to be predicted is situated. The latter term cannot be reduced for the clustering algorithm used – we consider it as a kind of theoretical minimum error for a given clustering algorithm, prediction sub-model and training samples size. However, one can delete clusters with lower prognostic values in order to reduce the former. The totality of procedures aimed at reducing the second summand (at estimating prognostic values of clusters [hyperparameters]) is termed 'quality assessment' for predictive clustering.

The present paper introduces a 'quality assessment' of clusters generated by a predictive clustering algorithm, and proposes several methods to solve this problem. To compare different methods, we utilize a contribution of the first summand to the total prediction error, as well as the number of non-predictable observations for a testing set [7, 8], that is the observations the algorithm is unable to predict due to the lack of the appropriate cluster. Let us stress, that the ability of any algorithm to detect non-predictable observations is its great advantage. Actually, it is much better if an algorithm 'honestly' indicates that it is unable to predict properly at a certain point and does not try to predict 'forcibly' - without indicating risk to use such predicted values.

Of fundamental importance is the ability of, and necessity for, a predictive clustering algorithm to generate clusters, using not only the series to be predicted but also a group of similar series that contains it.

Conventionally, predictive clustering researchers pursue two avenues of inquiry [1]. The first proposes that a time series is a single entity and a set thereof may be clustered using various clustering techniques. The second one looks for typical dynamical patterns (known as typical sequences [7–10], motifs [27], chunks [29], shapelets [30], subsequences [1], etc.) either in a time series observed, or in a group of similar time series. In what follows, we restrict our attention to the second line of investigation.

As discussed by E. Keogh and J. Lin [18], it serves no purpose to use the single time series to be predicted to generate clusters; it is essential to utilize a set of all other similar series. Papers concerned with the algorithms of pattern discovery, usually explore techniques to generate a training set, using a series at hand, and to cluster it. These parts of a predictive clustering algorithm are associated with concepts of data-adaptation and algorithm-adaptation [21]. The data-adaptation concept allows use of raw data, feature-based transformation of the data, and model-based transformation of the data as well, to generate samples [1, 21]. Algorithm-adaptation places the primary emphasis on clustering algorithms and their adaptation to the forecasting problem: A large part of previous studies deals with k-means, c-means (crisp and fuzzy) and the like.

Huang et al. [12] employ k-means in order to adjust it to seek for similar sections in chaotic time series; the modified algorithm is dubbed TSkmeans (*Time Series k-means*). Martinez-Alvarez and his colleagues [24] also uses k-means to predict chaotic time series; the paper summarizes results by various investigators for forecasting of Australia's national electricity market prices – this bunch of series seems to become a sort of benchmark to test various prediction algorithms for chaotic time series; an extended version of the results may be found in [7]. Papers [13, 14] analyse spatio-temporal data using a clustering technique grounded on the modified Euclidean distance capable of taking into account hidden space and time patterns. Benitez et al. [3] examine ways to extract typical patterns from series amassed by generating company; it is aimed at designing algorithms of rational energy consumption; the authors use various modifications of k-means.

The trouble with such algorithms is that, on the one hand, the structure of clusters depend heavily on the metric used and, on the other hand, it, for most cases, requires knowledge of the number of clusters before clustering [6]. The methods that employ concepts and methods of graph/complex network theory are free, in some sense, of these drawbacks. Ferreira and Zhao [6] propose to map time series sections into graph vertices in order to apply then community detection algorithms. Gromov and Borisenko [7] employ the modified Wishart algorithm to cluster sequences of observations [20]; the authors point out to correlation between clusters obtained and phase space regions with higher values of invariant measure of the respective dynamical systems.

3   Time Series Prediction Problem

Given a set S of chaotic time series $S = \left\{ y^{(s)} \right\} = \left\{ y_0^{(s)}, y_1^{(s)}, \ldots, y_{t_s}^{(s)} \right\}$, $s = 1..|S|$, where t_s is the size of the s series, $y_i^{(s)}$ is i-th observation of s-th series, and a series $y = \{y_t\}$, estimate the value of an observation y_{t+K} to minimise the prediction error.

$$I = minE(y_{t+K} - \hat{y}_{t+K})^2 \qquad (1)$$

It is supposed that we know all observations of y up to and inclusive y_t. In particular, if $K > 1$, then the problem is called the multi-step (ahead) prediction problem.

If $S = \varnothing$, then one obtains a more conventional definition of prediction problems. The definition (1) appears to be more convenient for predictive clustering as it allows utilizing information from various time series. Actually, any predictive clustering algorithm implies that one seeks motifs in the time series considered. A motif is a typical sequence that emerges from time to time in a series. We assume here that all transient processes in the system that generate the time series in hand have been completed, and the time series reflects the trajectory movement in the neighbourhood of the attractor of the dynamical system that generates the series. It is worth emphasizing that neither the system nor its attractor is known, and the problem to reconstruct them is usually a much more complicated problem than the prediction problem. For chaotic time series, an attractor is usually a complex geometrical (fractal) set, called strange attractor. The second assumption is that the series meets Takens theorem conditions, and respectively, one can analyse the attractor structure, using time series observations [16, 22].

As the trajectory of the system moves along the same area of the attractor frequently, one can meet similar sequences in the time series. These sequences resemble the motif associated with the respective area. If one reveals these areas, describes corresponding motifs, and develops the simplest prediction models for each one, one makes it possible to predict chaotic time series up to a considerable time limit [9]. The clustering method presented below is employed to collect together sequences belonging to the same cluster. The motifs are usually centres of such clusters. It is straightforward to extend this approach to a set of time series S, just using all motifs that can be found in them.

4 Non-successive Observations

Usually, to ensure that Takens theorem conditions are satisfied, vectors are composed from time series observations (z-vectors) [16, 22]: a d-dimensional z-vector is defined as $z_i^{(s)} = \left(y_i^{(s)}, y_{i+1}^{(s)}, \ldots, y_{i+d-1}^{(s)} \right)$. Conventional practice is to compose z-vectors from successive observations. Surprisingly, z-vectors composed of non-successive observations according to a certain pattern, proved more efficient [7]. For the best prediction, one should run over all or, at least, over a considerable portion of all reasonable patterns, and single out the most appropriate clusters. Different attractor areas are associated with different clusters and corresponding motifs. The pattern is defined as a pre-set sequence of distances between positions of observations, such that these (non-successive) observations are to be placed on the successive positions in a newly generated sample vector.

The vector, thus concatenated, generalises a conventional z-vector [16, 22], which corresponds to the pattern $(1, 1, \ldots, 1)$ (m times). Thus, each pattern is a $S-1$-dimension integer vector $(p_1, \ldots, p_{S-1})$, $p_j \in \{1, \ldots, P_{max}\}, j = 1 .. S - 1$; the parameter P_{max} dictates the maximum distance between positions of observations that become successive in the vector to be generated. Thereby, the quantity $S \cdot P_{max}$ refers to a kind of a memory depth.

For predictive clustering, samples selected from the vectors of concatenated successive observations (z-vectors), prove less efficient than those based on the vectors concatenated according to various patterns [7]. This is attributed to the fact that vectors of non-successive observations are able to store information about salient observations: minima, maxima, tipping points and so on.

One should emphasize that each model mentioned above is an averaged representation of the clustered time series sequences, or alternatively, trajectories belonging to the respective attractor area. Consequently, it leads to a decrease in the prediction error due to averaging (the predicted values are obtained by using the cluster centres), and simultaneously, to its increase, in virtue of the fact that the 'chaotic' exponential growth is alleviated. The clustering method used strikes a compromise between these two tendencies.

5 Prediction Algorithm

A predictive clustering algorithm is usually subdivided into three parts. The first part analyses a group of time series at hand in order to cluster sequences made of its observations, according to predefined patterns, and then to use cluster centres as typical sequences. The second, estimates clusters' prognostic values and deletes clusters with low values. Finally, the third provides a prognosis for the time series with the employment of the obtained typical sequences (cluster centres).

The series are considered to be normalized. We used two different normalization techniques. The first one suggests that an entire time series is normalized with the employment of its maximum and minimum values, whereas the second technique implies that sample vectors are normalized separately, using their own maxima and minima. Hereafter, we refer to these techniques as global (G) and local (L) respectively. The latter makes it possible to cluster, not typical amplitudes (as it takes place for the former), but rather typical profiles.

To cluster generalised z-vectors, we employ the Wishart clustering method [31] as modified by A. V. Lapko and S. V. Chentsov [20]. This method employs graph theory concepts and a non-parametric probability density function estimator, of k-nearest neighbours. Some problems associated with application of the algorithm to predict time series are discussed in [7]. The algorithms to estimate clusters' prognostic values are discussed in the next section.

To predict time series values in the framework of the third part of an algorithm, the centres of clusters (motifs) are calculated for all used patterns and obtained clusters. For a given position to be predicted (for the time series in question), and for a given cluster, one should take the following steps. Firstly, one composes a vector from time series observations, according to the pattern used to generate the cluster, with the position associated with the last vector element (respectively, undefined). Secondly, truncate the vector and the cluster centre - all elements but the last ones are included in the truncated vectors. Thirdly, calculate the Euclidian distance between the truncated observation vector and the truncated cluster centre. One searches over all patterns and clusters in order to find the cluster with the minimum distance. If the distance is less than a predefined vigilance threshold, then the centre of this cluster is employed to predict the observation, namely, the last element of the centre is used as a predicted value for the position in question. Otherwise, if the distance to any cluster available exceeds the threshold, the dynamics are considered unidentifiable, and the observation is appended to the set of non-predictable observations.

6 Non-predictable Points

Employing clustering techniques to reveal typical sequences and to predict time series using the revealed sequences, the predictive clustering methods are sometimes unable to find, for a given point to be predicted, any appropriate typical sequences to predict value at this position. This happens when there are no cluster centres matching observations from the time series section preceding this position. Hereafter such observations are called unpredictable, and their number (related to the testing set size) is taken to be a measure of prediction quality, along with a prediction error averaged over all other (predictable) observations of the testing set. It is worth stressing that this feature is conventionally regarded as a limitation of predictive clustering, but it seems that it is much better if an algorithm 'sincerely' warns that the point is unpredictable, than it generates an erroneous prediction without warning.

7 Quality Assessment

The total prediction error can be broken down into the two terms. The first term results from the incorrect choice of the active cluster, that is a cluster which centre is used to predict. Consequently, it is possible to state the problem of *estimating clusters' prognostic values* in order to minimize the term associated with incorrect choice of the active cluster, that is, the cluster engaged to predict the current observation (the first term). The problem involves selecting a subset of clusters such that the total prediction error (on the testing set) corresponding to the forecasting routine that employs this subset only, is either minimal (the first statement) or less than a predefined threshold (the second statement). Mathematically, the problem is formulated as follows. Let Λ is the set of clusters employed to predict the time series in question; $\Im \equiv \{G : \Lambda \to R^1\}$; $\tilde{\Lambda}(G, \beta) = \{\lambda \in \Lambda : G(\lambda) \geq \beta\}$. The problem is to find the estimator $G^* \in \Im$ and the threshold value $\beta^* \in R^1$, $\beta^* > 0$ (the first statement) in order to minimize prediction error (on the testing set):

$$\min I(\tilde{\Lambda}(G, \beta)) \tag{2}$$

The second statement implies that one minimizes the number of clusters belonging to $\tilde{\Lambda}(G, \beta)$:

$$\min \left| \tilde{\Lambda}(G, \beta) \right| \tag{3}$$

subject to constraint

$$\left| I(\tilde{\Lambda}(G, \beta)) \right| \leq \gamma, \tag{4}$$

where γ is a parameter of the algorithm.

In the framework of the first statement, one places emphasis on the minimum prediction error, while the second statement is concerned primarily with the speed to obtain prediction results. In either case, this suggests reducing the number of clusters, or to put it differently, the overall complexity of the prediction model under study (while maintaining prediction accuracy). One cannot but make analogies of various methods to reduce the complexity of regression models (for instance, AIC, BIC, GIC, and so on [19]).

To solve the problem, an additional set (the validation) is introduced, under the assumption that it differs from both the training and testing ones, and all three of them are drawn from the same universal set.

8   The Problem of Estimating Clusters' Prognostic Values (Quality Assessment)

Two techniques to estimate the values in question are considered. The first one suggests that the prognostic value of k-th cluster is calculated as follows:

$$Q_k(\beta) = \sum_{i \in S_k} \frac{\bar{e}_i}{e_{ik}} \frac{1}{|V_i|}, \tag{5}$$

where $\bar{e}_i = \frac{1}{|V_i|} \sum_{i \in V_i} e_{ij}$, V_i is a set of clusters able to predict i-th observation with an error less than β; S_k is the set of observations predicted by k-th cluster with an error less than β; e_{ij} is a prediction error for i-th observation if j-th cluster is used to predict.

The second method to perform quality assessment, offers not to use a single characteristic, but rather to extract knowledge from data about prediction errors for observations of the validation set.

Namely, we define for k-th cluster (over the validation set):

d_{ij} is the minimum Euclidian distance between i-th observation and elements of k-th cluster;

$S_i^{(d)}(\beta) = \left\{ y_i^{(s)} : d_{ij} \leq \beta \right\}$ is the number of observations with the distance less than β from j-th cluster;

m_j is the number of times the cluster has been active;

n_j is the number of times the use of the cluster would lead to the minimum possible error.

Algorithm 2. The quality assessment routine with the replacement of the active cluster.

1. Initialization: For each $S_i^{(d)}(\beta) \neq \varnothing$, $S_i(\beta) \neq \varnothing$: $m_j \leftarrow 0, n_j \leftarrow 0, i \leftarrow 0, j \leftarrow 0$.
2. If $d_{ij} \leq \beta$ then $S_i^{(d)}(\beta) = S_i^{(d)}(\beta) \cup y_i$.
3. If $e_{ij} \leq \beta$ then $S_i(\beta) = S_i(\beta) \cup y_i$.
4. Find $d_{imin} = d_{ik} = \min_j d_{ij}$; $m_k \leftarrow m_k + 1$.
5. Find $e_{imin} = e_{ip} = \min_j e_{ij}$ and the distance of d_{ip}; $n_k \leftarrow n_k + 1$.
6. $j \leftarrow j + 1$. If the list of clusters is not exhausted, then go to step 3.
7. $i \leftarrow i + 1$. If the list of observations is not exhausted, then go to step 2.

In what follows, we refer to these algorithms as to 1st and 2nd.

9   Numerical Results

The aforementioned clustering algorithm is applied to generate samples with the employment of all possible patterns of four elements with the maximum (minimum) distance between neighbouring positions in the pattern equal to 10. So the number of patterns used amounts to 10000. Each sample produces its own set of clusters, and then all sets of clusters are merged into a single set.

The method discussed in the previous section, is applied to a time series generated by the Lorenz system, to a set of noisy Lorenz series, and to a set of Australia's national electricity market price series too. Throughout the paper, we stick to single-step prediction. The highest Lyapunov exponent was calculated for all studied time series, with the employment of the analogue method [16, 22].

To measure prediction error, we used three measures. They are the root mean square error (*RMSE*), the mean average error (*MAE*), and the percentage of non-predictable observations. All three measures are averaged over the testing set, which is used neither for training nor for quality assessment.

The results obtained are presented in a uniform way for any series analysed. Namely, after introductory information about the series, we present prediction errors for different method versions in the form of a table. The table shows prediction errors corresponding to various choices of normalization, clustering, and quality assessment routines. The first column indicates a size of the validation set (the size of training set is usually the same); the next two columns present information about the method used.

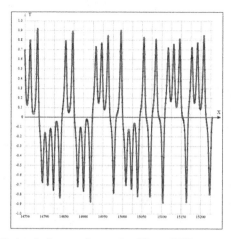

Fig. 1. Single-step prediction for Lorenz time series. Blue solid lines are associated with observed data, whereas red dashed lines are associated with predicted values. Green discs represent non-predictable points.

Namely, the second and third columns correspond to a normalization technique (G is global and L is local), and a method to estimate clusters' predictive values (quality assessment; 1 is the quality assessment method based upon a scalar estimate of clusters' prognostic value; 2 is the one based upon a replacement of the active cluster). The next three columns present RMSE, MAE, and the percentage of non-predictable observations. Finally, the last two columns display (for comparison) MAE and RMSE for the case, when the true active cluster is known in advance ('theoretical minimum').

The method under study was applied to the series generated by the Lorenz system [15, 22]. The Lorenz system with standard 'chaotic' parameters $\sigma = 10, b = \frac{8}{3}, r = 28$ integrated with the employment of Runge–Kutta's fourth-order method (integration step is equal to 0.05), yields a time series hereafter referred to as the Lorenz series.

The series in question, on the one hand, is a typical chaotic series (the highest Lyapunov equals to 0.92 that is in agreement with results by Malinetskii and Potapov [22]

Table 1. Prediction errors for the Lorenz series

Size	N	QA	RMSE ($*10^{-2}$)	MAE ($*10^{-2}$)	Non (%)	MMAE ($*10^{-2}$)	MRMSE ($*10^{-2}$)
10^4	G	1	1.82	1.2	0.73	0.358	0.367
10^5	G	1	1.023	0.89	0.61	0.358	0.364
10^6	G	1	0.89	0.81	0.59	0.358	0.361
10^7	G	1	0.83	0.79	0.52	0.358	0.359
10^4	G	2	1.45	1	0.74	0.358	0.367
10^5	G	2	1.027	0.78	0.64	0.358	0.364
10^6	G	2	0.87	0.73	0.6	0.358	0.361
10^7	G	2	0.78	0.72	0.57	0.358	0.359
10^4	L	1	0.96	0.73	0.43	0.207	0.229
10^5	L	1	0.79	0.69	0.34	0.207	0.227
10^6	L	1	0.64	0.52	0.31	0.207	0.224
10^7	L	1	0.48	0.48	0.3	0.207	0.221
10^4	L	2	0.84	0.72	0.38	0.207	0.229
10^5	L	2	0.78	0.63	0.36	0.207	0.227
10^6	L	2	0.53	0.51	0.29	0.207	0.224
10^7	L	2	0.46	0.45	0.26	0.207	0.221

Size is the size of a training set; N is a normalization technique; QA is a quality assessment algorithm; RMSE is a root-mean-square error; MAE is a mean absolute error; Non is the percentage of non-predictable observations (for the testing set); MMAE is theoretically minimal mean absolute error; MRMSE is theoretically minimal root-mean-square error.

[see on p. 217]) and, on the other hand, is a conventional benchmark to test forecasting procedures for chaotic time series.

For the Lorenz series, the first 3000 observations are discarded in order to ensure that trajectory moves in the neighbourhood of the respective strange attractor. The testing set for the series consists of 100000 observations, the training set consists of 100000, while a validation set size is varied and, actually, are crucial parameters for the method considered.

Figure 1 presents single-step prediction results for the Lorenz time series. The first figure displays a typical time series section (of the testing set) and the respective predicted values; blue solid lines are associated with observed data, whereas red dashed lines are associated with predicted values. Green circles represent non-predictable observations.

The size of the training set is 100000 observations, that of the validation set is 10^7. The percentage of non-predictable observations is 0.26%, RMSE is about 0.46%, while the average prediction error for predictable observations is equal to 0.0045%. Table 1 shows prediction errors.

The Wishart clustering technique, in conjunction with a local normalization routine and the quality assessment method based upon a scalar estimate of clusters' prognostic values, proves the most efficient; however, it also proves the most time-consuming. Another point of interest is the fact that the percentage of the clusters to be discarded to obtain the best prediction, converges to a certain limit (around 19%) as the size of the validation set increases.

To explore the potential to use clustering results obtained for a certain group of series in order to predict distinct but similar series, we consider a set of noisy Lorenz series. The training set is generated with the employment of the standard Lorenz series (see above) of 100000 observations, while the validation and testing is generated using noisy series. To generate these series, we add the white noise to a normalized standard Lorenz series and then normalize again. The noise amplitude is a normal random variable with a mean equal to 0.0 and a variance equal to 0.3. The series prove chaotic with the highest Lyapunov varying from 0.98 to 1.23. The size of the training set is 100000; the size of the testing set is 100000 (Table 2).

Table 2. Prediction error for a noisy series

Size	N	QA	RMSE (*10^{-2})	MAE (*10^{-2})	Non (%)	MMAE (*10^{-2})	MRMSE (*10^{-2})
10^4	G	1	21.82	16.37	18.69	4.05	4.21
10^5	G	1	16.83	14.38	18.51	4.05	4.15
10^6	G	1	13.89	9.32	15.13	4.05	4.12
10^7	G	1	11.63	7.56	14.69	4.05	4.09
10^4	G	2	17.45	15.29	16.54	4.05	4.21
10^5	G	2	12.64	13.26	15.34	4.05	4.15
10^6	G	2	11.87	8.74	14.97	4.05	4.12
10^7	G	2	10.87	6.87	13.78	4.05	4.09
10^4	L	1	23.48	15.98	15.31	3.89	4.19
10^5	L	1	18.64	15.33	14.11	3.89	4.11
10^6	L	1	15.17	13.69	13.68	3.89	4.01
10^7	L	1	12.77	12.83	12.97	3.89	3.94
10^4	L	2	19.89	15.67	14.84	3.89	4.19
10^5	L	2	18.21	14.88	13.72	3.89	4.11
10^6	L	2	14.63	13.15	13.03	3.89	4.01
10^7	L	2	12.35	12.19	12.56	3.89	3.94

The abbreviations are the same as for Table 1.

For that case, the best combination of techniques appears to be that of Wishart clustering and the quality assessment by replacement of the active cluster. The optimal percentage of clusters to be deleted for the quality assessment routine based upon a scalar estimate, in contrast to the previous case, does not converge to a fixed value. This may be attributed to the fact that the training and the validation sets are of a different nature (usual and noisy Lorenz series).

Finally, the method under study is applied to time series generated by electricity prices in various settlements of the Commonwealth of Australia (Table 3).

Table 3. Prediction error for Australia's national electricity market price

Size	N	QA	RMSE ($*10^{-2}$)	MAE ($*10^{-2}$)	Non (%)	MMAE ($*10^{-2}$)	MRMSE ($*10^{-2}$)
10^4	G	1	0.98	0.701	0.35	0.449	0.462
10^5	G	1	0.83	0.662	0.29	0.449	0.460
10^6	G	1	0.76	0.627	0.25	0.449	0.456
10^7	G	1	0.73	0.617	0.17	0.449	0.451
10^4	G	2	0.87	0.674	0.37	0.449	0.462
10^5	G	2	0.78	0.631	0.34	0.449	0.460
10^6	G	2	0.74	0.623	0.29	0.449	0.456
10^7	G	2	0.67	0.608	0.23	0.449	0.451
10^4	L	1	0.76	0.587	0.29	0.287	0.314
10^5	L	1	0.72	0.518	0.25	0.287	0.307
10^6	L	1	0.68	0.509	0.19	0.287	0.301
10^7	L	1	0.66	0.503	0.14	0.287	0.296
10^4	L	2	0.74	0.521	0.27	0.287	0.314
10^5	L	2	0.72	0.514	0.26	0.287	0.307
10^6	L	2	0.65	0.507	0.17	0.287	0.301
10^7	L	2	0.51	0.492	0.15	0.287	0.296

The abbreviations are the same as for Table 1.

10   Comparison with Published Results

Tables 4 and 5 exhibit results obtained by various methods; the tables are partially borrowed from [24]; see also [7]. Let us stress, that prediction error for algorithms proposed is lower than that of conventional soft-computing algorithms, provided the points classified as non-predictable by the algorithm are excluded (their percentage is usually lower than 1%), and is comparable with it, if these non-predictable observations are predicted forcibly.

Table 4. MER for some days of the year 2004 (Australia's national electricity market – Price)

Day	5th June	17th June	20th June	21th June	Average
ARIMA(%)	32.31	29.09	33.73	24.18	29.82
SVM(%)	18.09	13.31	17.11	19.2	16.93
PSF(%)	16.72	8.31	14.23	18.93	14.55
PCW(%)	1.94	1.72	1.32	1.94	1.73(0.42%, 1.78)
PCW(1)(%)	0.87	0.78	0.64	0.84	0.74 (0.18%, 0.77)
PCW(2)(%)	0.76	0.72	0.58	0.83	0.69 (0.24%, 0,71)

ARIMA – the best ARIMA model; SVM – support vector machine; PSF – pattern sequenced-based forecasting; PCW – predictive clustering using the Wishart algorithm [31]; PCW(1) – predictive clustering using the Wishart algorithm with quality assessment based upon clusters' prognostic values; PCW(2) – predictive clustering using Wishart algorithm with quality assessment based upon active cluster replacement; last column in parentheses is a percentage of non-predictable observations and the error calculated provided the non-predictable observations are predicted forcibly.

Table 5. MER for some weeks of the year 2004 (Australia's national electricity market – Price)

Week	First of January	First of July	First of August	Third of December	Average
DWT(%)	12.94	12.2	16.17	10.01	12.84
SVM(%)	23.37	15.0	36.18	33.74	27.08
PSF(%)	15.62	9.12	13.98	10.23	12.23
PCW (%)	1.33	1.47	1.28	1.11	1.30 (0,38%, 1,34)
PCW(1)(%)	0.96	0.78	0.83	0.62	0.76 (0,21%, 0,79)
PCW(2)(%)	0.89	0.81	0.74	0.59	0.72 (0,19%, 0,74)

The abbreviations are the same as for Table 4.

11 Conclusions

1. Predictions that uses already predicted values, the concept of non-predictable points, and quality assessment of clusters employed, taken together, direct the way to solution of the multi-step chaotic time series prediction problem.
2. Quality assessment procedure aimed at estimating clusters' prognostic values and deleting clusters with low ones (in the framework of predictive clustering) decreases essentially predictive error both for benchmark and for real-word data.
3. A wide-ranging simulation suggests that the error term associated with prediction sub-model used (provided that clusters used to predict are chosen correctly) vanishes as a validation set size tends to infinity. Similarly, the error term associated with incorrect choice of clusters used to predict decreases when a validation set size increases.

4. Prediction error for algorithms proposed is lower than that of conventional soft-computing algorithms, provided the points classified as non-predictable by the algorithm are excluded (their percentage is usually lower than 1%), and is comparable with it, if these non-predictable observations are predicted forcibly. The best variant is Wishart clustering algorithm in conjunction with local normalization and replacement of the active cluster.
5. The approach discussed allows one to separate calculation into two parts: the first, essentially larger, is performed off-line, the second, immediate prediction routine, is performed on-line. This makes possible to design fast and efficient prediction algorithms.

Acknowledgements. The author is deeply indebted to Mr. Joel Cumberland, HSE for the manuscript proof-reading and language editing.

References

1. Aghabozorgi, S., Shirkhorshidi, A.S., Wah, T.Y.: Time-series clustering – a decade review. Inf. Syst. **23**, 16–38 (2015)
2. Al Zoubi, O., Awad, M., Kasabov, N.K.: Anytime multipurpose emotion recognition from EEG data using a Liquid State Machine based framework. Artif. Intell. Med. **86**, 1–8 (2018)
3. Benítez, I., Díezb, J.L., Quijanoa, A., Delgado, I.: Dynamic clustering of residential electricity consumption time series data based on Hausdorff distance. Electr. Power Syst. Res. **140**, 517–526 (2016)
4. Blockeel, H., De Raedt, L., Ramon, J.: Top-down induction of clustering trees. In: 15th International Conference on Machine Learning, pp. 55–63 (1998)
5. D'Urso, P., De Giovanni, L., Massari, R.: GARCH-based robust clustering of time series. Fuzzy Sets Syst. **305**, 1–28 (2016)
6. Ferreira, L.N., Zhao, L.: Time series clustering via community detection in networks. Inf. Sci. **326**, 227–242 (2016)
7. Gromov, V.A., Borisenko, E.A.: Chaotic time series prediction and clustering methods. Neural Comput. Appl. **2**, 307–315 (2015)
8. Gromov, V.A., Konev, A.S.: Precocious identification of popular topics on Twitter with the employment of predictive clustering. Neural Comput. Appl. **28**(11), 3317–3322 (2016). https://doi.org/10.1007/s00521-016-2256-1
9. Gromov, V.A., Shulga, A.N.: Chaotic time series prediction with employment of ant colony optimization. Expert Syst. Appl. **39**(9), 8474–8478 (2012)
10. Gromov, V.A., Voronin, I.M., Gatylo, V.R., Prokopalo, E.T.: Active cluster replacement algorithm as a tool to assess bifurcation early-warning signs for von Karman equations. Artif. Intell. Res. **6**(2), 51–56 (2017)
11. Goodfellow, I., Bengio, Y., Courville, A.: Deep Learning. MIT Press, Cambridge (2015)
12. Huang, X., Ye, Y., Xiong, L., Lau, R.Y.K., Jiang, N., Wang, S.: Time series k-means: a new k-means type smooth subspace clustering for time series data. Inf. Sci. **367–368**, 1–3 (2016)
13. Izakian, H., Pedrycz, W.: Agreement-based fuzzy c-means for clustering data with blocks of features. Neurocomputing **127**, 266–280 (2014)
14. Izakian, H., Pedrycz, W., Jamal, I.: Clustering spatiotemporal data: an augmented fuzzy c-means. IEEE Trans. Fuzzy Syst. **21**(5), 855–868 (2013)

15. Jackson, E.A.: The Lorenz system: I. The global structure of its stable manifolds. Physica Scripta **32**(5), 469–475 (1985). https://doi.org/10.1088/0031-8949/32/5/001

16. Kantz, H., Schneider, T.: Nonlinear Time Series Analysis. Cambridge University Press, Cambridge (2004)

17. Kattan, A., Fatima, S., Arif, M.: Time-series event-based prediction: an unsupervised learning framework based on genetic programming. Inf. Sci. **301**, 99–123 (2015)

18. Keogh, E., Lin, J.: Clustering of time-series subsequences is meaningless: implications for previous and future research. Knowl. Inf. Syst. **8**(2), 154–177 (2004). https://doi.org/10.1007/s10115-004-0172-7

19. Konishi, S., Kitagava, G.: Information Criteria and Statistical Modeling. Springer, New York (2008)

20. Lapko, A.V., Chentsov, S.V.: Nonparametric information processing systems. Science, Novosibirsk (2000)

21. Liao, T.W.: Clustering of time series data-a survey. Pattern Recogn. **38**(11), 1857–1874 (2005)

22. Malinetskii, G.G., Potapov, A.P.: Modern problems of non-linear dynamics. Editorial URSS, Moscow (2002)

23. Martınez-Alvarez, F., Troncoso, A., Riquelme, J.C.: Data science and big data in energy forecasting. Energies **11**, 3224 (2018)

24. Martınez-Alvarez, F., Troncoso, A., Riquelme, J.C., Riquelme, J.M.: Energy time series forecasting based on pattern sequence similarity. IEEE Trans. Knowl. Data **23**(8), 1230–1243 (2011)

25. Obodan, N.I., Adlucky, V.J., Gromov, V.A.: Prediction and control of buckling: the inverse bifurcation problems for von Karman equations. In: Dutta, H., Peters, J.F. (eds.) Applied Mathematical Analysis: Theory, Methods, and Applications. SSDC, vol. 177, pp. 353–381. Springer, Cham (2020). https://doi.org/10.1007/978-3-319-99918-0_11

26. Obodan, N.I., Adlucky, V.J., Gromov, V.A.: Rapid identification of pre-buckling states: a case of cylindrical shell. Thin-Walled Struct. **124**, 449–457 (2018)

27. Palit, A.K., Popovich, D.: Computational Intelligence in Time Series Forecasting. Theory and Engineering Applications. Springer, New York (2005). https://doi.org/10.1007/1-84628-184-9

28. Pérez-Chacón, R., Luna-Romera, J.M., Troncoso, A., Martínez-Álvarez, F., Riquelme, J.C.: Big data analytics for discovering electricity consumption patterns in smart cities. Energies **11**(3), 683 (2018)

29. Phu, L., Anh, D.: Motif-based method for initialization the k-means clustering for time series data. In: Wang, D., Reynolds, M. (eds.) AI 2011. LNCS (LNAI), vol. 7106, pp. 11–20. Springer, Heidelberg (2011). https://doi.org/10.1007/978-3-642-25832-9_2

30. Widiputra, H., Kho, H., Pears, R., Kasabov, N.K.: A novel evolving clustering algorithm with polynomial regression for chaotic time-series prediction. Neural Inf. Process. **5864**, 114–121 (2009)

31. Wishart, D.: A numerical classification methods for deriving natural classes. Nature **221**, 97–98 (1969)

32. Zakaria, J., Mueen, A., Keogh, E.: Clustering time series using unsupervised shapelets. In: 12th International Conference on Data Mining, pp. 785–94. IEEE Computer Society (2012)

Machine Learning and Value Generation in Software Development: A Survey

Barakat J. Akinsanya, Luiz J. P. Araújo$^{(\boxtimes)}$, Mariia Charikova, Susanna Gimaeva, Alexandr Grichshenko, Adil Khan, Manuel Mazzara, N. Ozioma Okonicha, and Daniil Shilintsev

Innopolis University, Innopolis 420500, Russia
l.araujo@innopolis.university

Abstract. Machine Learning (ML) has become a ubiquitous tool for predicting and classifying data and has found application in several problem domains, including Software Development (SD). This paper reviews the literature between 2000 and 2019 on the use the learning models that have been employed for programming effort estimation, predicting risks and identifying and detecting defects. This work is meant to serve as a starting point for practitioners willing to add ML to their software development toolbox. It categorises recent literature and identifies trends and limitations. The survey shows as some authors have agreed that industrial applications of ML for SD have not been as popular as the reported results would suggest. The conducted investigation shows that, despite having promising findings for a variety of SD tasks, most of the studies yield vague results, in part due to the lack of comprehensive datasets in this problem domain. The paper ends with concluding remarks and suggestions for future research.

Keywords: Machine learning · Software engineering · Literature review

1 Introduction

The software has become an essential part of modern everyday life and has a ubiquitous presence in diverse sectors including manufacturing, agriculture and health industries, to mention a few [9]. Efficient software development is, therefore, essential for organisations and requires proper planning and execution to generate high-quality software at appropriate time and cost. There are several activities involved in this developmental process of software such as coding, testing and management of the software development cycle. Not surprisingly, issues may arise during the software life-cycle, including underestimation of necessary programming effort, poor code and external aspects that implicate in risks to the project [39]. These challenges hinder the growth of businesses since it is considered the top priority for most organisations. The prediction, mitigation

© Springer Nature Switzerland AG 2021
A. Kalenkova et al. (Eds.): TMPA 2019, CCIS 1288, pp. 44–55, 2021.
https://doi.org/10.1007/978-3-030-71472-7_3

and identification of response actions to issues during software development are complex tasks often performed by human agents who use the information and employ subjective expertise [19]. The support and automating of such tasks have gained increasing attention in the literature. Researchers over the years have produced different ideas to enhance software development by introducing statistical and regressional models. Some of the prevalent statistical models used for this purpose include Bayesian networks [30], fuzzy logic [15] and system dynamics and discrete event simulation-based models [42].

The use of machine learning (ML) techniques has become increasingly popular in the context of software development [36]. ML is a subfield of artificial intelligence (AI) in which mathematical models identify patterns in the input data and reach a conclusion judging by the data. Thus, such algorithms can learn some information from the input (training data) and afterwards predict the answer for new data (test data). ML techniques include supervised learning, an approach characterised by the existence of prior knowledge of the input-output mapping for a training set; unsupervised learning, which algorithms proceed with no labelled data, and reinforcement learning (reward-based approach) [23]. There are two tasks supervised learning handles: regression (predicting a continuous numerical value) and classification (assigning a label to an item).

Software development is a very complicated process which includes many non-obvious things to consider when developing products. Reducing the number of software failures is one of the most challenging problems in software production. This survey aims to investigate different approaches and applications for the use of ML in the software development process.

The remaining of this paper is summarised as follows. Section 2 presents the main ML techniques employed for predicting and estimating programming effort. Section 3 shows how these techniques can be used to mitigate risks to the software project. Identifying software defects is performed in the Defects Section (Sect. 4). A discussion of the main findings from studies on ML embedded into software development processes is presented in Sect. 5. Suggestions for future work is shown in Sect. 6.

2   Predicting Programming Effort

Software effort estimation has received attention since the late 1970s and has been noticed to affect the workflow of the project and its overall success significantly. Moreover, programming effort underestimation often leads to missed deadlines and deterioration of the software quality. Effort overestimation, on the other hand, is one of the reasons for project deceleration [28]. Many software effort estimation methods have been proposed to accurately estimate effort as a function of a large number of factors. The most widely employed methods [36] include expert models and logical, statistical models (parametric models SLIM, COCOMO; regression analysis), traditional machine learning algorithms (Fuzzy Logic, Genetic Algorithms and Regression Trees) and Artificial Neural Networks. According to [36], the coding effort is most often estimated in lines of code (LOC), function points (FP) [13]; use case points (UCP) [1] or in labour hours [45]. This section depicts the most common approaches for software development effort estimation (SDEE) in the literature, as well as their characteristics.

The importance of accurate effort predictions and the demand for automation of the estimation process have motivated the researchers to propose first parametric models in the early 80s. These models were then tested on the software datasets comprised of the real industrial data of completed projects [21]. According to Srinivasan and Fisher, the three most prominent models are COCOMO, SLIM and Function Points [39]. COCOMO and SLIM models rely almost exclusively on source lines of code (SLOC) as a major input, while the function point approach utilises the number of transactions and other few additional processing characteristics (online updating and transaction rates). Despite being evaluated on the available historical data (COCOMO dataset), the above models have been proven to suffer from inconsistent performances due to the noisy nature of software datasets [2]. Bayesian Networks (BN) is a statistical model used for estimating Agile development effort [14]. Dragicevic, Celar and Turic outlined the benefits of BNs, which include the capability of handling vast uncertainties caused by the shortage of relevant information, subjective nature of a number of metrics and difficulties in gathering them [14].

Another common technique for predicting effort is expert estimation, which is suitable when the domain knowledge is not leveraged by the models [17]. Despite its popularity, expert systems exhibit considerable human bias. One example of such system is Planning Poker, a gamified baseline strategy for SDEE in Agile environments in which developers make estimates by playing numbered cards. In a study by Moharreri et al. Planning Poker was proven to overestimate in 40% of instances and was shown to have a very high MMRE score of 106.8% [27]. Parametric models and expert systems are still widely used in industry and studies; however, the need for better generalisation and overall performance has driven the researchers to apply machine learning methods [39].

Case-based reasoning (CBR) and decision trees (DT) have been among the most effective and researched ML models for SDEE [44]. Results of these models are highly interpretable and are recognised as superior or at least compatible with those of parametric and effort estimation models [5]. It was also asserted by Wen et al. that CBR is more suitable than DTs for this task since it is favourable towards smaller datasets, which is one of the biggest limitations in SDEE research [44]. It is worth mentioning that ensemble models that different methods are often used to gain even better precision. Moharreri et al. presented experimental evidence that DT, coupled with Planning Poker, produce better estimations than these models do on their own [27]. Genetic algorithms and fuzzy logic have been used in ensemble models, primarily handling feature selection and imprecise information provided in the datasets [44].

The idea of Artificial Neural Networks (ANNs, or simply NNs), a model that has proven its potential and outperformed traditional ML methods in many areas, was first proposed in the 1940s and inspired by biological neurons. ANNs are an attractive approach due to their remarkable computational power: an ability to learn nonlinear relations, high parallelism, noise tolerance, learning and generalisation capabilities [4]. The drawbacks of applying Neural Networks are as follows: a necessity of large datasets, computational expensiveness and the fact that the results are significantly less interpretable compared to traditional machine learning methods [22]. However, there are some methods to overcome this limitation of interpretability [40].

Comparative study of techniques such as regression tree, k-nearest neighbour, regression analysis and neural networks when applied for software development effort estimation has shown neural networks' best estimation ability [22]. Further consideration was given to neural networks by various researchers to emphasize their superior capabilities in effort prediction [13]. Thus, neural networks based models most often provide the best effort estimation compared to traditional ML and their accuracy increases with the amount of data supplied [3].

3   Predicting Risks to the Project

Several aspects can affect and abuse the software development cycle. Predicting risks is important because it helps to mitigate delays and unforeseen expenses and dangers to the project. As it was mentioned in [12], software development projects are more vulnerable to risks than other management projects as they have more technical uncertainty and complexity. Most developers look for a methodology to minimize the critical threats because the risk factor affects the success or failure of any project.

Hu et al. identified the four main types of risks [16]: schedule: the wrong schedule may break the development even at its very first stage; budget: the correct financing is a process that requires a careful consideration to avoid the risks in software development; technical: developers changing or fixing the unexplored code tend to make relatively large amount of mistakes before the details of the task become crystal clear. Even if the damage of one mistake is minor, a number of such errors can be a critical fact for the project; and management risks: risks which may include the bad working environment, insufficient hardware reliability, low effectiveness of the programming etc.

Wauters and Vanhouke proposed a method for continuously assessing schedule risks which uses support vector regression which reads periodic earned value management data from the project control environment, resulting in a more reliable time and cost forecasts [43]. The parameters of the Support Vector Machine were tuned using a cross-validation and grid search procedure, after which a large computational experiment was conducted. The results showed that the Support Vector Machine Regression outperforms the currently available forecasting methods. Additionally, a robustness experiment has been set up to investigate the performance of the proposed method when the discrepancy between training and test set becomes larger.

Wauters and Vanhouke proposed a method for continuously assessing schedule risks which uses support vector regression which reads periodic earned value management data from the project control environment, resulting in a more reliable time and cost forecasts [43]. The parameters of the Support Vector Machine were tuned using a cross-validation and grid search procedure, after which a large computational experiment was conducted. The results indicated that Support Vector Machine Regression is superior to the currently utilizes techniques for schedule risks prediction. The performance of the method has been checked with a robustness experiment in which the discrepancy between training and test set becomes larger.

Even a small number of technical mistakes could be a critical factor for the project. In [38], machine learning classifiers have emerged as a way to predict the existence of bugs in a change made to a source code file. The classifier is first trained on software history data and then used to predict bugs. Large numbers of features adversely impact scalability and accuracy of the approach. This technique is applied to predict bugs in software changes, and performance of Naive Bayes and Support Vector Machine classifiers is characterized.

Management risks in software development are one of the most global types of risks because if they exist, most of the time, they present the most prominent damage. [12] aimed to predict the risks in software development projects by applying multiple logistic regression. The logistic regression was used as a tool to control the software development process. The logistic regression analyses can grade and help to point out the risk factors, which were considerable problems in development processes. These analytic results can lead to the creation and development of strategies and highlighted issues, which are necessary to manage, control and reduce the risks of error.

4   Predicting Defects

Software fault prediction is a process which involves the use of software metrics and algorithms to detect software components prone to error. Testing is one of the most crucial steps of the software development life cycle as it involves a lot of time and effort. It is desirable to detect faults in software early in the software development life cycle in order to reduce software testing costs. In recent years, researchers have considered different approaches from machine learning to improve the effectiveness of software testing. [29] introduces a model of software testing which uses fault prediction to estimate cost-effectiveness.

In machine learning, the task of predicting which part of software prone to fault is known to be a classification task. Classification is the process in which the computer program learns from the data input given to it, alongside algorithms known as machine learning algorithms and then uses this learning to classify new observations. The idea behind these machine learning algorithms is for machines to learn and be able to predict faults in the future. For this learning to happen, they have first to identify the defects then classify them. In research, software metrics are put in place to help identify the faults and test the machine learning models. A lot of metrics are used, either method level metric or class level metric. Among them are lines Of code (LOC), weighted methods for class (WMC), coupling between objects (CBO), response for class (RFC), branch count, unique operand and total operand.

In the work of [11], Artificial Immune Recognition System (AIRS), an immune-inspired supervised learning algorithm, was used to create a defect model based on method-level metrics and Chidamber-Kemerer metrics suite. [10] on other research work examined nine classifiers for each of the five public NASA datasets. According to the research, the Naive Bayes algorithm provides the best prediction performance for small datasets, while Random Forest is the best prediction algorithm for large datasets. [35] compared four classifiers (Naive Bayes, K-star, Random Forest and SVM). Random Forest classifier showed better results for method level metric and SVM for class level metric. [24] used Random Forest, Adaboost, Bagging, Multilayer Perceptron, VM, Genetic Programming. Prediction models to estimate fault proneness using the dataset of Open Source "Apache POI" (pure Java library for manipulating Microsoft documents). The best result is shown by Random Forest and bagging algorithm.

An important issue in designing machine learning models for software fault detection is the imbalance of data sets. Most researchers focus on developing models which solve this imbalance either by directly influencing the data or not. [33] used the Asymmetric Kernel Principal Component Analysis Classification (AKPCAC) method based off of the kernel principal component regression algorithm proposed by [34] and Asymmetric Kernel Partial Least Squares Classier (AKPLSC) method. [25] use Fuzzy decision tree, a hybrid of fuzzy logic and decision tree which proves better than the decision tree approach.

In fault prediction studies, class level metric show better prediction performance compared to method level metric [20]. The primary machine learning algorithms used are Fuzzy Decision Trees, Random Forest, Bagging, AKPCAC, SVM, Naive Bayes, Regression Trees and K-Star. SVM and Random Forests provide best fault prediction models as SVM produces the best accuracy in detecting faults, and Random Forest is known to be suitable for massive datasets. On the whole, a lot of research uses various software metrics and improved machine learning algorithms to detect and predict faults.

Within development philosophies, DevOps is becoming an increasingly adopted approach, and attention is rising in both industry and academia giving rise to new projects, conferences and training programs [6–8,26]. Considering that the DevOps toolchain generates a large quantity of data allowing the extraction of information regarding the status and the evolution of a project, this domain is emerging as particularly suitable for ML applications for SD. Our team is currently working on the implementation of and an ML-based Anomaly Detection System (ADS), and we expect the research community to focus on this aspect increasingly.

5   Discussion

Machine learning techniques have been consistently used in the last decades to provide some assistance for generating high-quality software and a smoother development process. An overview of the literature shows that most of the research has been focusing on the task of predicting both software quality or error appearance. As a result, the software life-cycle is often shortened, and the maintaining costs reduced. Moreover, by predicting the occurrence of risks, project managers can mitigate delays and reduce the chances of project failures. The implications and limitations of the use of these computational techniques are discussed as follows.

The survey of the scientific papers on predicting programming effort has shown that machine learning models are continuously gaining popularity in the academic community. The complexity of applied algorithms is rising as more researchers focus on Deep Learning and continue refining less sophisticated ML models with optimisation algorithms [2]. The obtained results challenge the claims of [18] that expert estimation is the most reliable method of effort estimation. Instead, the study confirms the potential of ML models to provide reliable solutions to SDEE problem, which was first suggested by [39] as early as 1995. Empirical evidence of ML models' performance allows the developers to have greater freedom in selecting various models and tailoring them to a specific project. Subsequently, recent progress in the field encourages more and more publications on the topic. However, when it comes to direct applications in the industry, these models are not used as frequently as their reported performance would suggest. For instance, among Agile practitioners, 63% use Planning Poker as the primary estimation tool and 38% prefer expert estimation [41], despite the results of [27]. The reasons behind this phenomenon are a few limitations of the reviewed scientific papers that hinder the reliability of the results. Due to the lack of large software datasets to use as training data, the studies cannot confirm that their particular results will generalise to every real industrial project. Future studies should attempt to gather information about recent software projects, as the majority of currently considered datasets are outdated.

In the third section, we have wanted to consider the most popular types of risks related to software development, which we have chosen from [16], and decide which of them are more important for the development process. This information should be taken into account when considering how to manage a software project with minimal losses in the development process. We cannot decide which of these risks are most significant, so, as it was said in [12], developers and managers should take into account them all to design really good software project. Because of the big difference between considered risks, we should use different methods of Machine Learning. Further research is needed to observe a real IT project to find out which of the risks (schedule, budget, technical and management) may affect the development of the project the most negatively. We are also going to find out which risks can be predicted to the maximum extent using Machine Learning.

A substantial amount of research has been conducted with respect to predicting faults and defects using machine learning. The results of the survey undertaken show that in predicting faults, machine learning algorithms such as Naive Bayes, K-star, Random Forest and Support Vector Machine have proven to be very beneficial [20] and more favoured. Moreover, some researchers, such as [32] and [31] suggest that Case-based reasoning approach using similarity functions such as Euclidean distance and Manhattan distance to determine the most similar cases, yields encouraging results. While previous research failed to take into consideration the problem of dataset imbalance [37], the outcome of the survey demonstrates that the imbalance was accommodated. However, it is beyond the scope of this study to specify the metrics which are relevant in predicting faults. Further research has to make plans for generating new datasets as the available ones, mostly NASA and PROMISE, were used severally.

Table 1. Machine Learning for Software Development in academic literature.

Reference	Task	ML model	Data
Azzeh (2011)	SEE[a]	Decision Tree	PROMISE and ISBSG datasets
Bardsiri and Hashemi (2017)	SEE[a]	Regression Trees, ANN	ISBSG and NASA datasets
Baskeles, Turhan, and Bener (2007)	SEE[a]	Multilayer Perception, Regression Trees, Support Vector Regression	NASA and USC datasets
Catal, Diri, and Ozumut (2007)	SFP[b]	Artificial Immune Systems paradigm	PROMISE dataset
Ceylan, Kutlubay, and Bener (2006)	SFP[b]	Decision Trees, Multilayer Perception, Radial Basis Functions	NASA dataset
Clemente, Jaafar, and Malik (2018)	SFP[b]	ANN, Random Forest, Decision Trees, Naive Bayes, SVM	SeaMonkey, Mozilla Firefox
Dragicevic, Celar, and Turic (2017)	SEE[a]	Bayesian Network	Historical data
Hu et al. (2007)	SRP[c]	ANN, Support Vector Machine	Questionnaire based data
Joseph (2015)	SRP[c]	ANN	Oracle dataset
Karim et al. (2017)	SFP[b]	SVM, ANN, Naive Bayes, Random Forest	PROMISE dataset
Kim and Lee (2005)	SEE[a]	ANN, Regression Tree	ISBSG dataset
Marian et al. (2016)	SFP[b]	Fuzzy decision tree	JEdit(version4.2), Ant(version 1.7)
Moharreri et al. (2016)	SEE[a]	Decision Trees, Random Forest, Logistic Model Tree, Naive Bayes	IBM Rational Team Concert data
Nassif et al. (2016)	SEE[a]	ANN	ISBSG dataset
Panda, Satapathy, and Rath (2015)	SEE[a]	ANN	Zia dataset
Perkusich et al. (2015)	SFP[b]	Bayesian Networks	Case studies in software companies
Ren et al. (2014)	SFP[b]	Partial Least Squares and Kernel principal component analysis	NASA and SOFTLAB datasets
Sharma and Singh (2017)	SEE[a]	ANN, Fuzzy logic, Genetic Algorithms, Regression Trees	NASA, ISBSG, Desharnais and COCOMO datasets.
Shepperd and Schofield (1997)	SEE[a]	Case-Based Reasoning	Albrecht, Atkinson, Desharnais, Finnish and MM2 datasets
Wright and Ziegler (2019)	SEE[a]	Neural Hidden Markov Model, Deep Mixture Density Networks	LGTM dataset

[a]SEE: Software Effort Estimation
[b]SFP: Software Fault Prediction
[c]SRP: Software Risks Prediction

The overview of the literature shows that some ML techniques, namely case-based reasoning and neural networks, are particularly popular in this field, as shown in Table 1. Case-based reasoning is favoured due to its ability to produce high accuracy given limited data, while neural networks are popular due to their ability to learn complex functions and handle outliers [44]. The reported results build on existing evidence of the usefulness of ML embedded into the software development process. The reliability of such data, however, is affected by the limited available data and the lack of a united and shared dataset. These aspects indicate the need for the development of larger datasets that are representative of current tendencies in software engineering to provide researchers with quality training data and allow them to draw reliable conclusions. Future studies should take into account recent developments in the field of ML, such as reinforcement learning, convolutional and recurrent neural networks, providing their applications to software development, which have been scarce to the best of the authors' knowledge.

6   Conclusion and Future Research

The presented survey showcases considerable progress in the field over the last decades. Across three outlined subfields (effort estimation, risks and defects prediction) ML models have been deployed and achieved satisfactory results that are in the majority of cases comparable to traditional approaches or even surpass them. Literature analysis has also established that increasing research interest in this area provides practitioners with a variety of models to apply to their particular project. Given this abundance of models, comparative studies rarely reach consensus about whether traditional regression, classification or Deep learning approach is generally preferable in software development.

In the subfield of predicting risks to the software project regression models are considered dominant over other ML models as well as state-of-the-art non-ML methods. Expressly, the performance of Support Vector Machine is frequently noted in regards to predicting schedule and budget risks. On the other hand, defect prediction favours classification algorithms with Random Forest being one of the most reliable models. Research in programming effort estimation initially preferred regression models. However, recent breakthroughs confirmed superior accuracy by Cascade Correlation Neural Networks.

Notable gaps in the current state of the research on the topic include investigating the broader scope of applications for Artificial Neural Networks and reinforcement learning. Despite that ANNs have shown promising results in software effort estimation, the research about their applications in two other subfields have been rather scarce. A similar pattern is observed regarding Reinforcement learning, which was not yet applied to any of the software development tasks mentioned in this paper.

For future work, it is recommended that researchers attempt to use more massive datasets and those that are more representative of the current state of software engineering for the models' assessment to be complete and reliable.

Moreover, it is advised that closer interaction between academic and industrial communities needs to be established to facilitate deployment of ML models on real-world software projects.

References

1. Ajitha, S., Kumar, T.S., Geetha, D.E., Kanth, K.R.: Neural network model for software size estimation using use case point approach. In: 2010 5th International Conference on Industrial and Information Systems, pp. 372–376. IEEE (2010)
2. Azzeh, M.: Software effort estimation based on optimized model tree. In: Proceedings of the 7th International Conference on Predictive Models in Software Engineering, p. 6. ACM (2011)
3. Bardsiri, A.K., Hashemi, S.M.: Machine learning methods with feature selection approach to estimate software services development effort. Int. J. Serv. Sci. **6**(1), 26–37 (2017)
4. Basheer, I.A., Hajmeer, M.: Artificial neural networks: fundamentals, computing, design, and application. J. Microbiol. Methods **43**(1), 3–31 (2000)
5. Baskeles, B., Turhan, B., Bener, A.: Software effort estimation using machine learning methods. In: 2007 22nd International Symposium on Computer and Information Sciences, pp. 1–6. IEEE (2007)
6. Bobrov, E., Bucchiarone, A., Capozucca, A., Guelfi, N., Mazzara, M., Masyagin, S.: Teaching devops in academia and industry: reflections and vision. CoRR abs/1903.07468 (2019)
7. Bobrov, E., et al.: Devops and its philosophy: Education matters! CoRR abs/1904.02469 (2019)
8. Bruel, J.-M., Mazzara, M., Meyer, B. (eds.): DEVOPS 2018. LNCS, vol. 11350. Springer, Cham (2019). https://doi.org/10.1007/978-3-030-06019-0
9. Casale, G., et al.: Current and future challenges of software engineering for services and applications. Procedia Comput. Sci. **97**, 34–42 (2016)
10. Catal, C., Diri, B.: Investigating the effect of dataset size, metrics sets, and feature selection techniques on software fault prediction problem. Inf. Sci. **179**(8), 1040–1058 (2009)
11. Catal, C., Diri, B., Ozumut, B.: An artificial immune system approach for fault prediction in object-oriented software. In: 2nd International Conference on Dependability of Computer Systems (DepCoS-RELCOMEX 2007), pp. 238–245. IEEE (2007)
12. Christiansen, T., Wuttidittachotti, P., Prakancharoen, S., Vallipakorn, S.A.O.: Prediction of risk factors of software development project by using multiple logistic regression. ARPN J. Eng. Appl. Sci. **10**(3), 1324–1331 (2015)
13. Dave, V.S., Dutta, K.: Neural network based models for software effort estimation: a review. Artif. Intell. Rev. **42**(2), 295–307 (2012). https://doi.org/10.1007/s10462-012-9339-x
14. Dragicevic, S., Celar, S., Turic, M.: Bayesian network model for task effort estimation in agile software development. J. Syst. Softw. **127**, 109–119 (2017)
15. Engel, A., Last, M.: Modeling software testing costs and risks using fuzzy logic paradigm. J. Syst. Softw. **80**(6), 817–835 (2007)
16. Hu, Y., Huang, J., Chen, J., Liu, M., Xie, K.: Software project risk management modeling with neural network and support vector machine approaches. In: Third International Conference on Natural Computation (ICNC 2007), vol. 3, pp. 358–362. IEEE (2007)

17. Jørgensen, M.: A review of studies on expert estimation of software development effort. J. Syst. Softw. **70**(1–2), 37–60 (2004)
18. Jørgensen, M.: What we do and don't know about software development effort estimation. IEEE Softw. **31**(2), 37–40 (2014)
19. Jorgensen, M., Shepperd, M.: A systematic review of software development cost estimation studies. IEEE Trans. Softw. Eng. **33**(1), 33–53 (2006)
20. Karim, S., Warnars, H.L.H.S., Gaol, F.L., Abdurachman, E., Soewito, B., et al.: Software metrics for fault prediction using machine learning approaches: a literature review with promise repository dataset. In: 2017 IEEE International Conference on Cybernetics and Computational Intelligence (CyberneticsCom), pp. 19–23. IEEE (2017)
21. Kemerer, C.F.: An empirical validation of software cost estimation models. Commun. ACM **30**(5), 416–429 (1987)
22. Kim, Y., Lee, K.: A comparison of techniques for software development effort estimating. SYSTEM, p. 407 (2005)
23. Lison, P.: An introduction to machine learning. Lang. Technol. Group (LTG) **1**(35) (2015)
24. Malhotra, R., Jain, A.: Fault prediction using statistical and machine learning methods for improving software quality. J. Inf. Process. Syst. **8**(2), 241–262 (2012)
25. Marian, Z., Mircea, I.G., Czibula, I.G., Czibula, G.: A novel approach for software defect prediction using fuzzy decision trees. In: 2016 18th International Symposium on Symbolic and Numeric Algorithms for Scientific Computing (SYNASC), pp. 240–247. IEEE (2016)
26. Mazzara, M., Naumchev, A., Safina, L., Sillitti, A., Urysov, K.: Teaching DevOps in corporate environments. In: Bruel, J.-M., Mazzara, M., Meyer, B. (eds.) DEVOPS 2018. LNCS, vol. 11350, pp. 100–111. Springer, Cham (2019). https://doi.org/10.1007/978-3-030-06019-0_8
27. Moharreri, K., Sapre, A.V., Ramanathan, J., Ramnath, R.: Cost-effective supervised learning models for software effort estimation in agile environments. In: 2016 IEEE 40th Annual Computer Software and Applications Conference (COMPSAC), vol. 2, pp. 135–140. IEEE (2016)
28. Molokken-Ostvold, K., Jorgensen, M.: A comparison of software project overruns-flexible versus sequential development models. IEEE Trans. Softw. Eng. **31**(9), 754–766 (2005)
29. Monden, A., et al.: Assessing the cost effectiveness of fault prediction in acceptance testing. IEEE Trans. Softw. Eng. **39**(10), 1345–1357 (2013)
30. Perkusich, M., Soares, G., Almeida, H., Perkusich, A.: A procedure to detect problems of processes in software development projects using Bayesian networks. Expert Syst. Appl. **42**(1), 437–450 (2015)
31. Rashid, E., Patnayak, S., Bhattacherjee, V.: A survey in the area of machine learning and its application for software quality prediction. ACM SIGSOFT Softw. Eng. Notes **37**(5), 1–7 (2012)
32. Rashid, E.A., Patnaik, S.B., Bhattacherjee, V.C.: Machine learning and software quality prediction: as an expert system. Int. J. Inf. Eng. Electron. Bus. **6**(2), 9 (2014)
33. Ren, J., Qin, K., Ma, Y., Luo, G.: On software defect prediction using machine learning. J. Appl. Math. **2014** (2014)
34. Rosipal, R., Girolami, M., Trejo, L.J., Cichocki, A.: Kernel PCA for feature extraction and de-noising in nonlinear regression. Neural Comput. Appl. **10**(3), 231–243 (2001)

35. Shanthini, A., Chandrasekaran, R.: Applying machine learning for fault prediction using software metrics. Int. J. Adv. Res. Comput. Sci. Softw. Eng. **2**(6), 274–284 (2012)

36. Sharma, P., Singh, J.: Systematic literature review on software effort estimation using machine learning approaches. In: 2017 International Conference on Next Generation Computing and Information Systems (ICNGCIS), pp. 43–47. IEEE (2017)

37. Shatnawi, R.: Improving software fault-prediction for imbalanced data. In: 2012 International Conference on Innovations in Information Technology (IIT), pp. 54–59. IEEE (2012)

38. Shivaji, S., Whitehead Jr., E.J., Akella, R., Kim, S.: Reducing features to improve bug prediction. In: 2009 IEEE/ACM International Conference on Automated Software Engineering, pp. 600–604. IEEE (2009)

39. Srinivasan, K., Fisher, D.: Machine learning approaches to estimating software development effort. IEEE Trans. Softw. Eng. **21**(2), 126–137 (1995)

40. Sundararajan, M., Taly, A., Yan, Q.: Axiomatic attribution for deep networks. In: Proceedings of the 34th International Conference on Machine Learning, vol. 70, pp. 3319–3328. JMLR.org (2017)

41. Usman, M., Mendes, E., Börstler, J.: Effort estimation in agile software development: a survey on the state of the practice. In: Proceedings of the 19th International Conference on Evaluation and Assessment in Software Engineering, p. 12. ACM (2015)

42. Uzzafer, M.: A simulation model for strategic management process of software projects. J. Syst. Softw. **86**(1), 21–37 (2013)

43. Wauters, M., Vanhoucke, M.: Support vector machine regression for project control forecasting. Autom. Constr. **47**, 92–106 (2014)

44. Wen, J., Li, S., Lin, Z., Hu, Y., Huang, C.: Systematic literature review of machine learning based software development effort estimation models. Inf. Softw. Technol. **54**(1), 41–59 (2012)

45. Wright, I., Ziegler, A.: The standard coder: a machine learning approach to measuring the effort required to produce source code change. arXiv preprint arXiv:1903.02436 (2019)

The Conception of Strings Similarity in Software Engineering

Sergey Frenkel[(⊠)] and Victor Zakharov

Federal Research Center "Computer Science and Control" Russian Academy of Sciences,
Moscow, Russia
fsergei51@gmail.com, VZakharov@ipiran.ru

Abstract. Many tasks of modern software engineering, such as malware detection, attack recognition, Web Caching and Prefetching, etc., are based on the concept of distance between various data sets, e.g. between the strings of symbols. Such distances should express "similarity" between various data, e.g., the degree of similarity (or dissimilarity) between a suspected program and benign software.

In our previous works, some inequalities have been obtained that describe upper and lower bounds on Normalized Edit Distance (NED) values in terms of the Jaccard distance.

In this paper, based on this result we suggest and study the Averaged Normalized Edit Distance (ANED) as a new similarity metric which can be useful in classification-via-clustering problems. We show that ANED has well-interpreted properties, on the base of which it is possible to define a metric subspace on the strings space. The ANED based approximation can be used for various areas of data clustering, but in this paper we demonstrate the experiments showing the relevance of our approach to malware clustering for their detection issues. Traces used in our experiments come from the KVM hypervisor Runtime Execution Introspection and Profiling (REIP) system based on Virtual Machine Introspection (VMI) techniques to profile hooked Windows API calls.

Keywords: Similarity and distance · Software design for security · Malware detection

1 Introduction

The problem of assessing the similarity of data sets for classification purposes one way or another appears in various problems of informatics, such as web Cognitive Load analysis [1], web caching and Prefetching [2], web context analysis, malware detection, attacks recognition [3], etc. For the most part the similarity estimation is based on the concept of distance between the data sets, which expresses the degree of similarity (or dissimilarity), e.g. similarity of a suspected program to benign software [3]. Presently various similarity metrics were suggested and used in data classification through-clustering tasks [4], one of the most discussed is Jaccard distance J_D (or easily connected with J_D Jaccard similarity Index (JI) $J_S = 1 - J_D$) measure. Another metric is the Edit Distance (ED), namely,

A. Kalenkova et al. (Eds.): TMPA 2019, CCIS 1288, pp. 56–67, 2021.
https://doi.org/10.1007/978-3-030-71472-7_4

the minimal number of edit operations (delete, insert and substitute of a single symbol) required to convert one sequence (string) to the other [4, 13]. In order to normalize the ED to interval (0,1), the Normalized Edit Distance (NED) is often used [5, 6, 13].

The computational complexity of the NED is high, e.g., in comparison with the commonly used Jaccard distance. Moreover, when computing Jaccard measure, one can employ several approximation techniques, such as Locally-Sensitive hashing with MinHash [4], to dramatically speedup the clustering, classification and identification, what is absent for NED. Nevertheless, despite these difficulties, now ED/NED is seen as a highly desirable measure of similarity (distance) in such areas as optical character recognition, text processing, computational biology, cryptography etc., as it, from the point of view of the Machine Learning community, is a more acceptable measure for such complex structured information [7]. Note that ED-or-NED are often used not only as a characteristic of proximity, but as the cost of automatically converting one line to another for automatic language recognition/classification [8].

The analysis of the literature shows that although the researchers try to consider semantics in the tasks of assessing the similarity of texts [9], often in the tasks of programs developments, in particular, in the tasks of malware detection, the "similarity" regarding the difference of the data (e.g., in the benign-malicious behavior estimation) on an intuitive level only is considered, and accordingly, detection is carried out on the basis of numerical characteristics that have no obvious links with the property of being similar [9].

In the paper, we analyze some informal (and some formal as well) inferences from using of Jaccard-based similarity measure suggested in [10] which is based on JI approximation and reflects some properties of NED. We show, that under some insignificant updating suggested measure, it receives some property, enabling to reflect to some degree semantics of the compared string forms. The reason of why we can consider a relation between such different measures as Jaccard and NED is that the scope of our analytical results is so-called the representing strings, which is a result of original (raw) textual data shingling [4], taking into account that there is a solid evidence that these similarity estimation results can be applied to raw strings that have representation by n-gram with low repetitions (more explanations see in Sect. 3).

In general, the area of this paper refers to the range of such tasks for assessing and using similarity measures for which the effectiveness of using edit distance can be justified. Thus, what we do in this paper is to analyze to extent to which the applied approximation allows one to reflect the semantical differences of two strings.

Briefly, the contribution of this paper in comparison with [10, 11] is:

- it is shown that the average value obtained by averaging over the interval of possible NED values has specific properties that are different from both JD and NED, namely, the possibility to take into account the explicit dependence on the difference in sizes of the compared sets, the possibility of using the property of triangle inequality for clustering different subsets of strings,
- the relationship between the values of the true values, and the approximate values of JD, NED and their approximate estimates is shown, which can be useful when choosing threshold values for the conditions for assigning to clusters,

– we show, in fact, that well-known similarity measures, formally calculated without using any conditions for the semantics proximity of the objects being compared [9], can be transformed into measures more sensitive to semantic differences, with computational complexity similar to Jaccard metrics, with ability to reflect (a greater extent) the semantics differences of the compared data.

The rest of the paper is organized as follows. Section 2 is an analysis of the most popular metrics from the point of view of their ability to reflect the semantical differences of the data compared. Note that talking about "semantics" in this paper we mean simply the applied properties and goals of the compared data, without using any formal definitions of semantics (see, e.g. [12]). For example, if we deal with malware detection problem, we must think about how a similarity measure used for discrimination between malicious and benign behavior and results of their execution.

Section 3 explains and analyzes the measure of similarity suggested in [10]. A way to overcome the triangular inequality violation of traditional NED is shown. The technical aspects of the similarity measures computation are considered in Sect. 4. The results are discussed in the Sect. 5 and in Conclusion.

2 Data Similarity Conception

Before solving the problem of approximating a NED, let us consider what basic requirements the similarity estimates should meet. First of all, it must be based on a well-defined mathematically notion distance in a space. Formally, distance ("distance in a space") is a function D with nonnegative real values defined on the Cartesian product $X \times X$ such that D: $X \times X \to R^+$. It is called a distance metric on X if for every x, y, z $\in$ X:

$D(x, y) = 0$ iff_x = y (the identity axiom);
$D(x, y) + D(y, z) \geq D(x, z)$ (the triangle inequality);
$D(x, y) = D(y, x)$ (the symmetry axiom).

A set X, which is provided with a metric, is called a metric space.

The similarity $S(x, y)$ metrics considered as an inversion to the distance notion which must follow these rule, but be greater, the smaller the differences between the objects x, y, $S(x; x) > S(x; y)$, $x \neq y$, in particular.

Let us consider the case, when the data semantics imposes that the data to be some strings of ordered symbols. The traces of API system calls are an example.

From the practical viewpoint, the similarity definition problem is a combination of two subproblems: (i) what kind of similarity metric is most relevant to the compared data, and (ii) given a query string Q, how to use a similarity metric to search with suitable complexity (cost), in order to find all strings in a data set whose distances with Q is no more than a given threshold.

Let us consider two the most popular measures of similarity.

Jaccard Distance. The Jaccard distance J_D (or Similarity Index $J_S = 1 - J_D$) is often used for strings similarity estimation despite its intended use for simple (not multi-!) sets.

The Jaccard distance is $J_D(x, y) = |x \triangle y|/|x \cup y|$, where $\triangle$ denoted the symmetric difference between two sets x, y (that is x and y are considered as a unordered set of symbols from a given alphabet). Correspondingly, Jaccard similarity metrics $J_S(x, y) = 1 - J_D(x, y) = |x \cap y|/|x \cup y|$ is defind.

This metric can be interpreted as probability that random mapping by a hash-function h_i (different mappings for different i) do not repeat accidental collisions, that is probability $\Pr(h_i(x_i = y_i)) = J_S(x, y) + (1 - J_s)/2^k$ that a random permutation of the subsets (substrings, in particular) produces the same values, k is the number of bits mapped by the hash-function hi. The meaning of this consideration is that the probability that the Minhash function [4] for two sets equals the J_S of those sets, therefore there is a clear interpretation of similarity. It is important that J_S is a true metric in the space of sets with such distance, as the triangle inequality holds. This is why it may be effectively used in clustering algorithms. Moreover, in spite of obvious violation of the string's semantic, the using of Jaccard similarity is rather successful for clusterization of traces for malicious code detection [9]. The appropriate result in these applications is possible if the main difference between malicious and benign codes is the composition of system calls and their parameters.

However, in many cases, in view of the triviality of connection (noted above) between the similarity of J_S (or J_D) and the structure and semantics of program behavior data displayed in traces, an incorrect detection of the consequences of attacks is possible. For example, in the very topical problem of detecting Replacement Attacks [3], J_S of two traces can incorrectly reflect the change of control graph (representing dependencies between the system calls in the traces of the program execution [11]) because it takes into account the difference in the number of systems calls only but not the sequence of their interactions, since a significant change in the structure of the traces under the influence of attacks can only slightly change the value of J_S.

Most frequently, the text files are shingled into q-grams (sequences of q tokens/terms from the text) [4, 14], see an example in the Sect. 3, therefore, the distances/similarities are considered relatively to q-grams. That is Jaccard index on shingle sets S(d1), S(d2): $J_S(d1, d2) = |S(d1) \cap S(d2)|/|S(d1) \cup S(d2)|$ is used, where d1, d2 are the texts compared.

Edit Distance. Edit (Levenshtein) distance (ED) [13] takes into account (to a certain extent) the structure of compared symbol strings. It takes into account the location in a trace where the characters do not match (number of "insertion" edit operations), the location where the symbols of one string are missing in the other (number of "deletes" edit operations), and reflects more correctly, for example, the fact that with a given class of attacks, a slight change in the types of system calls (and, accordingly, a slight change in J_S) leads to a significant change in ED due to a change in the trace of structure. Thanks to this, it, for example, increases stemming from the input strings being "repetitive", which means that many of their substrings are approximately identical, while J_D may be insensitive to such specific features of the structure.

This string similarity metric captures both similarities in the overall structure of the two sentences being compared as well as some similarity between different word forms [15].

But in general, ordering of objects in the strings compared (e.g., the ordering of web objects in web caching and prefetching prediction task [2]) is not explicitly reflected in the ED. Further, although ED computes the distance for string of different lengths, the degree of influence of differences in these lengths on the value of ED is not reflected in any way in calculation models. Besides, the above-mentioned ability to interpret J_S as the probability of the hash coincidence of the two sections of the two compared traces, giving the possibility of a clear interpretation of their "similarity", is impossible for the ED.

So-called Normalized Edit Distance (NED) can enhance to some degree these aspects of ED using.

Normalized Edit Distance as Similarity Metric. Normalized Edit Distance of two strings x, y is [6]:

$$NED = ED(x, y)/\max(|x|, |y|) \tag{1}$$

and $SimNED(x, y) = 1 - ED(x, y)/\max(|x|, |y|)$, where $SimNED(x, y)$ is Normalized ED Similarity.

That is, a perfect match will have $SimNED(x, y)$ of 1.0, and completely dissimilar strings will be assigned a value of 0.0.

As it can be seen from (1), NED can be interpreted as a probability, that number of the transformation of the maximal (of two) strings (as well as minimal string to maximal one) requires $ED(x, y)$ edit operations.

However, strictly speaking, there is no the effective hashing algorithm to allow an interpretation of the probability as the probability of hash values (like for the J_S) [14], and the computation of ED and NED is time-consuming $O(n^2 \log\log n/\log^2 n)$, while there are efficient hashing based linear algorithms for approximating Jaccard distance for large data sets. But, what is important, the specific of ED computation (complexity increasing) is that in contrast to Jaccard (or Hamming) distance/similarity, when string comparison consists only in comparing string characters (without regard to their position, as in Jaccard, or standing at the same places in the strings, as for Hamming distance), it is necessary to consider the alignment operations, as associated with the requirement of minimal number of editing operations. This, in turn, ensures that a much larger specificity of the structure of strings is taken into account in terms of their similarity.

There is also the problem that in contrast to the J_D, the normalized edit distance NED does not satisfy to the triangle inequality, what may prevent computation-effective clustering of the maliciousness (or benign, depending on algorithm of machine learning based detection). Although so-called Generalized Edit (Levenshtein) Distance (GLD) was suggested [16], for which the triangle inequality is fulfilled, however, its calculation requires the selection of weights for the cost of performing editing operations, which can significantly increase the computational cost, which is significantly higher compared to J_D.

3   Jaccard Distance-Based NED Approximation

Let us assume that we know a Jaccard similarity (or distance) between strings x and y, which are considered as two sets of symbols corresponding their plain texts. How could we approximate normalized edit distance NED(x, y)? An obvious hurdle in the technique suggested, namely, using Jaccard as the basis for the approximation of NED is that these metrics are based on different mathematical concepts. Jaccard is defined over (unordered) sets, in which each different element appears only once, despite that it may occur many times in different parts of the set (document, in particular). Edit Distance is defined over strings and depends on the order of the symbols in the underlying strings.

In order to overcome the difficulties associated with this discrepancy, we confine the argument to certain types of sets and strings, both derived from the original documents (plain texts of the traces, in the case considered); the documents in question go through a shingling process (which collects all the substrings of certain length of appearing in the document), which is the first necessary stage in most of modern methods of similarity estimation [4, 9, 10]. The outcome of the shingling process is sets of n-grams (without repetitions), which will be used for computing Jaccard similarity (distance). Then, we create representing strings of the sets by sorting and concatenating their elements according to, say, lexicographic ordering, as described in Sect. 3.9.2 in [4]. As a result, we get strings of n-grams (string over the alphabet of the n-grams) that are sorted and has no repetitions.

For example, 3-gram of a fragment of API system calls trace, CreateFile, is.

`Cre rea eat ate teF e Fi Fil ile.`

These representing strings will be used for NED estimation. As it was shown in [10], the difference between NED on pairs of original texts (strings) and NED of their n-grams representation is decreased very fast as a function of the n-gram size, which proves the possibility to use the representing strings instead of the original texts.

Our experiment results showed that it is possible to choose n-grams (3-gram and more, we used up to 13-gram) that yield better than 7% average difference between the NED over the original documents, and the NED over the representing strings.

Thus, it justifies our choice to concentrate in analyzing the representing string as we do in the sequel. We note that in general, one may sample a given data set and tune the length of the n-grams for the given data set, taking into account the correspondence between the original document and representing strings, and then to proceeding with the clustering of the representing strings. Thus, such consideration allows to consider any data set as a string, and correspondingly, to define the problem of Jaccard based expression of NED.

This result is understandable as the more n-grams size the more symbols must be inserted/deleted/substituted on the same way as it requires ED computation algorithm for the plain text.

In [10] we received inequalities for the NED in terms of Jaccard metric that impose upper and lower bounds on the NED values:

$$1 - \alpha \le \text{NED}(x, y) \le (1 + \alpha)(J_D(X, Y)/(2 - J_D(X, Y)))$$

X, Y means the set of symbols, contained in the strings x, y (recall that we deal with representing strings $\{x, y\}$ obtained from original (raw) strings, that is J_D is distance between corresponding n-grams (Sect. 2), $\alpha = \min(|x|, |y|)/\max(|x|, |y|)$.

Let us average NED over the interval $[1 - \alpha, (1 + \alpha)J_D(x, y)/(2 - J_D(x, y))]$ (assuming the uniform NED distribution within this interval). Then we received the averaged NED depicted as ANED:

$$ANED(x, y) = (1 + \alpha(J_D(X, Y) - 1)/(2 - J_D(X, Y))) \qquad (2)$$

Leaving for now aside the question of the accuracy and usefulness of this averaging from the point of view of using strings for classification (for example, the traces classification as malicious and benign programs), the first significant result is that we express the average NED value through the values J_D which are computed by the hashing mentioned above.

ANED term α takes into account such an important factor of the editing distance as the fraction of characters that you need to "insert\delete\replace" to convert the string x to y (or vice versa). Accordingly, from the point of view of the program execution semantics, the magnitude of the similarity metric is not simply reduced to the ratio of the number of characters coinciding in them (n-grams, in particular), as is the case in the Jacquard distance metric.

The relationships between the ratio of the pair strings length, their Jaccard distance and the ANED are represented in Fig. 1.

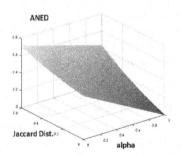

Fig. 1. Relationship between Average Normalized Edit Distance, ratio of strings pair α, and Jaccard Distance.

One of the very important Jaccard metric properties is *(d1, d2, P1, P2)-sensitivity* [15], that is:

if $J_D(x, y) \leq d1$ then Prob $[h(c) = h(y)] \geq P1$,
or, for Jaccard similarity:
$J_S(x, y) \geq d2$, then Prob$[h(x) = h(y)] \geq P2$.
where h(x), h(y) –hash-function implementing given permutation.

This property provides the ability to use the MinHashing algorithm to a good approximation of the estimate of the similarity of two sets [4]. Obviously, due to the uniformity relationship between the average NED and JD, we can find that our average Normalized editing distance (ANED) is also (d1, d2, P1, P2) -sensitive, which also indicates possibility of approximation based on LSH.

3.1 About Triangular Inequality for NED

As noted above, the triangle inequality does not hold for NED (unlike J_D and J_S), i.e. set of strings S with a given NED (also with SimNED) do not form a metric space. It means that for each strings x; y; z $\in$ S, it can be: SimNED(x, y) + SimNED(y, z) $\leq$ SimNEDD(x, z). Taking into account the formulae (1) we can formulate the requirement that the subset {x, y, z} be a metric space with the metric SimNED(x, y):

$$1 - ED(x, z)/\max(|x|, |z|) \leq 2 - ED(x, y)/\max(|x|, |y|) - ED(y, z)/\max(|y|, |z|)$$
(3)

We can rewrite the condition (3) relatively ANED (2) in an obvious way and can see that regarding ANED, a similar analysis for formula (2) shows that there are (continuous) regions {α, JD}, where, calculating $J_D(x, y)$, $J_D(y, z)$, $J_D(x, z)$ (and corresponding "alphas" for each pairs) we can find different subsets of triads {x, y, z} for which the triangular inequality is true. Note, that in practice the fact that for most pairs of traces there are always natural signs of their disagreement, for example, the J_S about zero (α is considerably less that 1 as well) allows us to exclude a significant number of cases from consideration, and increase the proportion of triads satisfying the triangle rule (see Sect. 4).

Correspondingly, it is possible to implement the effective clustering with ANED as a distance metric, say, using K-nearest Neighbour algorithm.

4   Similarity Model Validation

Now we demonstrate the rationality of our view on data set similarity estimation on an example dealing with traces of malicious programs recognition mostly represented in [10].

4.1 About Data Set

The data set is the records of the Windows API system calls of malware including a) the timestamp; b) the function name; c) all parameter values, and d) the return value.

We considered the traces subset (gathered in Taiwan National University [10]) focused on important and significant Windows API calls related to a) Files and I/O (Local file system), b) Windows System Information (Registry), c) Processes, and d) Dynamic-Link Libraries (DLLs). The order of the API system calls is perfectly preserved. There was access to two sets of malware traces and one set of benign traces are ready. The set has 272 malware samples (which fork 419 processes). According to VirusTotal, their first-seen dates were from August 2009 to October 2014. The benign data set contains about ten software (such as IE, Paint, Calc, CMD) of Windows XP and Win7's built-in software.

4.2 Similarity Metrics Measurement Issue

Similar traces can be grouped together using Locality Sensitive Hashing (LSH) in linear time with only a small increase in false negative results, hashes items into buckets several times, such that:

– similar items are hashed into the same bucket with high probability,
– items that are not similar enough are hashed into a common bucket with low probability.

Hence, there is a benefit of using a large number of buckets for maximizing the probability of collision of similar items.

4.2.1 Similar Traces Finding

In accordance with LSH technique [4] items that are mapped to the same bucket are considered as candidates for being similar. But there are no any strong methods to compute probabilities of real semantically-grounded similarity. In fact, J_S is just the probability that LSH maps two Jaccard-similar traces in the same bucket. When computing Jaccard measure, one can employ several approximation techniques, such as MinHash, to dramatically speedup the clustering, classification and identification.

The use the ANED estimation allows us to supplement the clustering technique outlined in the next section, by a scheme, where LSH provides Jaccard similar strings (traces) in the same clusters, (that allows us to check the NED for any item in the cluster, without accurate ED computation), and another technique we use is MinHashing [4] which is a compression method for sets of items that preserves the Jaccard similarity, that allows to work with much shorter same-length MinHash signatures.

5 Experimental Results of ANED-Based Approximation and Their Discussion

Figure 2 contains the main validation and explanatory data on topic of this paper. These results were obtained for 55 pairs of malware trace by LSH with Minhash [10].

For improved efficiency the text items are MinHashed into signatures, then LSH is performed on these signatures (integer vectors) using the banding technique [4].

First of all, note that ANED was computed by formula 2 not by accurate J_D values, but via its LSH-Minhash approximation. Certainly, this is more interesting from the practical point of view as LSH with Minhash allows reducing essentially J_D computation cost, that meet to the requirement to reduce NED cost computation as much as possible. It can be seen, that the behavior of ANED (regarding the pairs of compared trace s and ratios of their lengths α), computed by suggested approximation by ANED (star line), is the same the accurate NED values (solid line) in terms of increasing and decreasing values of both variables relative to the numbers of pairs and values to the ratio of their lengths. Moreover, Fig. 2 shows a rather good approximation of the NED by ANED.

Let's see how the given data allows to evaluate the fulfillment of the basic properties of NED in its approximation of ANED, and also how it allows understanding some

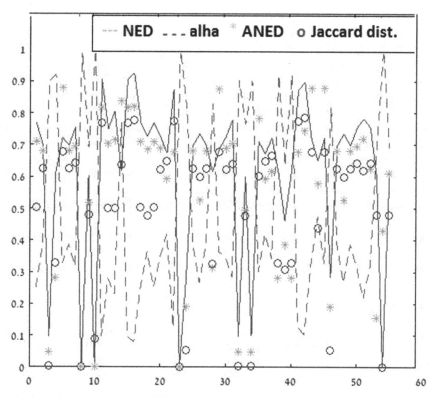

Fig. 2. J_D-based approximation of Normalized Edit Distance by ANED calculated through LSH estimations of J_D given the relationship between length of strings α.

possibilities to display certain properties of the semantics of words contained in the compared lines in ANED. Since, for strings of approximately equal length, the number of operations required to convert one string to another should be greater than the number of mismatched words (characters) in both strings (since, replacing one character with another (operation "substitution") also requires the operation "delete"), it is obvious that $J_D \leq$ NED. As we can see for Fig. 2, for the pair of traces with lengths for pairs of strings whose lengths are not dramatically different from each other (say, $\alpha > 0.8$) this relation also holds for ANED, in spite of that for ANED computation by formula (2) LSH Minhash approximations of J_D were used, not the J_D exact values. It means that the use of ANEDs corrects the situation when the use of Jaccard for sets with the same character set but organized as strings of different lengths gives a zero distance value, i.e., a complete match. At the same time, computational costs are equivalent to Jaccard computational cost.

As mentioned in Sect. 2, the main question of our study is to preserve the semantics of the similarity of the ED based measures despite the use of J_D for ANED computation. For example, API system calls "RegQueryValue" is often called sequentially in the Windows program and without taking into account the values of its arguments, it may not be possible to compare the equivalence of the traces of two different programs to detect possible malicious behavior. In this case, the parameters may differ more than a few characters, and the Jaccard distance for their n-gram representation can be close to zero, while the NED will give significantly higher distance values, i.e. the probability that one string (trace) transforms into another with probability which is equal to NED. As a result, using ANED can provide clustering that learns from the malicious dataset without any explicit descriptions of each malware or its class. Each hash table bucket, obtained during J_D computing as it mentioned above, is selected and used as its representative, then the binary (malicious/benign) decision by comparing each trace query against all medoids m_1, m_2,.., m_k (corresponding to the buckets mentioned above). If its maximal similarity to one of the medoids exceeds a predefined threshold t chosen as $max_{i=1, ...,:k}$ (ANED), then it is classified as malicious, otherwise it is classified as benign.

Some examples of buckets with computed average value of Jaccard and NED distances (as a threshold to be include in the bucket) and corresponding NEDs of shingled and original texts:

Bucket #290, has 6 traces: $J_D = 0.320966$, NED $= 0.320051$, NED(Orig. Text) $= 0.290116$, Bucket #437, has 5 traces: $J_D = 0.575048$, NED $= 0.575708$, NED(Orig Text) $= 0.613325$.

6 Conclusion

Many approaches to the similarity of different symbolic structures estimation are based on edit Edit Distance notion. In this paper we showed that the average value obtained by averaging over the interval of possible NED values has specific properties, namely, the possibility to take into account the explicit dependence on the difference in sizes of the compared sets, the possibility of using the property of triangle inequality for clustering subset of strings, in dependence on ratio of their length and the mutual features of pair of strings, expressed by Jaccard distance. That is the pairs $(\alpha, J_D(x, y))$ can characterize some semantical important properties of the string pairs, e.g., that the similarity of two traces x, y, is less than simple fraction of coincided symbols, as it takes place in the Jaccard distance metric. It means that for the tasks for which the effectiveness of using edit distance-based similarity have been justified, the edit distance-like measure can be transformed into measure more sensitive to semantic differences, with computational complexity like to Jaccard.

Acknowledgements. Research partially supported by the Russian Foundation for Basic Research under grants RFBR 18–07-00669, 18–07-00576 and 18–29-03100.

References

1. Tracy, J.P.: Measuring cognitive load to test the usability of web sites. University of Memphis, Memphis, USA (2007)
2. Kallurkar, P., Sarangi, S.: pTask: a smart prefetching scheme for OS for intensive applications. In: 49th Annual IEEE/ACM - International Symposium on Microarchitecture (MICRO-49), 15–19 October 2016, pp.1–12 (2016)

3. Ming, J., Xin, X., Lan, P., Liu, D., Mao, B.: Replacement attacks: automatically impeding behavior-based malware. In: Malkin, T., Kolesnikov, V., Lewko, A., Polychronakis, M. (eds.) ACNS 2015. LNCS, vol. 9092, pp. 497–517. Springer, Cham (2015). https://doi.org/10.1007/978-3-319-28166-7_24

4. Leskovec, J., Rajaraman, A., Ullman, J.D.: Mining of Massive Datasets. Cambridge University Press, Cambridge (2014)

5. Vidal, E., Marzal, A., Aibar, P.: Fast computation of normalized edit distances. IEEE Trans. Pattern Anal. Mach. Intell. **17**(9), 899–902 (1995)

6. Abdulalah, N., Arslani, I.: Efficient algorithms for normalized edit distance (2000). https://citeseerx.ist.psu.edu/viewdoc/download;jsessionid=00C048E4B2B4BD190985960DC69FED7F?doi=10.1.1.63.8070&rep=rep1&type=pdf

7. Kim, C.W.: NtMalDetect: a Machine learning approach to malware detection using native API system calls. arXiv:1802.05412v2, 19 (2018)

8. Chakraborty, I., Das, D., Goldenberg, E., Koucky, M.: Saks, V.: Approximating edit distance within constant factor in truly sub-quadratic time. arXiv:1810.03664 (2018)

9. Jang, J., Brumley, D., Venkataraman, B.S.: BitShred: feature hashing malware for scalable triage and semantic analysis. In: Proceedings of the 18th ACM Conference on Computer and Communications Security, CCS 2011, 17–21 October 2011, pp. 309–320 (2011)

10. Dolev, S., Ghanayim, M., Binun, A., Frenkel, S., Sun, Y.S.: Relationship of Jaccard and edit distance in malware clustering and online identification. In: Proceedings of NCA2017, pp. 369–373 (2017)

11. Frenkel, , Zakharov, V.: Brief Announcement: Graph-based and probabilistic discrete models used in detection of malicious attacks. In: Dinur, I., Dolev, S., Lodha, S. (eds.) CSCML 2018. LNCS, vol. 10879, pp. 184–187. Springer, Cham (2018). https://doi.org/10.1007/978-3-319-94147-9_15

12. Dennal, A., Benslimane, S.M.: A New measure of the calculation of semantic distance between ontology concepts. Int. J. Inf. Technol. Comput. Sci. **7**, 48–56 (2015)

13. Levenshtein, V.I.: Binary codes capable of correcting deletions, insertions and reversals. In: Soviet Physics Doklady, pp. 10–707 (1966)

14. Das, S., Pakray, P., Gelbukh, A.: Identifying semantic similarity using Levenshtein ratio. In: Proceedings of 10th International Workshop on Semantic Evaluation SemEval-2016, 1 January 2016, pp. 702–705 (2016)

15. Yuana, P., Wang, H., Chea, J., Ren, S., Xu, H.: Dechang approximate string similarity join using hashing techniques under Edit Distance constraints. J. Softw. **10**(9), 2721–2730 (2014)

16. Yujian, L., Bo, L.: A Normalized Levenshtein distance metric. IEEE Trans. Pattern Anal. Mach. Intell. **6**(29), 1091–1095 (2007)

Multi-perspective Process Mining with Embedding Configurations into DB-Based Event Logs

Sergey A. Shershakov$^{(\boxtimes)}$ (iD)

National Research University Higher School of Economics,
20 Myasnitskaya st., 101000 Moscow, Russia
sshershakov@hse.ru
http://pais.hse.ru

Abstract. Process mining is a research discipline that offers methods and tools for analyzing various processes. There are a variety of process mining techniques that have in common the use of an event log as a starting point for research. In most cases, it is a flat event log (for example, in the form of a text file) containing prepared information about events. Most information systems that work with large data use the technology of relational database management systems (RDBMS) for their effective storage and processing. Recently, there has been a trend towards greater integration of RDBMSs with process mining tools. With the direct interaction of a process mining tool with a database, it becomes possible to transfer part of the "costly" data preparation operations directly to the RDBMS level. This work represents an approach in which an arbitrary database is considered as a direct data source for process mining; that is, data are extracted without using intermediate flat logs and processed directly by process mining algorithms. An approach is proposed for translating event logs represented using RDBs into their abstract representation. There is described a novel method for embedding translation schemes inside a database in the form of so-called configurations, each of which corresponds to one data perspective/process view. This allows getting instrumented self-described DB event logs and switching between different embedded perspectives without rebuilding the logs.

Keywords: Process mining · DB event logs · RDBMS · Multi-perspective models

1 Introduction

Process mining is a research discipline that offers methods and tools for analyzing various processes [2,10]. Process mining is successfully applied in various

This work is supported by the Basic Research Program at the National Research University Higher School of Economics and the study was funded by RFBR according to the Research project No. 18-37-00438 "mol_a".

fields: research and optimization of business and technological processes, software development [5,6,16,17,20], education, medicine, etc.

Currently, a large number of different process analysis techniques have been developed in such disciplines as data mining (DM), machine learning (ML), business process management (BPM), etc. All these techniques are united by several key points. The most common are the use of an *event log* as a source of data with which they work, and a *process model*, which can be both the resulting and the input component of such a technique.

An *event log* is an entry point of any process mining task. Depending on a specific task, a log can be used more or less intensively. Two types of event logs are usually considered. 1) *Artificial event logs* are usually used in the development of new algorithms or to study the behavior of existing algorithms, they are generated in a special way (manually or with the help of special tools [13]) and contain data that have certain specific features. 2) *Real-life event logs* are the result of the work of information systems that support a particular process, or accumulate data that can be used for analysis after preprocessing. Real-life event logs tend to contain a huge amount of data. This leads to the presence of a number of issues, which should be considered while designing a log subsystem.

In most cases, the event log is a text file containing prepared information about events. Examples of formats used to represent such files are: MXML [1], XES [9], CSV, etc. Most of the tools currently developed for process mining are focused on event logs and are presented in this form. However, some tools use an internal representation to optimize the work with such logs. For example, such systems accept a log file for input, import data from it, and store these data in RAM. One of the main side effects of this approach is data duplication and size limitation determined by the size of RAM available for the process.

Most information systems (IS) working with large data use various technologies for their efficient storage and processing. One of the most common approaches is the use of *relational database* (RDB) technologies supported by various DBMS systems. Such databases may contain information that allows the analysis of related processes in various ways. This makes them an indispensable source of data for process mining.

Formerly, the approaches associated with the use of databases in process mining included various techniques for extracting and preparing these data in the form of so-called *flat event logs* [4], that is, performing controllable *export* of data from a database to an event log. Such flat logs could be directly used by process mining tools. Recently, there has been a trend towards greater integration of databases and RDBMSs with process mining tools. This is due to the fact that with the direct interaction of the process mining tool with a database, it becomes possible to transfer part of the "costly" data preparation operations directly to the RDBMS level, while using well-established and time-tested approaches for efficient storage and manipulation of large amounts of data.

In addition, the use of databases containing more information than required for the "traditional" process mining expands the possibility of a *multi-perspective process analysis*, which considers various aspects of a process or behavior of a certain system from different sides [12]. Further we will call such databases *enriched databases* (EDBs).

This work is devoted to the study of an approach in which an arbitrary database is directly a data source for process mining, that is, data are extracted without using intermediate models (flat logs) and processed directly by process mining algorithms. A key feature of this work is the development of an approach to translate *event logs represented using RDBs* into their *abstract representation* used by process mining algorithms. Moreover, the translation of EBD into an abstract event log can be carried out in many different ways, which generates various abstract logs. A review of each such abstract log provides a separate perspective for consideration, and many such abstract logs provide many perspectives used for multi-perspective analysis.

Another important feature of the work that distinguishes it from other works on this topic is a new way of *embedding* translation schemes directly into a database itself in the form of so-called *configurations*, which makes such an event log self-describing and self-contained. This allows the end user to simplify the work with such an event log by choosing an appropriate prepared configuration in a tool that supports such event logs. Developing and adding new configurations, in turn, is not a difficult task and can be performed directly by a data analyst without the need to write software extensions.

The approach proposed in this paper is focused on the specific SQLite RDBMS. However, it can be easily adapted to any other RDBMS with minor modifications or even without them.

The remaining part of the paper is organized as follows. Section 2 gives an overview of related work in the context of applying databases in the process mining domain. Section 3 introduces main idea of relating a DB-based log and an abstract log representation. An approach to embed perspective configurations into DB logs together with some implementation details is discussed in Sect. 4. Finally, Sect. 5 concludes the paper and discusses some directions for future work.

2   Related Work

One of the first works on relating logs presented in the form of relational databases to process mining techniques was [22]. It proposes a method for extracting a dataset for building *fuzzy maps* by preparing SQL queries and executing them with the help of the embedded SQLite DBMS. In the work, the SQLite database itself acts as an event log. The data generated and prepared by SQL queries are available for the algorithm of construction of fuzzy maps through independent components of the VTMine framework [11]. Such components are part of the general scheme of DPMine [18,19] preprocessing and data processing for building resulting fuzzy models.

In [22] there are is also an approach proposed for using the Cartesian product operator of a data set extracted from a DBMS and mapped onto an abstract event log to obtain event relations, a particular case of which is also known as direct follow relations (DFR). Thus, for the first time an attempt was made to transfer part of the resource-intensive operations performed by a certain process mining algorithm from a tool with which data analysis is performed to an auxiliary component, which a DBMS is.

The work [4] describes a comprehensive theoretical relationship between databases and flat event logs. This relationship is represented as an abstract model based, in particular, on *UML class* models, *Entity-Relationship* models and *Object-Role Modeling* models.

In [20], the authors use an event log presented in the form of a database. To do this, the flat event log is converted to the SQLite database format, and the database is normalized taking into account the subject area. The use of the database is determined by the flexibility that it gives when performing projection of the event log relative to some perspective. The generated database is used in the work in two ways. The first allows extracting a required perspective from the database by executing a corresponding SQL query. The extracted data are saved as a *flat event log* and analyzed using process mining tools: violations of expected behavior are detected through examining the model. Such violations are expressed in the form of anti-patterns and formulated in terms of metrics that determine numerical relationships between individual events. The found *anti-pattern* candidates are then "checked" by executing generalized SQL queries. These queries are based on the technique of obtaining event relations/DFR described in [22].

The work [15] considers the use of process mining to study processes that occur as a result of working with databases. Here, as the main data source are used so-called database redo logs stored by some DBMSs for the purpose of tracking a database operations that alter its state. This paper discusses a configurable concept of a *case* or a *process instance* by setting relations between a DBMS data model and an event log. *Flat event logs* are used as the latter. The proposed method is elaborated in a subsequent paper [14]. There, the authors propose a meta-model that allows combining a database and an abstract event log. The implementation of such a metamodel is based on SQLite, which is similar to how it was previously done in [22] and [20].

In [8], the authors discuss limitations of the then major XES standard [9] for exchanging event logs and propose a new approach, *Relational XES* (RXES), which completely maps a XES metamodel onto a relational database. The proposed database meta-model takes into account the specifics of the event logs from the point of view of process mining, but it is artificial, and the proposed RelationalXES framework allows working only with databases of such a structure.

The previous work continues with [23]. It proposes a scheme according to which the database is considered not only as a data source but also performs preliminary processing of event logs: it determines DFR in a way similar to that in [22] and [20]. In the subsequent work [7], the proposed approach for determining DFR was refined to a special DBMS operator H2, which allows optimization of SQL queries at the level of the DBMS engine.

One novelty of the paper as compared with the previous works is a definition of a set of queries that instrument a DB with event data to turn it into a prepared event log. Such an event log can be used with any process mining algorithm in a general manner in contrast with [22], where defined queries extract specific datasets to build only fuzzy map models. Another novelty is a method for embedding a number of different perspective configurations inside a DB. This allows switching between pre-defined perspectives by determining only a simple query.

3   A Database Approach for Representing Event Logs

There are possible different strategies for extracting data from event logs. These strategies are closely related to a specific problem and an algorithm used to solve it. We highlight some points that influence a strategy for storing data in and extracting data from an event log.

Slow IO Operations and Caching. For instance, some algorithms read an event log sequentially and do not need to go back to the previous point. In this case event data can also be extracted and processed from a serialized form of a log sequentially. In contrast, other algorithms use the same event data multiple times; thus, the use of the previous approach becomes inefficient from a time perspective due to repetitive IO operations. This problem can be eliminated by caching the event data, once read from a log, in RAM. Nevertheless, such an approach also has its overheads; generally, the amount of RAM is much more limited than the amount of persistent storage. Huge event logs simply cannot be mapped onto RAM, so a more sophisticated approach is needed here.

Filtering and Making Projections. Event logs often contain data that can be considered from different perspectives. Extracting a desirable perspective from a log usually includes the following operations.

(1) Attribute mapping. The abstracted representation of an event log is a multiset of traces, where each trace is an ordered sequence of events. Normally, a trace corresponds to a single instance of a process described by the log, and each event corresponds to some activity in the context of such a process; finally, ordering of events is done according to some time perspective.

   At the same time, in reality, an event log is often given in the form of a table with a number of various attributes related to the underlying process. So, at this step, mapping of real attributes onto those related to the process mining domain is needed. Three main attributes are *case number/trace*, *activity class* and *timestamp*. More specific problem domains also provide their attribute extensions. For instance, in the context of software process mining [17], a number of additional attributes (related to method invocations, classes, services and so on) can be requested.

(2) Events filtering. According to a context, only some classes of event activities have to be presented in an abstracted object model of a log [3]. Such filtering

Table 1. A fragment of an event log

Inv_ID	Unit_name	Action	Start_timestamp	Complete_Timestamp
17	office	init	2015-05-19 14:06:27	2015-05-19 14:16:13
17	acc	doc	2015-05-19 14:20:01	2015-05-19 14:43:31
20	office	mail	2015-05-19 14:25:49	2015-05-19 14:26:18
17	office	decide	2015-05-19 14:45:27	2015-05-19 14:48:04
20	mng	decide	2015-05-19 14:50:38	2015-05-19 14:55:36
21	mng	init	2015-05-19 15:17:24	2015-05-19 15:19:07
21	office	mail	2015-05-19 15:21:31	2015-05-19 15:24:58
21	acc	check	2015-05-19 15:22:04	2015-05-19 15:23:19

is referred to as a *horizontal projection*. Another type, *vertical projection*, is given by filtering only those traces that satisfy some criteria, for instance, being not older than some timestamp. It is also possible to define a more complex projection, which takes into account additional attributes. Filtering can be quite an expensive operation, especially when the related data (e.g. different events belonging to the same trace) are scattered along the whole log.

3.1 An Abstract Event Log and an DB-Event Log

In process mining, the event log is usually treated in an abstract form. Since one of the goals of this work is to compare the abstract form of the event log and its specific representation using the DBMS, herefrom follow basic concepts related to event logs and some other notations that are needed for explaining the approach.

Definition 1 (Trace, Event Log). *Let $\mathcal{B}(X)$ be the set of all multisets over some set X. Let A be a set of activities. A* trace *is a finite sequence $\sigma = \langle a_1, a_2, ..., a_i, ..., a_n \rangle \in A^+$. By $|\sigma|$ we denote trace length. $L \in \mathcal{B}(A^+)$, such that $|L| > 0$, is an* event log. *Here, $|L|$ is the number of all traces.*

Thus, we consider the abstract event log as a multiset of traces. In real life, an event log is represented using a set of attributed events. As a running example, we consider a fragment of an event log (Table 1). The columns of the table correspond to the attributes of the *events*, the rows correspond to the individual *events*. Such a table can be obtained in different ways. For example, it can naturally correspond to a CSV file in which one text line corresponds to one table row and represents an *event*, while the attributes of the events inside the line are separated using a *separator*. Another way to get such a table is to *linearize* the event log in XES format. In this case, one row of the table corresponds to one **event** element of a XES file, and the event attributes correspond to the children of the **event** element. Finally, such a table can correspond to a relation in a relational database, which in turn can be represented using a *DB table* or a *DB view*. Further, we consider exactly such an approach. To do this, we introduce some notations from relational algebra.

Definition 2 (Attribute, schema, relation). *Let Λ be a set of all possible strings. Then, $\alpha = (\lambda, D)$ is an* attribute, *where $\lambda \in \Lambda$ is the name of the attribute α and D is its domain. By $\xi = (\alpha_1, \alpha_2, ..., \alpha_n)$ we denote a* schema, *which is an (ordered) set of attributes α_i.*

Let $D_1, D_2, ..., D_n$ be domains (not necessarily distinct) of attributes $\alpha_1, \alpha_2, ..., \alpha_n$ of the schema ξ. Then $R = (\xi, D)$ is a relation *of these n attributes, where ξ is the relation schema and $D \subseteq D_1 \times D_2 \times ... \times D_n$ is a subset of the Cartesian product of the set of domains.*

That is the relation R is a combination of a schema and a set of n-tuples, each of which has its first element from the set D_1, its second element from D_2 and so on. By $e = R[i]$ we will denote the i-th tuple $e \in D$, starting with 1, and e_λ will refer to the value of the attribute λ of tuple e.

The event log (Table 1) is represented in the database as a relation $R_{L_1} = (\xi, D)$ (which can be either a DB table, a DB view or a result of executing some SQL query), with the *scheme* $\xi = ((\text{Inv\_ID}, \mathbb{N}), (\text{Unit\_name}, \Lambda), (\text{Action}, \Lambda), (\text{Start\_timestamp}, Datetime), (\text{Complete\_timestamp}, Datetime))$, where $\mathbb{N}$ is the set of natural numbers, used as a domain for the attribute "invocation id"; Λ is used as a string domain for the attributes "unit name" and "action"; *Datetime* represents a domain for the attributes "start timestamp" and "complete timestamp". The set of tuples D of the relation R is as follows: $R[1] = (\text{17}, \text{"office"}, \text{"action"}, \text{2015/05/19 14:06:27}, \text{2015/05/19 14:16:13})$, $R[2] = (\text{17}, \text{"acc"}, \text{"doc"}, \text{2015/05/19 14:20:01}, \text{2015/05/19 14:43:31})$, and so on. The order in which tuplets of D appear matters.

3.2 Relating DB Event Logs and Abstract Event Logs

The mapping of a specific set of event data recorded in the database onto an abstract event log is performed by executing SQL queries that prepare a dataset of a certain structure.

Let $DB = (R_1, R_2, ...)$ be a database including the relations $R_1, R_2, ...$, each of which can be represented using a *DB Table* or a *DB View*. In this example (Table 1), the database consists of a single relation: $DB_{L_1} = (R_{L_1})$. Let Q be an SQL query executed on a set of relations $\bar{R} \in \mathcal{B}(DB)$ of the database DB such that $R' = Q(\bar{R})$. The result of this query is a (possibly empty) relation R'.

To map the database $DB_{L_1} = (R_{L_1})$ onto the abstract event log L_1, one needs to set a *perspective* in it by defining a set of SQL queries and to determine which attributes of the relation R_{L_1} will act as a *case/trace identifier, activity* and *timestamp*. The latter is needed to organize the events within the trace.

Suppose that in the relation R_{L_1} each tuple represents one event record, that is, a set of attributes associated with some event $a \in A$. For definiteness, we assume that the table contains all 8 events that are available in the event log.

Next, we define the *Perspective 1* as follows. Let attribute $(\text{Inv\_ID}, \mathbb{N})$ serve as a process case and, hence, determine a *trace key*. Thus, the relation R_{L_1} contains three cases, namely the cases #17, #20 and #21, which are considered as three log traces. The trace #17 contains three events, the trace #20 contains two events and, and finally, the trace #21 also contains three events.

Then we map one of the attributes onto *activity* and choose another one to determine the order of events. This can be done in a number of possible ways. For instance, let *Perspective 1* be defined for the attribute Action as an *activity* and the attribute Start_timestamp as an *ordering key*. The resulting abstracted log viewed from *Perspective 1*, hence, will be as follows (we provide action names and by the indexes we denote tuple numbers of the corresponding events):

$$L_{p1} = [\langle init_1, doc_2, decide_4 \rangle, \langle mail_3, decide_5 \rangle, \langle init_6, mail_7, check_8 \rangle] \qquad (1)$$

To obtain specific data sets corresponding to components of this abstract log L_{p1}, we define the following SQL queries. Since an event log is a collection of traces, there is a query Q_1 (named qry1_traces) to extract such a collection:

```
SELECT Inv_ID FROM Events GROUP BY Inv_ID
```

The result of the query Q_1 is the relation $R_{Q_1} = (\text{Inv\_ID}, \mathbb{N})$, where $R_{Q_1}[1]_{\text{Inv\_ID}} = 17$, $R_{Q_1}[2]_{\text{Inv\_ID}} = 20$, $R_{Q_1}[1]_{\text{Inv\_ID}} = 21$ (hereinafter for brevity we will denote the values of the relations tuple by tuple, e.g. $[R_{Q_1}] = ((17), (20), (21))$, or simply $[R_{Q_1}] = \langle 17, 20, 21 \rangle$, if this does not create ambiguity). This set can be enumerated by values of its elements. Each element of the set is a key to extracting a corresponding trace by using the following query Q_2 (named qry1_get_trace_events):

```
SELECT Inv_ID as CaseID, Action as Activity, Start_timestamp as
   Timestamp FROM Events WHERE CaseID = ?1 ORDER BY Timestamp
```

Here we use *vertical projection*—the selection of necessary attributes with their renaming, and *horizontal*—filtering by event instance identifier (CaseID). Then, the Start_timestamp attribute in ORDER BY clause specifies the order of events in every case. Using time-related attributes for this purpose is straightforward. There is a single parameter ?1 in WHERE clause. The parameter is assigned where a specific trace is requested. For instance, by putting 17 as a value for this parameter, the query returns a dataset containing the following events: $[R_{Q_2}] = ((17, \text{"init"}, 2015\text{-}05\text{-}19\ 14\!:\!06\!:\!27), (17, \text{"doc"}, 2015\text{-}05\text{-}19\ 14\!:\!20\!:\!01), (17, \text{"decide"}, 2015\text{-}05\text{-}19\ 14\!:\!45\!:\!27).)$ The inclusion of the Inv_ID and Start_timestamp attributes in the resulting query is redundant, since, according to Definition 1, the trace is an ordered sequence of events. This is achieved by the following qry1_get_trace_events query:

```
SELECT Action as Activity FROM Events
WHERE Inv_ID = ?1 ORDER BY Start_timestamp
```

The result of its execution is a relation consisting of one attribute with the values $\langle \text{"init"}, \text{"doc"}, \text{"decide"} \rangle$.

To make available all operations applicable to the abstract event log, it is necessary to define 15 named SQL queries and 3 parameters (the attribute names *trace*, *activity* and *timestamp*). They return the total number of all events and traces, some individual attributes of events, a trace or the log itself and so on.

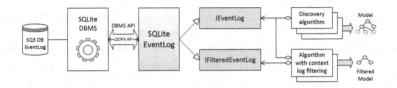

Fig. 1. The *EventLog* subsystem of the LDOPA library

The complete list of them can be found on the website[1] of the LDOPA library [21] implementing the proposed approach.

4   Implementation

The idea presented above is implemented as a part of the library LDOPA [21] called *EventLog*.

The setting using the SQLite DB as an event source is illustrated in Fig. 1. Here, the API of *SQLite*[2], which is implemented as a small library, is embedded directly to the *EventLog* subsystem of the LDOPA project. The most convenient feature is that an individual database is represented as a single file; this rather correlates to the "log as a file" idea.

The abstracted interface for event logs is represented as the IEventLog component. This interface is implemented by the SQLiteEventLog component, which uses the SQLite API for querying and extracting event data prepared in desirable projections. Then, these data are provided to algorithms in a standard form, namely a log as a multiset of traces, a trace as a sequence of events, an event as a collection of attributes.

There are several points behind this approach.

(1) Any complex structure of an existing database can be adapted to a desirable process mining projection without any data transformation. This is achieved by applying flexible features of SQL queries, which allows to apply attribute mapping, record filtering, to join separate tables etc. Moreover, it is a rather natural way to switch between different projections by applying different SQL queries.

(2) All steps of the preprocessing stage are moved out from the LDOPA library to a DPMS engine, for instance to the SQLite engine. It is rather clear that all mature DPMSs are suited to manipulate big amounts of data in the most effective way with the least overhead costs. In this way, instead of profiling home-grown filtering implementations, one can apply a well-tuned DBMS tool and simply use prepared datasets in process mining algorithms.

(3) It is possible to improve performance aspects of extracting data directly at the DB side without any changes at the tool side, i.e. in a transparent

---

[1] Available at https://prj.xiart.ru/projects/ldopa.
[2] Available at sqlite.org.

way. This is achieved by creating additional indices for attributes that are used in mapping to a process mining perspective (case id, activity, etc.). Moreover, table indexing allows obtaining a logarithmically fast access to random data in a log in comparison with the slow linear access provided by plain text structures (including XML/XES and CSV files). Overhead here is additional disk space to store the indices, but this cost is specifically cheap.

(4) Storing persistent data in a database is much more compact than in any text format, due to the binary representation of data and avoiding storing structure-handling elements.

4.1   Embedding Configurations into DB-Based Event Logs to Obtain Multi-perspective Process Mining

We consider again the example discussed in Sect. 3.2. In expression (1) we have an abstracted form of an event log projected to the *Perspective 1*. The standard approach based on a *flat event log* implies the necessity to export data from Table 1 as an individual log file, for instance `persp1.xes`. This log can also be projected in another way. Let *Perspective 2* this time use `Unit_name` as an activity and `Complete_timestamp` as an ordering key. Note, not only this projection provides different attributes extracted from events, but the order of events (7 and 8) is also changed:

$$L_{p2} = [\langle office_1, acc_2, office_4 \rangle, \langle office_3, mng_5 \rangle, \langle mng_6, acc_8, office_7 \rangle] \qquad (2)$$

Following the *flat event log* approach there is a need to export another projection from Table 1 as another file, `persp2.xes` correspondly. On the contrary, by using an instrumented DB-event log, we only need to ajust a perspective configuration only. To obtain data in accordance with this perspective, the `qryl_get_trace_events` query will change as follows:

```
SELECT Unit_name as Activity FROM Events
WHERE Inv_ID = ?1 ORDER BY Complete_timestamp
```

In general, for each perspective, one may need to redefine all of the above SQL queries and the parameters associated with them. Above we gave an example of such parameters, namely `qryl_traces` and `qryl_get_trace_events`. These parameters can be configured/set directly in the SQLite EventLog component, which allows certain flexibility. Nevertheless, configuring parameters in such a way is a bit complicated and, what is worse, it separates an event log configuration from event data. In order to eliminate this issue, we implemented an ability to embed a *log configuration* directly into the DB log.

We define the perspective configuration as a relation of the form: $R_C = (\xi_C, D_C)$ with the schema $\xi_C = ((\texttt{param}, \Lambda), (\texttt{value}, \Lambda))$ and the set of tuples D_C of the form: $\langle(\texttt{"qryl\_trace"}, \texttt{"SELECT Inv\_ID FROM Events GROUP BY Inv\_ID"}), \ldots\rangle$

Technically, this goal can be achieved by adding to the log's database a special table (e.g., named `Config`) containing such a configuration as a collection of param-value pairs (Table 2). Any dataset that consists of at least two columns with strings is suitable for this role. Such attributes must have predefined names

Table 2. Configuration table `Config`

param	value	persp
...	...	0
qryl_traces	SELECT Inv_ID FROM Events GROUP BY Inv_ID	0
qryl_get_trace_events	SELECT **Action** FROM Events WHERE Inv_ID = ?1 ORDER BY **Start_timestamp**	0
ev_act_attr_id	**Action**	0
...	...	
qryl_traces	SELECT Inv_ID FROM Events GROUP BY Inv_ID	1
qryl_get_trace_events	SELECT **Unit_name** FROM Events WHERE Inv_ID = ?1 ORDER BY **Complete_timestamp**	1
ev_act_attr_id	**Unit_name**	1
...	...	1

"param" and "value". This approach allows defining more than one perspective configuration, for example, by setting the number or name of a perspective as a separate attribute. For example, in Table 2, two configurations are defined with numbers 0 and 1, which can be queried from the database as follows (here the parameter `persp = 0` determines the perspective number):

```
SELECT param, value FROM Config WHERE persp = 0
```

The proposed approach underlies the following scheme for preparing and instrumenting an event log in the form of a database using the *SQLite EventLog* component of the *LDOPA* library.

1. Defining one or more process perspectives for extracting data from a specific database in the form of a set of SQL queries and related parameters.
2. Creating a configuration table that stores the parameters of (a) perspective(s).
3. Connecting a database using the *EventLog* component by setting two configuration parameters: the *name of the database file* and the *SQL configuration query* which extracts parameters of the current working perspective.

5   Conclusion

A new approach is proposed for the representation of data recorded in a database in the form of an abstract event log. The data are retrieved according to a specified process perspective set by the user. The perspectives are embedded directly in the event log in the form of *perspective configurations*, and then switching between them is carried out at the stage of connecting the event log to process mining algorithms by setting a simple SQL query. The proposed approach is implemented as a component of the LDOPA library, for the configuration of which two parameters are set: the database file name and the SQL configuration query. Further work on the topic includes development of an appoach for inheriting perspective configurations, which allows defining new configurations by overriding only necessary parameters instead of specifying a complete set.

References

1. van der Aalst, W.M.P., et al.: Business process mining: an industrial application. Inf. Syst. **32**(5), 713–732 (2007). https://doi.org/10.1016/j.is.2006.05.003
2. van der Aalst, W.: Process mining (2016)
3. van der Aalst, W.M.P.: Decomposing Petri nets for process mining. A generic approach (2012)
4. van der Aalst, W.M.P.: Extracting event data from databases to unleash process mining. In: vom Brocke, J., Schmiedel, T. (eds.) BPM - Driving Innovation in a Digital World. MP, pp. 105–128. Springer, Cham (2015). https://doi.org/10.1007/978-3-319-14430-6_8
5. Davydova, K.V., Shershakov, S.A.: Mining hierarchical UML sequence diagrams from event logs of SOA systems while balancing between abstracted and detailed models. Proc. Inst. Syst. Programm. RAS **28**(3), 85–102 (2016)
6. Davydova, K.V., Shershakov, S.A.: Mining hybrid UML models from event logs of SOA systems. Proc. Inst. Syst. Program. RAS **29**(4), 155–174 (2017)
7. Dijkman, R., Gao, J., Syamsiyah, A., van Dongen, B., Grefen, P., ter Hofstede, A.: Enabling efficient process mining on large data sets: realizing an in-database process mining operator. Distrib. Parallel Databases **38**(1), 227–253 (2019). https://doi.org/10.1007/s10619-019-07270-1
8. van Dongen, B.F., Shabani, S.: Relational XES: data management for process mining, pp. 169–176 http://ceur-ws.org/Vol-1367/#paper-22
9. Günther, C.W., Verbeek, E.: XES. Standard definition. TU/e, Den Dolech 2, 5612 AZ Eindhoven, P.O. Box 513, 5600 MB Eindhoven, 2.0 edn., 28 March 2014
10. van der Aalst, W., et al.: Process mining manifesto. In: Daniel, F., Barkaoui, K., Dustdar, S. (eds.) BPM 2011. LNBIP, vol. 99, pp. 169–194. Springer, Heidelberg (2012). https://doi.org/10.1007/978-3-642-28108-2_19
11. Kim, P., Bulanov, O., Shershakov, S.: Component-based VTMine/C framework: not only modelling. In: Kamkin, A., Petrenko, A., Terekhov, A. (eds.) Proceedings of the 8th Spring/Summer Young Researchers' Colloquium on Software Engineering, SYRCoSE 2014, pp. 102–107. ISP RAS (2014). http://syrcose.ispras.ru/2014/files/SYRCoSE2014_Proceedings.pdf
12. Mannhardt, F.: Multi-perspective process mining. Ph.D. thesis, Department of Mathematics and Computer Science, February 2018. proefschrift
13. Mitsyuk, A.A., Shugurov, I.S., Kalenkova, A.A., van der Aalst, W.M.P.: Generating event logs for high-level process models. Simul. Model. Pract. Theory **74**, 1–16 (2017)
14. de Murillas, E.G.L., Reijers, H.A., van der Aalst, W.M.P.: Connecting databases with process mining: a meta model and toolset. In: Schmidt, R., Guédria, W., Bider, I., Guerreiro, S. (eds.) Enterprise, Business-Process and Information Systems Modeling, pp. 231–249. Springer, Cham (2016)
15. de Murillas, E.G.L., van der Aalst, W.M.P., Reijers, H.A.: Process mining on databases: unearthing historical data from redo logs. In: Motahari-Nezhad, H.R., Recker, J., Weidlich, M. (eds.) BPM 2015. LNCS, vol. 9253, pp. 367–385. Springer, Cham (2015). https://doi.org/10.1007/978-3-319-23063-4_25
16. Rubin, V., Günther, C.W., van der Aalst, W.M.P., Kindler, E., van Dongen, B.F., Schäfer, W.: Process mining framework for software processes. In: Wang, Q., Pfahl, D., Raffo, D.M. (eds.) ICSP 2007. LNCS, vol. 4470, pp. 169–181. Springer, Heidelberg (2007). https://doi.org/10.1007/978-3-540-72426-1_15

17. Rubin, V., Mitsyuk, A.A., Lomazova, I.A., van der Aalst, W.M.P.: Process mining can be applied to software too! In: Proceedings of the 8th ACM/IEEE International Symposium on Empirical Software Engineering and Measurement. ACM, New York (2014)

18. Shershakov, S.: DPMine/C: C++ library and graphical frontend for DPMine workflow language. In: Kamkin, A., Petrenko, A., Terekhov, A. (eds.) Proceedings of the 8th Spring/Summer Young Researchers' Colloquium on Software Engineering, SYRCoSE 2014, pp. 96–101. ISP RAS (2014). http://syrcose.ispras.ru/2014/files/SYRCoSE2014_Proceedings.pdf

19. Shershakov, S.A.: DPMine graphical language for automation of experiments in process mining. Autom. Control. Comput. Sci. **50**(7), 477–485 (2016). https://doi.org/10.3103/S014641161607018X

20. Shershakov, S.A., Rubin, V.A.: System runs analysis with process mining. Model. Anal. Inf. Syst. **22**(6), 818–833 (2015)

21. Shershakov, S.: Enhancing efficiency of process mining algorithms with a tailored library: design principles and performance assessment. Technical report, National Research University Higher School of Economics (2018). https://www.researchgate.net/publication/332869308_Enhancing_Efficiency_of_Process_Mining_Algorithms_with_a_Tailored_Library_Design_Principles_and_Performance_Assessment_Technical_Report

22. Shershakov, S.A.: VTMine framework as applied to process mining modeling. Int. J. Comput. Commun. Eng. **4**(3), 166–179 (2015)

23. Syamsiyah, A., van Dongen, B.F., van der Aalst, W.M.P.: DB-XES: enabling process discovery in the large. In: Ceravolo, P., Guetl, C., Rinderle-Ma, S. (eds.) SIMPDA 2016. LNBIP, vol. 307, pp. 53–77. Springer, Cham (2018). https://doi.org/10.1007/978-3-319-74161-1_4

On DB-Nets and Their Applications

Marco Montali[ID] and Andrey Rivkin[(✉)][ID]

Free University of Bozen-Bolzano, Piazza Domenicani 3, 39100 Bolzano, Italy
{montali,rivkin}@inf.unibz.it

1 Introduction

The recent developments in the Business Process Management (BPM) community demonstrate a paradigmatic shift in the way complex systems are perceived [2,4,11]. Now, the "language" for describing such systems should not only consider both processes and (master) data dimensions, but also should be expressive enough to talk about their interplay. The recently introduced formalism of DB-nets [9] is an example of such language. DB-nets provide a new conceptual way of modelling complex dynamic systems that equally account for the aforementioned dimensions, and where the data dimension considers both local and persistent data. To correctly represent process and data dimensions in one model, DB-nets combine two conventional approaches such as coloured Petri nets (CPNs) with name creation and management, and relational databases. More specifically, in a DB-net: *(i)* master data are represented using full-fledged relational databases with constraints; *(ii)* the process logic as well as local data are captured using a variant of CPNs extended with special places whose content corresponds to a view on top of the underlying database; *(iii)* the task logic conceptually defines how the underlying database is updated. In this short paper we briefly introduce the formalism of DB-nets, showcase its currently existing applications and briefly discuss its future perspectives.

2 The Formalism

Here we provide a simplified definition of a DB-net by formalizing intro thee conceptual layers the three abstractions described above. For a more detailed definition refer to [9]. A *db-net* is a tuple $\langle \mathfrak{D}, \mathcal{P}, \mathcal{L}, \mathcal{N} \rangle$, where:

- $\mathfrak{D}$ is a type domain – a finite set of pairwise disjoint *data types* $\mathcal{D} = \langle \Delta_{\mathcal{D}}, \Gamma_{\mathcal{D}} \rangle$, where $\Delta_{\mathcal{D}}$ is a *value domain*, and $\Gamma_{\mathcal{D}}$ is a finite set of domain-specific (rigid) *predicates*.
- $\mathcal{P}$ is a $\mathfrak{D}$-typed persistence layer – a pair $\langle \mathcal{R}, \mathcal{E} \rangle$ where: *(i)* $\mathcal{R}$ is a $\mathfrak{D}$-typed database schema, i.e., a set of $\mathfrak{D}$-typed relation schemas $R(\mathcal{D}_1, \ldots, \mathcal{D}_n)$, with $\mathcal{D}_i \in \mathfrak{D}$ for $i \in \{1, \ldots, n\}$; *(ii)* $\mathcal{E}$ is a finite set $\{\Phi_1, ..., \Phi_k\}$ of $FO(\mathfrak{D})^1$ sentences (or queries) over $\mathcal{R}$, modelling *constraints over* $\mathcal{R}$.

---

[1] First-order (FO) logic extended with data types.

© Springer Nature Switzerland AG 2021
A. Kalenkova et al. (Eds.): TMPA 2019, CCIS 1288, pp. 81–87, 2021.
https://doi.org/10.1007/978-3-030-71472-7_6

- $\mathcal{L}$ is a $\mathfrak{D}$-typed data logic layer over $\mathcal{P}$ – a pair $\langle \mathcal{Q}, \mathcal{A} \rangle$, where $\mathcal{Q}$ is a finite set of $\texttt{FO}(\mathfrak{D})$ queries over $\mathcal{R}$, and $\mathcal{A}$ is a finite set of parametric atomic actions specifying which facts to delete from (and/or to add to) the persistent storage.[2]
- $\mathcal{N}$ is a $\mathfrak{D}$-typed control layer – a tuple $\langle P, T, F_{in}, F_{out}, F_{rb}, \texttt{color}, \texttt{query}, \texttt{guard}, \texttt{act} \rangle$, such that:
  - $P = P_c \cup P_v$ is a finite set of *places* partitioned into control places P_c and view places P_v (decorated as ⦿, connect to transitions only with read arcs).
  - T is a finite set of *transitions*, such that $T \cap P = \emptyset$.
  - F_{in} is an input flow from P to T assigning multisets of inscriptions (over $\mathfrak{D}$-typed variables) to input arcs.[3]
  - F_{out} and F_{rb} are respectively an *output* and *rollback flows* from transitions T to places P assigning multisets of inscriptions to output arcs.
  - $\texttt{color}$ is a color type assignment over P, mapping each place $p \in P$ to a cartesian product of $\mathfrak{D}$-types.
  - $\texttt{query}$ is a query assignment mapping each view place $p \in P_v$ to a query $Q \in \mathcal{Q}$, s.t. the color of p component-wise matches with the types of the free variables in Q.
  - $\texttt{guard}$ is a transition guard assignment over T assigning to each transition $t \in T$ a $\mathfrak{D}$-typed guard φ (i.e., a quantifier- and relation-free $\texttt{FO}(\mathfrak{D})$ formula), that is defined over t's input inscriptions.
  - $\texttt{act}$ is a partial function assigning actions from $\mathcal{A}$ to transitions from T.

While the input flow contains inscriptions that match the components of colored tokens present in the input places, the output/roll-back flow can also contain constants and special kind of variables called *fresh*, allowing to generate data values not already present in the net, nor in the underlying database instance. Elements of inscription tuples can be referenced in transition guards and action assignments (for instantiating action formal parameters with inscription bindings).

Example 1. To demonstrate a simple DB-net model, let us consider a simplified accommodation booking process in a travel e-commerce website. Using the website, a user should be able to search for various options by specifying a city and a period of stay. As soon as a suitable option is found, she is offered to complete a booking form. Upon its completion, selected accommodation is getting booked. Note that the website supports multiple user sessions running at the same time. This can create a situation in which two users are completing forms for the same accommodation option, but one of them is faster. The slower user then loses her chance to get accommodation and has to search for another one.

The persistence layer stores background data as well as data that persist across cases. In our scenario the website database comprises two relation

---

[2] As in STRIPS, we assume that when the same fact is asserted to be added and deleted during the same step, the higher priority is given to the addition.

[3] An inscription is a tuple $\langle e_1, \ldots, e_n \rangle$ of $\mathfrak{D}$-typed elements, where each e_i can be either a variable or a constant.

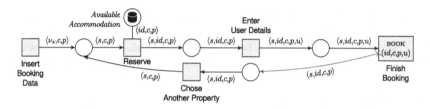

Fig. 1. The control layer of a DB-net for online booking. Here, ν_s is a fresh variable corresponding to a newly created session on the website, whereas c and p are two unbounded variables simulating user input for selected city and period of stay. The rollback output arc (corresponds to the rollback flow) is in red and decorated with an "x".

schemas: *Available*($\underline{\text{ID}}$: **int**, city : **string**, period : **string**) lists available accommodation options, whereas *Booked*($\underline{\text{ID}}$: **int**, city : **string**, period : **string**, data : **string**) lists the booked ones. Each relation is equipped with a primary key constraint defined on ID attributes.

We use view places to expose a portion of the persistence layer in the control layer, so that each token in every view place represents one of the answers produced by the query attached to the place. Such tokens are not directly consumed, but only read by transitions, so as to match the input inscriptions with query answers. In our scenario we would like to have access to available accommodations from the website database. To this end, we use a query that is formally defined as $Q_{\text{ava}}(id, c, p)$:- *Available*(id, c, p). Its SQL counterpart is **SELECT** id, c, p **FROM** *Available*. This query is then assigned to view place *Available Accommodation* in Fig. 1.

A transition in the control layer may bind its input inscriptions to the parameters of an action attached to the transition itself, thus providing a mechanism to trigger a database update upon transition firing (and, maybe, consequently change the content of view places). Here, the data logic layer provides a functionality for booking accommodation for specified period p using action BOOK(id, c, p, u) (with four formal parameters) that, upon execution, removes chosen accommodation with identifier id from the *Available* table, and then adds a new entry with the same id and customer data u to the *Booked* table. Formally it is specified using the following notation: BOOK·del = {*Available*(id, c, p)} and BOOK·add = {*Booked*(id, c, p, u)}. In Fig. 1, BOOK assigned to transition **Finish Booking** graphically appears in the grey transition box.

Note that **Finish Booking** has one rollback arc connected to it. This arc essentially models the aforementioned case of at least two users trying to book the same accommodation. Indeed, when consequently firing **Finish Booking** with two tokens carrying identical identifiers that correspond to the same accommodation option, the second triggered update of BOOK will violate the primary key constraint of *Booked*, and the net will follow the compensation flow.

Execution Semantics. Let us briefly recall the execution semantics of DB-nets, that has to simultaneously capture the progression of both persistence and control layers. To this end, at each point in time, the persistence and control layers are respectively associated with database instance $\mathcal{I}$ and marking m, in which content of view places must be compatible with that of $\mathcal{I}$ (i.e., it is aligned via queries assigned to view places). We shall refer to this as a DB-net snapshot, denoted as $\langle \mathcal{I}, m \rangle$. Next we informally define a transition enablement and a transition firing in a given snapshot.

By analogy with CPNs, the firing of a transition t in a snapshot is defined w.r.t. a so-called binding σ for t that substitutes all variables in the inscriptions on the arcs incident to t and, possibly, formal parameters of an action signature assigned to t with values from $\mathfrak{D}$. However, to properly enable the firing of t, the binding σ must satisfy three conditions: (i) there should be enough of tokens that mach inscriptions on the corresponding input arcs; (ii) the guard attached to t has to be satisfied; (iii) all fresh variables should be substituted with values that are pairwise distinct, and also distinct from all the values present in the current marking, as well as in the current database instance.[4] Now, if a transition is enabled, it can be fired. The firing, instead, has a threefold effect. First, all tokens in control places P_c are consumed according to matching input inscriptions. Second, the instantiated action assigned to t is applied on the current database instance $\mathcal{I}$. Since actions are atomic (i.e., the respect transactional semantics), one proceeds as follows. If the application is successful (i.e., the resulting instance of the persistence storage satisfies the constraints from $\mathcal{E}$), the database instance is updated (*commit*); if not, it is kept unaltered (*rollback*). Third, tokens are populated in target places according to output arc inscriptions and an output flow, that is going to be F_{out} in the case of commit and F_{rb} otherwise. Note that the latter is virtually an example of how a net can alter its behavior based on the manipulations with the persistent data.

All in all, the execution semantics of a DB-net is captured by a possibly infinite-labeled state transition system that accounts for all possible executions starting from their initial markings. While transitions in such LTSs model the effect of firing nets under given bindings, their states are represented with DB-net snapshots.

3   Current and Prospective Applications

DB-Nets for EAI. [12] studies an application of DB-nets to Enterprise Application Integration (EAI). EAI defines a set of technologies and services for integrating various applications in an enterprise using compositions of Enterprise Integration Patterns (EIPs) and their extensions. EIPs are adopted by various EAI system vendors in their proprietary integration scenario modelling languages. However, such languages are not grounded in any formalism, and thus may produce integration models that are prone to design flaws. To minimize the manual errors and allow for automatic analysis of the pattern correctness, EIPs should be formalised.

---

[4] Fresh variables is a typed analogue of ν-variables of ν-Petri nets [13]. They can appear only in actions as well as inscriptions of output and rollback flows.

Our work revealed that more versatile modelling formalisms are in high demand and, given growing interest in complex enterprise scenarios in which several inter-related business processes are linked together via shared data objects and events, DB-nets are very appreciated thanks to the conceptual tradeoffs they realize. Moreover, it appeared that DB-nets exhaustively cover all the requirements for EIPs and their extensions mentioned in the most recent classification suggested in [12]. We demonstrated how to model EIPs using DB-nets and showed how such models can become operational in a prototype based on CPN Tools (http://cpntools.org/) and its extension library Access/CPN. Unfortunately, our work revealed that the verification of EIP models created in CPN Tools using the state exploration tool falls short, since the latter becomes non-operational in the presence of data generating third party extensions (i.e., those that populate data/tokens into the net model). In order to still guarantee some form of correctness, we opted for the validation via simulation. This, in turn, proved to be quite efficient since CPN Tools offers a range of analytic features (e.g., a generation of simulation performance reports) based on the simulation toolkit.

One of the drawbacks of this approach is that the functionality provided by CPN Tools and Access/CPN is rather limited and hampers fast and agile modelling of data-aware processes. For example, there is no approach that would allow for the on-the-fly specification of data acquisition functions (that, essentially, model data injection via unbounded variables appearing in output flows as well as action formal parameters of DB-nets). They must be implemented per DB-net model directly in the Java code of its extension. In order to overcome such limitations one could use Renew (http://www.renew.de/), proviso that modelling and simulation remain the main objectives. Notably, Renew supports high-level Petri nets and provides tighter integration with Java.

Formal Verification. It is easy to see that our formalism is Turing-complete. Nevertheless, given that DB-nets conceptually separate different aspects of a dynamic system, the formalism itself becomes an interesting model for fine-grained studies on how such aspects impact on undecidability and complexity of verification tasks, and how should they be controlled to guarantee decidability/tractability. For example, it is known that (un)decidability of reachability can be affected by the presence of ordered vs. unordered data types as well as (globally) fresh inputs [7], or by the presence of of negation in the queries used to inspect the persistence layer as well as the arity of relation schemas contained in it [1]. DB-nets do not only provide a comprehensive model to fine-tune all such parameters, but also allow to study how they interact with each other. We also consider the case in which, under certain *state-boundedness* restrictions that apply both to the database and the net (a state-bounded DB-net is still allowed to visit infinitely many different snapshots along its runs), one could show that by following a similar procedure used in [8], decidability results are derivable for model checking properties expressed in first-order variant of μ-calculus. Alternatively, one can leverage results on the verification of infinite-state systems using Satisfiability Modulo Theories (SMT) techniques. While these techniques typically only support verification of (variants of) safety properties, a large amount of available tools can be used for testing DB-net encodings in different FO theories. We are currently working on the realization of both ideas. It would be also interesting to study how to check or guarantee, using modeling strategies, that a DB-net is state-bounded.

In [10] we have shown that one can isolate a fragment of DB-nets (with the querying language being restricted to SELECT-FROM-WHERE SQL queries with WHERE clauses using only conjunctions of atomic formulas) for which there exists a bisimilar class of CPNs with prioritized transitions, name creation and management, and provided a translation for constructing the latter. Even though such class of CPNs differs from the more conventional one of Jensen [5] by allowing variables range over infinite domains, one can realize the injection of possibly fresh data values (the way it is done in DB-nets) directly in CPN Tools using the Comms/CPN library. Note that one can then exploit the translation to automatically construct a bisimilar CPN and inspect its state space using CPN Tools, proviso that the generated state space is finite. The finitness can be achieved by implementing a special abstraction technique directly in the net.

Finally, the formalism of DB-nets paves the way towards the formal analysis of additional properties, which only become relevant when CPNs are combined with relational databases. In particular two families of properties could be of high interest. The first is related to rollbacks, so as to check whether it is always (or never) the case that a transition induces a failing action. The second is related to the true concurrency present in a DB-net, which may contain transitions that appear to be concurrent by considering the control layer in isolation, but have instead to be sequenced due to the interplay with the persistence layer (and its constraints).

Modelling and Beyond. From the modeling point of view, DB-nets incorporate all typical abstractions needed in data-aware business processes. And existing tool support makes this formalism even more attractive for scenarios that also require simulation. For example, considering that a simulation of DB-nets produces a database instance populated by executing the control layer (and thus implicitly reflecting its footprint), the formalism could provide novel insights into the problem of data benchmarking [6], especially in the context of data preparation for process mining. Another interesting scenario has been recently proposed by Lomazova and Carrasquel [3], in which they aim at using a variant of DB-nets for modelling and validating trading systems. Interestingly, as the basis for their validation approach, they suggest to use simulation together with conformance checking from the domain of process mining. The latter is very challenging as it considers a multi-perspective approach in which one has to take into account the interplay between the net in the control layer (including its local data) and the persistent storage.

4   Conclusions

In this paper we provided a short summary of the formalism of DB-nets. This formalism can be seen as the marriage of colored Petri nets and relational databases, and can be used for modelling, enactment and verification of data-aware processes. We also discussed current and prospective applications. Given the preliminary theoretical results as well as studied use cases, we believe that the formalism could find multiple applications in different modelling and simulation settings, and also could be investigated towards more fine-grained verification scenarios.

References

1. Abdulla, P.A., Aiswarya, C., Atig, M.F., Montali, M., Rezine, O.: Recency-bounded verification of dynamic database-driven systems. In: Proceedings of PODS. ACM Press (2016)
2. Calvanese, D., De Giacomo, G., Montali, M.: Foundations of data aware process analysis: a database theory perspective. In: Proceedings of PODS (2013)
3. Carrasquel, J.C., Lomazova, I.A.: Modelling and validation of trading and multi-agent systems: an approach based on process mining and petri nets. In: Proceedings of the ICPM Doctoral Consortium (2019). http://ceur-ws.org/Vol-2432/paper4.pdf
4. Hull, R.: Artifact-centric business process models: brief survey of research results and challenges. In: Meersman, R., Tari, Z. (eds.) OTM 2008. LNCS, vol. 5332, pp. 1152–1163. Springer, Heidelberg (2008). https://doi.org/10.1007/978-3-540-88873-4_17
5. Jensen, K., Kristensen, L.M.: Coloured Petri Nets - Modelling and Validation of Concurrent Systems. Springer, Heidelberg (2009). https://doi.org/10.1007/b95112
6. Lanti, D., Rezk, M., Xiao, G., Calvanese, D.: The NPD benchmark: reality check for OBDA systems. In: Proceedings of EDBT, pp. 617–628. OpenProceedings.org (2015)
7. Lasota, S.: Decidability border for petri nets with data: WQO dichotomy conjecture. In: Kordon, F., Moldt, D. (eds.) PETRI NETS 2016. LNCS, vol. 9698, pp. 20–36. Springer, Cham (2016). https://doi.org/10.1007/978-3-319-39086-4_3
8. Montali, M., Rivkin, A.: Model checking petri nets with names using data-centric dynamic systems. Formal Aspects Comput. **28**(4), 615–641 (2016)
9. Montali, M., Rivkin, A.: DB-Nets: on the marriage of colored Petri Nets and relational databases. Trans. Petri Nets Other Model. Concurr. **12**, 91–118 (2017)
10. Montali, M., Rivkin, A.: From DB-nets to coloured petri nets with priorities. In: Donatelli, S., Haar, S. (eds.) PETRI NETS 2019. LNCS, vol. 11522, pp. 449–469. Springer, Cham (2019). https://doi.org/10.1007/978-3-030-21571-2_24
11. Reichert, M.: Process and data: two sides of the same coin? In: Meersman, R., et al. (eds.) OTM 2012. LNCS, vol. 7565, pp. 2–19. Springer, Heidelberg (2012). https://doi.org/10.1007/978-3-642-33606-5_2
12. Ritter, D., Rinderle-Ma, S., Montali, M., Rivkin, A., Sinha, A.: Formalizing application integration patterns, pp. 11–20 (2018)
13. Rosa-Velardo, F., de Frutos-Escrig, D.: Name creation vs. replication in petri net systems. Fundam. Inform. **88**(3), 329–356 (2008)

Pre-processing Network Messages of Trading Systems into Event Logs for Process Mining

Julio C. Carrasquel[1(✉)], Sergey A. Chuburov[2], and Irina A. Lomazova[1]

[1] National Research University Higher School of Economics, Myasnitskaya ul. 20, 101000 Moscow, Russia
{jcarrasquel,ilomazova}@hse.ru
[2] Exactpro Systems, Lenina ul. 20, 156013 Kostroma, Russia
sergey.chuburov@exactprosystems.com

Abstract. Process mining is emerging as an important discipline for the analysis, monitoring, and improvement of business and software processes. Methods from process mining are based on the use of formal models and event logs, i.e., describing respectively the expected and observed behavior of system processes. This approach can be leveraged by the software testing industry for the log-based analysis of trading platforms. In this light, this paper presents an approach to extract event logs for process mining from network messages of trading systems. In particular, these messages are Financial Information Exchange (FIX) protocol messages, which are related to trading sessions in order books.

Keywords: Process mining · Trading systems · Financial information exchange (FIX) protocol · Event logs · Data pre-processing

1 Introduction

The reliability and robustness of stock trading platforms [10] is widely recognized to be crucial for the stability and integrity of global financial markets [21]. The rapid increase in the volume of transactional data, and the growing complexity of the market rules and infrastructures have turned automated exchanges into very large distributed systems, which present significant testing challenges [9].

Moreover, quality standards to meet, such as the minimization of latency and overhead, make difficult the deployment of intrusive testing instrumentation within trading platforms. This is the reason why logs of these systems are often employed as an alternative to analyze their behavior [12]. A recent endeavor in this direction can be found in [11], where the authors propose a (user-assisted) log analysis framework, powered by different *data science* techniques. The framework is aimed to be a support for test engineers, providing

This work is supported by the Basic Research Program at the National Research University Higher School of Economics.

them an understanding of system states and possible behavior deviations. As an example, a practical experience using text analysis and clustering was also introduced in [11] for the diagnosis of *settlement* and *clearing* systems.

The usage of logs for analyzing the behavior of trading systems matches with the approach of process mining [4]. Methods from process mining take as input the so-called *event logs*. An event log is related to a system process, and it records a set of *cases*, such that each case represents an execution of the process (a process instance). A case consists of *events*, where each event is related to some process activity. Fueled by event logs, process mining methods allow to construct process models from *observed behavior* (process discovery), to diagnose deviations comparing logs against *expected behavior* described by formal models (conformance checking) [3,5,14], and to analyze process performance [13,15], among other capabilities. Research works have employed process mining to analyze software systems behavior and the interaction of users [18–20].

Thus, process mining can be integrated within the analysis framework of trading systems introduced in [11]. However, as Fig. 1 depicts, it is firstly required to pre-process system data sources (either from logging components or captured from network interfaces) into well-structured event logs that process mining methods may leverage afterwards.

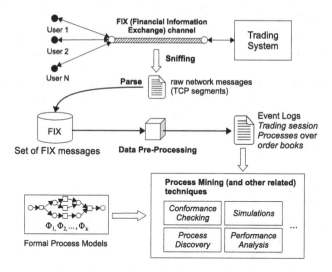

Fig. 1. The research scheme: from FIX messages to event logs for process mining.

This paper presents an approach to extract event logs for process mining from network messages of trading systems. In particular, we consider Financial Information Exchange (FIX) protocol messages [7]. FIX is a communication standard widely adopted in large-scale trading systems. Besides, in this work we focus on trading session processes in order books. These processes are carried out within trading system cores, and their correct execution is determining. In order books, submitted orders to buy or sell securities from market participants are ranked and crossed for trading, typically supported by a matching engine (see [10] for a detailed description of such processes). In such context, we present the approaches for extracting two types of event logs, each of them with a different notion of a case:

- **Order-based event logs:** Each case refers to the observed trace of an individual order submitted by a market participant, i.e., from an event when an order is submitted until an event in which such order is discarded, i.e., because it is *filled, canceled*, etc. Each case is identified by an order identifier.
- **Order-Book-based event logs:** Each case refers to the trading session of a financial security in an order book, i.e., from a first to a last event during a trading day related to orders trading a specific security. Each case is identified by a security identifier.

In this way, process mining methods can leverage *order-based* event logs to diagnose the behavior of executed orders, whereas using *order-book-based* event logs it is possible to analyze states of order books. Based on the approaches provided in this paper, we have developed a toolset (in Java programming language) to extract these two types of event logs from FIX messages; the toolset is available via [1]. The toolset includes a graphical interface to replay order-book-based event logs. The interface also can be used for simulation purposes. The results provided in this paper can be replicated to extract event logs for process mining to analyze other components of trading systems, as well as using other protocols similar to FIX.

The remainder of this paper is structured as follows. Section 2 introduces some basics about the FIX protocol, as well as some basic features of the message set used as input for extracting event logs. Section 3 describes the approaches to extract event logs for process mining from FIX messages. Finally, Sect. 4 presents some conclusions and future work.

2   The Financial Information Exchange (FIX) Protocol

The Financial Information Exchange (FIX) protocol [7] is a point-to-point communication standard for exchanging trading-related messages. It operates at the application layer over the TCP/IP stack. FIX is employed in many large-scale trading systems operating worldwide such as in the National Association of Securities Dealers Automated Quotation (NASDAQ) [16], or in the London Stock Exchange (LSE) [2]. In the following, we describe some basics of the protocol, as well as we present an example of some basic features of a set of FIX messages.

Message format. A FIX message is a sequence of ASCII-encoded tag-value pairs separated by the 0x01 control character; tags are integers indicating the meaning of the value. Figure 2 depicts a message from a trader, with identifier User1 (tag 49), to the trading system; The message can be read as follows: Tag 35 refers to the activity (message type) performed by the sender, i.e., the value

8=FIXT1.1	9=90	35=D	49=User1	56=FGW
version	*message length*	*message type*	*sender*	*receiver*
34=2	55=VTB24	54=1	40=2	
seq. number	*instrument*	*side (buy,sell)*	*order type (market,limit,....)*	
38=40	59=0	44=100	11=ORD1	10=197
order size	*time in force*	*price*	*order id*	*checksum*

Fig. 2. Example of a Financial Information Exchange (FIX) protocol message.

D stands for submit an order; tag 40 indicates which order type (*market, limit, stop, pegged*, etc.) is submitted—in this case, it is a limit order (2); tag 59 refers to the validity, i.e., how long this order will be alive—the value 0 stands for a day order; tag 54 indicates whether the user wants to buy (1) or sell (0). Thus, the user is submitting a `day limit order` configured to buy 40 stocks (tag 38) of the security VTB24 (tag 55) at a stock price of 100 (tag 44).

Table 1. A subset of some FIX messages related to the handling of orders [7].

Message type ⟨code⟩	*Description*
Client-initiated messages	
New order - single ⟨D⟩	*Submit* an order
Order cancel request ⟨F⟩	*Cancel* an order
Order cancel mass request ⟨q⟩	*Cancel multiple* orders
Order replace request ⟨G⟩	*Replace* an order
System-initiated messages (notifications)	
Execution report ⟨8⟩	Notifies a performed activity over an order
Order cancel reject ⟨9⟩	A cancel/replace request has been rejected
Order mass cancel report ⟨r⟩	A mass cancel request has been accepted/rejected

Protocol Layers and Message Types. The FIX protocol is divided in two layers: a session and an upper application layer. The session layer handles the maintenance of a session between a user and the system. Once a session is established, the upper application layer in each entity is enabled to transmit. FIX messages can be either session-level messages (*logon, logout, heartbeat*, etc.) or application specific. The message type is indicated in tag 35 (as depicted in Fig. 2). Trading systems provide a large set of application-related message types, i.e., for order handling, quote negotiation, market data subscriptions, etc. For instance, Table 1 presents a subset of application message types related to the order handling between clients and a trading system.

Message set for extracting *event logs*. As shown by Fig. 1, FIX messages used to extract event logs are captured from a system network interface during

Table 2. Some features of a network message set captured during a trading day.

TCP Segments (including just control segments)	988803
Valid FIX Messages	552935
First message (*event*) sent at	18-02-2019 02:14:31
Last message (*event*) sent at	18-02-2019 17:29:06
Number of individual orders to buy or sell	64539
Number of financial securities being traded	1144
Number of distinct market participants	593
FIX *Execution report* messages	138392

a trading day. The messages are encapsulated in network packet payloads, i.e., TCP segments. For this reason, we implemented a parser used in the toolset we developed (available via [1]) to extract FIX messages from TCP payloads. As Table 2 exemplifies, it is possible to extract basic information from a set of FIX messages, captured during a trading day, such as the total amount of orders executed, number of securities traded, number of market participants, etc.

3   Extracting Event Logs for Process Mining from FIX Messages

In this section we present approaches to extract event logs for process mining from a set of FIX messages. A set of FIX messages captured during a trading day contains the observed behavior of several trading system components, so event logs of different processes may be extracted. In this work, we consider specifically event logs related to the trading session process in *order books*, where orders from market participants to buy or sell securities are submitted, ranked and crossed [10]. We present techniques for extracting two types of event logs—*order-based* and *order-book-based* event logs. On the one hand, in *order-based* event logs each case is related to the trace of an individual order, so they allow to diagnose the observed behavior of a given set of orders. On the other hand, in *order-book-based* event logs each case refers to the trading session of a financial security in an order book, so this type of event logs can be useful to analyze states of order books. We point out that the performance in practice of these approaches depends on the number of input FIX messages. Notice that we consider a set of already captured messages (*post-mortem* data) and not online pre-processing, which can be instead a subject for further research.

In the following, we introduce some basic definitions related to event logs for process mining. Afterwards, we describe in detail the techniques for extracting the two mentioned types of event logs.

3.1   Basic Definitions

An *event log* L is a finite set of *cases* $\{c_1, c_2, ..., c_{|L|}\}$ related to a specific process. Each case $c \in L$ represents an execution of the process, and it consists in an *ordered sequence of events* $\{e_1, e_2, ..., e_{|c|}\}$. Each *event* e is related to the occurrence of an *activity* $a \in \mathcal{A}$, where $\mathcal{A}$ is the set of all activities. An event may have a timestamp t and other domain-specific attributes. Below we define the set of activities $\mathcal{A}$ for both types of event logs presented in this work. It represents some of the activities executed over orders. The set is defined using the values of the FIX tag 150 (of *execution report* messages) plus a *submit* activity (executed when a participant submits an order using a *new order* $\langle D \rangle$ message).

$$\mathcal{A} = \{new, replace, reject, cancel, expire, trade, trade\_cancel\} \cup \{submit\}$$

3.2   Extraction of Order-Based Event Logs

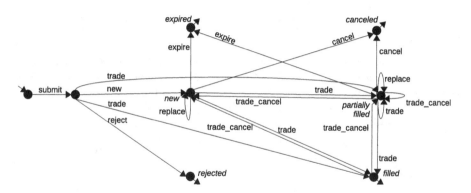

Fig. 3. *Order handling process* as a *transition system*; the node with a small inbound arrow represents the initial state, whereas nodes with small outbound arrows represent the final states.

We consider the extraction of order-based event logs. An order-based event log is related to handling process of individual orders. Each case in this log is an observed trace for a specific order—from an initial event when an order was submitted by a participant until an event when the order was discarded (because it was *filled, canceled*, etc.). Figure 3 depicts the order handling process as a *transition system*—nodes represent states of an order, whereas transitions denote *activities* fired over such order. Each activity a belongs to the set $\mathcal{A}$ presented previously indicating an activity fired over a specific order.

Algorithm 1 presents the procedure we implemented to extract an order-based event log L given a time ordered set $\mathcal{M}$ of FIX messages. We extract orders trading the same financial security, whose identifier *secId* is given as input. We consider a relationship 1:1 between a FIX message and an *event*, so in each iteration through the set $\mathcal{M}$ (ll. 2-35), a message m is used to create an

---

Algorithm 1: Extraction of Order-based Event Logs

    Input: $\mathcal{M}, secId$;
    Output: L;
1 $\mathcal{D} \leftarrow \emptyset,\; L \leftarrow \emptyset,\; I \leftarrow \emptyset$;
2 **foreach** $m \in \mathcal{M}$ **do**
3   **if** $secId \neq m.securityId$ **then**
4   **continue**;
5   **endif**
6    $t \leftarrow m.transactTime$;   `// timestamp (tag 60)`
7    $\mathfrak{s} \leftarrow m.side$;   `// tag 54`
8    $cid \leftarrow m.clOrdId$;   `// client-side order identifier (tag 11)`
9    $p \leftarrow m.ordType =$ *"market"* ? *"market"* : $m.price$;   `// tag 44`
10 $msgType \leftarrow m.msgType$;   `// tag 35`
11 **if** $msgType =$ *"D"* **then**
12    $a \leftarrow$ *"submit"*;
13    $s \leftarrow$ *" − "*;
14    $q \leftarrow m.qty$;   `// stock quantity to trade (tag 38)`
15    $e \leftarrow (cid, a, s, t, q, p, \mathfrak{s})$;
16    $\mathcal{D} \leftarrow \mathcal{D} \cup \{e\}$;   `// storing` *submit* `events to be added to cases`
17 **endif**
18 **if** $msgType =$ *"8"* **then**
19    $id \leftarrow m.orderId$;   `// (system-side) order identifier (tag 37)`
20    $a \leftarrow m.execType$;   `// an activity from the set` $\mathcal{A}$ `(tag 150)`
21    $s \leftarrow m.ordStatus$;   `// current order state (tag 39)`
22    $q \leftarrow m.leavesQty$;   `// current stock quantity (tag 151)`
23    $tr \leftarrow$ **null**;
24   **if** $a =$ *"trade"* $\vee$ $a =$ *"trade_cancel"* **then**
25      $tr \leftarrow m.trdMatchId$;   `// trade identifier (tag 880)`
26   **endif**
27   **if** $L.contains(id) =$ **false then**
28      $c \leftarrow$ **new** $case()$;
29      $L.put(id, c)$;
30      $I \leftarrow I \cup \{(id, cid)\}$;   `// relation of system and client order ids.`
31   **endif**
32    $e \leftarrow (id, a, s, t, q, p, \mathfrak{s}, tr)$;   `// create an event related to order` id
33    $L.get(id).add(e)$;   `// add the event into its corresponding case`
34 **endif**
35 **endfor**
36 **foreach** $e \in \mathcal{D}$ **do**
37   **foreach** $(id, cid) \in I$ **do**
38   **if** $e.id = cid$ **then**
39        $e.id \leftarrow id$;
40        $L.get(id).add(0, e)$;   `// place` *submit* `event at the case start`
41   **break**;
42   **endif**
43   **endfor**
44 **endfor**
45 **return** L;

---

event e. Thus, we use tag fields contained in the FIX messages to indicate states and attributes of orders when events occur.

Two kind of messages are used in Algorithm 1: *new orders⟨D⟩* and *execution reports⟨8⟩* (see Table 1). For each processed message m (ll. 2-35), if m is a *new order* message, then a *submit* event is created with some initial order attributes. Otherwise, if m is an *execution report*, then an event e is created, and added to its respective case c in the log L identified by the order identifier (tag 37).

Each event e is structured as a tuple $(id, a, s, t, p, q, \mathfrak{s}, [tr])$ where: id is a case (order) identifier (tag 37); $a \in A$ is an *activity* executed (tag 150); t is a timestamp (tag 60); s, q and p are the current *state*, *size*, and *price* of the order after activity a fired (tags 38, 151, and 44); and $\mathfrak{s} \in \{buy, sell\}$ indicates an order side (tag 54); an event e also may have a *trade identifier* tr (tag 880) if the activity a is a *trade* or a trade cancel—the motivation is to relate two events referring to the same trade (or trade cancellation) in two distinct cases.

Notice that *new order ⟨D⟩* messages do not contain the system-side order identifiers that we use as case identifiers (tag 37), but just a client-side identifier (tag 11). In Algorithm 1, both identifiers are extracted from *execution report ⟨8⟩* messages to relate to which case each new order message (*submit* event) belongs. Thus, *submit* events are added at the beginning of each case (ll. 36-44). Table 3 presents an event log extracted by Algorithm 1. It describes the execution history of 4 *limit* buy orders and 1 *market* sell order in an order book. Figure 4 depicts a *directly-follows graph*, obtained using Disco [8], which summarizes the observed behavior of orders in the event log of Table 3.

Table 3. An order-based event log consisting of 5 individual orders.

case	order (id)	activity (a)	state (s)	timestamp (t)	size	price	side	trade_id
1	Pl	submit	–	07.536000	100	9.0	*buy*	
1	Pl	new	*new*	07.537557	100	9.0	*buy*	
1	Pl	trade	*filled*	07.581175	0	9.0	*buy*	VE
2	Pm	submit	–	07.544000	100	8.9	*buy*	
2	Pm	new	*new*	07.545718	100	8.9	*buy*	
2	Pm	trade	*filled*	07.581175	0	8.9	*buy*	VF
3	Pn	submit	–	07.565000	100	8.57	*buy*	
3	Pn	new	*new*	07.566645	100	8.57	*buy*	
3	Pn	trade	*filled*	07.581175	0	8.57	*buy*	WG
4	Po	submit	–	07.572000	100	8.45	*buy*	
4	Po	new	*new*	07.573880	100	8.45	*buy*	
4	Po	cancel	*canceled*	11.236553	0	8.45	*buy*	
5	Pp	submit	–	07.579000	400	market	*sell*	
5	Pp	trade	*partially_filled*	07.581175	300	market	*sell*	VE
5	Pp	trade	*partially_filled*	07.581175	200	market	*sell*	VF
5	Pp	trade	*partially_filled*	07.581175	100	market	*sell*	WG
5	Pp	cancel	*canceled*	07.536000	0	market	*sell*	

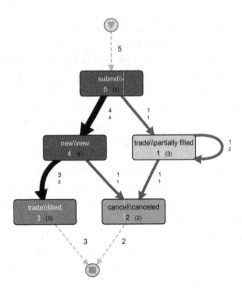

Fig. 4. Directly-follows graph describing execution of orders recorded in Table 3.

Thus, order-based event logs are suitable to analyze the behavior of a set of individual orders. Using this type of event logs it is possible to detect deviations of specific orders, i.e., to detect non-allowed transition movements checking against some reference model like the transition system in Fig. 3. Desired properties can be specified based on order attributes, i.e., using temporal logics [3], to verify whether or not orders in an event log meet these properties.

3.3   Extraction of Order-Book-Based Event Logs

Order-based event logs are limited to diagnose the behavior of individual orders, rather than capturing together how orders interact in an order book. The latter is useful to analyze states of order books. Hence, in this part we consider *order-book-based* event logs. In this type of logs, each case refers to a trading session of a financial security in an order book, i.e., from a first to a last event during a trading day involving the trading of a specific security. Each case is identified by a security identifier (FIX tag field 48). Thus, the trade of several financial securities during a trading day, each of them in a different order book, can be recorded in an event log.

Each event e in an order-book-based event log L_{OB} is defined as a tuple $(secId, a, t, o_1, [o_2], [tr])$ where: $secId$ is a case (security) identifier; $a \in \mathcal{A}$ is an activity fired; t is a timestamp; o_1 is an order involved in e, whereas o_2 an optional second order for events where two orders interact, i.e., in *trade* or *trade_cancel* activities; and finally, tr—an optional trade identifier. Orders o_1 and o_2 are tuples of the form $(id, s, q, p, \mathfrak{s})$ indicating an order identifier id, a current state s, size q, price p, and a side $\mathfrak{s}$. For these attributes, we use the same correspondence of FIX tags previously described for order-based event logs.

Let L be an order-based event log, i.e., obtained from a set $\mathcal{M}$ of FIX messages as explained in Sect. 3.2. Algorithm 2 extracts an order-book-based event log L_{OB} given L as input. We assume that orders in L may trade different securities, so events in L also have an attribute $secId$ indicating the securities that orders trade. As an example, Table 4 shows an event log L_{OB} extracted by Algorithm 2. This event log consists of just one case, the trading of a single financial security in an order book, since it used the same data of orders for the log of Table 3.

Algorithm 2: Extraction of Order-Book-based Event Logs

Input: L;
Output: L_{OB};
1   $\mathcal{E} \leftarrow \emptyset,\ L_{OB} \leftarrow \emptyset$;
2   **foreach** $c \in L$ **do**
3   **foreach** $e \in c$ **do**
4       $o_1 \leftarrow (e.id, e.s, e.q, e.p, e.\mathfrak{s})$;
5       $o_2 \leftarrow$ **null**;
6       $\mathcal{E} \leftarrow \mathcal{E} \cup \{\ (e.secId, e.a, e.t, o_1, o_2, e.tr)\ \}$;   `// assume secId in e`
7   **endfor**
8   **endfor**
9   $\mathcal{E} \leftarrow sort(\mathcal{E})$;   `// sort all events by timestamp and activity priority`
10 **foreach** $e_1 \in \mathcal{E}$ **do**
11   **if** $e_1.tr \neq null$ **then**
12   **foreach** $e_2 \in \mathcal{E}$ **do**
13   **if** $e_1.a = a_2.a \wedge e_1.tr = e_2.tr$ **then**
14          $o_2 \leftarrow (e_2.id, e_2.s, e_2.q, e_2.p, e_2.\mathfrak{s})$;
15          $e_1.o_2 \leftarrow o_2$;   `// merge together orders o1 and o2 in trade event`
16          $\mathcal{E} \leftarrow \mathcal{E} - \{e_2\}$;
17   **break**;
18   **endif**
19   **endfor**
20   **endif**
21   **if** $L.contains(e_1.secId) =$ **false then**
22      $c \leftarrow$ **new** $case()$;
23      $L.put(e_1.secId, c)$;
24   **endif**
25    $L.get(e_1.secId).add(e_1)$; `// add event to corresponding trading session`
26 **endfor**
27 **return** L_{OB};

Table 4. Order-book-based event log, using the data of orders in Table 3. In this example, there is just one case consisting of 14 events where 5 orders interact.

secId	a	t	order 1 (o_1)					[order 2 (o_2)]				
			id_1	s_1	q_1	p_1	s_1	$[id_2]$	$[s_2]$	$[q_2]$	$[p_2]$	$[s_2]$
1	submit	07.536000	Pl	–	100	9.0	buy					
1	new	07.537557	Pl	new	100	9.0	buy					
1	submit	07.544000	Pm	–	100	8.9	buy					
1	new	07.545718	Pm	new	100	8.9	buy					
1	submit	07.565000	Pn	–	100	8.57	buy					
1	new	07.566645	Pn	new	100	8.57	buy					
1	submit	07.572000	Po	–	100	8.45	buy					
1	new	07.573880	Po	new	100	8.45	buy					
1	submit	07.579000	Pp	–	400	market	sell					
1	trade	07.581175	Pp	partially_filled	300	market	sell	Pl	filled	0	9.0	buy
1	trade	07.581175	Pp	partially_filled	200	market	sell	Pm	filled	0	8.9	buy
1	trade	07.581175	Pp	partially_filled	100	market	sell	Pn	filled	0	8.57	buy
1	cancel	11.236553	Po	canceled	0	8.45	buy					
1	cancel	11.236553	Pp	canceled	0	market	sell					

3.4   Replay of Order-Book-Based Event Logs

We have developed a graphical interface (see Fig. 5) to replay order-book-based event logs, providing a convenient visualization of order book states (available via [1]). For example, event number 10 in the event log of Table 4 presents the situation of four buy limit orders, and a market sell order trading with the highest ranked buy order. While order-book-based event logs do not present directly such order book state, the replay capabilities of the interface show directly such situation. The interface operates in two modes: either reading event logs from a file, or receiving events in stream via sockets. The latter allows to connect the interface with modelling and simulation tools.

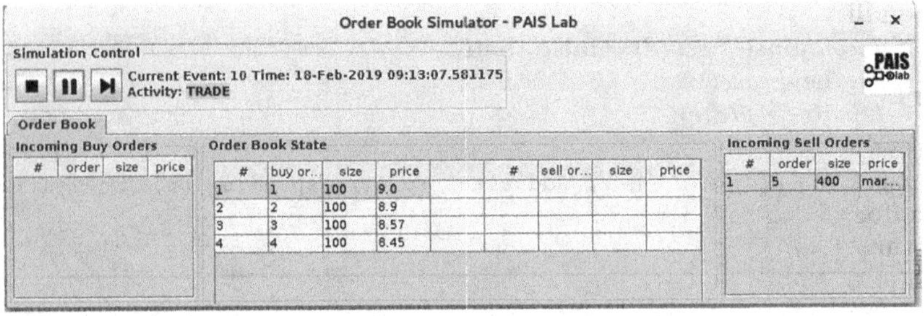

Fig. 5. Interface prototype for replay and visualization of order book states.

4 Conclusions and Future Work

In this paper, we presented an approach to extract event logs for process mining from Financial Information Exchange (FIX) protocol messages of trading systems. We present the extraction of two types of event logs: *order-based* and *order-book-based* event logs. In order-based event logs each case refers to the trace of an order. This allows to synthesize order behavior in process models, and to verify if these orders hold some desired properties. In order-book-based event logs, each case represents a trading session in an order book (related to a single security). Order-book-based event logs can be replayed to analyze order book states. We assumed independence between securities (isolated cases) for reducing the complexity when analyzing and replaying order books states [17]. We selected as event attributes some major order features (state, size, price, side, etc.). We studied event logs with two order types—limit orders and market orders (the latter behave as aggressive limit orders). We also developed a program (available via [1]) for extracting order book trading sessions such that all orders involved are exclusively limit or market orders. Our research is dealing with the construction of event logs for more complex scenarios integrating other order types, i.e., pegged orders, orders with stop conditions, or with non-visible quantities. Finally, it is of interest to integrate explicitly the behavior of market participants in the logs. In such context, a line of our research [6] addresses the development of a formal modelling language that can be suitable to describe the dynamics of trading sessions in order books, integrating the interaction of market participants. On the one hand, models based on such formalism may be useful for simulation. On the other hand, the models are aimed to be compared against event logs, like the ones presented in this paper, for conformance checking.

References

1. Laboratory of Process-Aware Information Systems (PAIS Lab) - Projects - Modelling and Validation of Trading Systems. https://pais.hse.ru/en/research/projects/tradingsystems
2. London Stock Exchange - MIT 202 - FIX Trading Gateway Issue 11 September 2018
3. van der Aalst, W.M.P., de Beer, H.T., van Dongen, B.F.: Process mining and verification of properties: an approach based on temporal logic. In: Meersman, R., Tari, Z. (eds.) OTM 2005. LNCS, vol. 3760, pp. 130–147. Springer, Heidelberg (2005). https://doi.org/10.1007/11575771_11
4. van der Aalst, W.: Process Mining: Data Science in Action, 2nd edn. Springer, Heidelberg (2016). https://doi.org/10.1007/978-3-662-49851-4
5. Carmona, J., van Dongen, B., Solti, A., Weidlich, M.: Conformance Checking: Relating Processes and Models. Springer, Heidelberg (2018). https://doi.org/10.1007/978-3-319-99414-7
6. Carrasquel, J.C., Lomazova, I.A.: Modelling and validation of trading and multi-agent systems: an approach based on process mining and petri nets. In: van Dongen, B., Claes, J. (eds.) Proceedings of the ICPM Doctoral Consortium. CEUR Workshop Proceedings, vol. 2432 (2019)

7. FIX Community - Standards. https://www.fixtrading.org/standards/
8. Fluxicon: Disco. https://fluxicon.com/disco/
9. Government Office for Science (United Kingdom): The Future of Computer Trading in Financial Markets: An International Perspective. Final Project Report (2012)
10. Harris, L.: Trading and Exchanges: Market Microstructure for Practitioners. Oxford University Press, Oxford (2003)
11. Itkin, I., et al.: User-assisted log analysis for quality control of distributed fintech applications. In: IEEE International Conference On Artificial Intelligence Testing (AITest), pp. 45–51. IEEE (2019)
12. Itkin, I., Yavorskiy, R.: Overview of applications of passive testing techniques. In: Lomazova, I., Kalenkova, A., Yavorsky, R. (eds.) Modeling and Analysis of Complex Systems and Processes (MACSPro). CEUR Workshop Proceedings, vol. 2478 (2019)
13. Jaisook, P., Premchaiswadi, W.: Time performance analysis of medical treatment processes by using disco. In: 13th International Conference on ICT and Knowledge Engineering (ICT Knowledge Engineering 2015), pp. 110–115 (2015)
14. Kalenkova, A.A., Ageev, A.A., Lomazova, I.A., van der Aalst, W.M.P.: E-government services: comparing real and expected user behavior. In: Teniente, E., Weidlich, M. (eds.) BPM 2017. LNBIP, vol. 308, pp. 484–496. Springer, Cham (2018). https://doi.org/10.1007/978-3-319-74030-0_38
15. Mannhardt, F., Arnesen, P., Landmark, A.: Estimating the impact of incidents on process delay. In: 1st International Conference on Process Mining (ICPM), pp. 49–56. IEEE (2019)
16. NASDAQtrader (FIX). https://www.nasdaqtrader.com/Trader.aspx?id=FIX
17. Protsenko, P., Khristenok, A., Lukina, A., Alexeenko, A., Pavlyuk, T., Itkin, I.: Trading day logs replay limitations and test tools applicability. In: International Conference on Tools and Methods of Program Analysis (TMPA 2014), pp. 46–53 (2014)
18. Rubin, V., Mitsyuk, A., Lomazova, I., van der Aalst, W.: Process mining can be applied to software too! In: Proceedings of the 8th ACM/IEEE International Symposium on Empirical Software Engineering and Measurement. ACM (2014)
19. Sahlabadi, M., Muniyandi, R., Shukur, Z.: Detecting abnormal behavior in social network websites by using a process mining technique. J. Comput. Sci. 10, 393–402 (2014)
20. Shershakov, S., Rubin, V.: System runs analysis with process mining. Model. Anal. Inf. Syst. 22, 818–833 (2015)
21. U.S Securities and Exchange Commission: Commission Roundtable on Technology and Trading: Promoting Stability in Today's Markets (2012). https://www.sec.gov/news/otherwebcasts/2012/ttr100212.shtml

Time Series Classification Based on Visualization of Recurrence Plots

Lyudmyla Kirichenko$^{(\boxtimes)}$ (ID) and Petro Zinchenko (ID)

Kharkiv University of Radio Electronics, Nauki ave. 14, Kharkiv 61166, Ukraine
`lyudmyla.kirichenko@nure.ua`

Abstract. Ordered data sets such as time series are found in almost all areas of human activity from cardiograms and to cyberattacks. Classification of time series is one of the most difficult tasks in data mining. In the article, a new method of time series classification based on the construction of recurrence plots is considered. The time series is transformed into a matrix, which characterizes the recurrence of the time series states, and the matrix is presented as a black-and-white image. Further, the convolutional neural network is used to classify the image. The application of the method is demonstrated by examples of simulated time series. A comparative analysis of the classification of noisy time series is carried out. The dependences of the classification accuracy on the noise level of time series are obtained. The results showed that the considered method has a high enough classification accuracy at high noise levels.

Keywords: Time series · Noise · Classification · Recurrence plot · Convolutional neural network

1 Introduction

Most of the processes occurring in the human body, nature, society, science and technology are complex, partly or completely random and have non-linear relationship. In practice, processes are presented in the form of corresponding time series, the properties of which make it possible to judge the properties of the generating process. The task of time series classification is one of the most difficult tasks of data mining. There are a number of approaches to the classification of time series, most of which are based on the calculation of various metrics between time series [1–5].

In the last few years, a number of studies have appeared in which the method of recurrent plots is used to classify time series. The recurrence analysis is based on such a property of the process as state repeatability, i.e. recurrence. In this case the recurrent properties of a time series are represented in the form of geometric structures and allow you to visualize the dynamics of the series. Methods of recurrence analysis were originally proposed in [6].

Over the past years, the recurrence plot method has been widely used for analyzing stochastic time series of various nature [7–11]. With the development of machine learning, recurrence characteristics calculated from time series began to be used as features for classification tasks [12–14].

© Springer Nature Switzerland AG 2021
A. Kalenkova et al. (Eds.): TMPA 2019, CCIS 1288, pp. 101–108, 2021.
https://doi.org/10.1007/978-3-030-71472-7_8

Another approach to the application of recurrence methods for classification is the time series recognition directly from the images of recurrence plots. Since the best tools for recognition and classification of images are deep neural networks, a number of researchers use them to classify recurrence plots [4, 15].

However, since such studies are fairly new, there has still not been enough attention paid to classify noisy time series. The purpose of the presented work is to conduct a comparative classification of noisy time series based on the visualization of recurrence plots.

2 Method of Recurrence Plots

In recent decades, the traditional methods for studying time series has been significantly replenished with the methods of the theory of nonlinear dynamics and chaos. In this case, the time series is considered as the evolution trajectory of some nonlinear system. The main point of application of nonlinear dynamics methods to the analysis of the dynamic system trajectory is what the system attractor, containing all the information about the dynamics and properties of the system, can be restored by only time realization [16, 17].

Recurrence analysis is one of such nonlinear dynamics methods used for time series and it is a tool for detecting not obvious dependencies in the dissipative dynamics. A recurrence analysis investigates the m-dimensional trajectory of a pseudo-phase space constructed by time realization. The well-known Packard-Tackens procedure [16] for constructing a pseudo-phase space from only realization allows one to restore the attractor of a dynamic system:

$$F(t) = [x(t), x(t + \tau), ..., x(t + m\tau)],$$

where $F(t)$ is m-dimensional pseudo-phase space, $x(t)$ is time realization, τ is delay time.

In turn, the recurrence plot is a projection of m-dimensional pseudo-phase space onto a plane. Let the point x_i corresponds to the phase trajectory $x(t)$ that describes the dynamical system in m-dimensional space at the time moment $t = i$ for $i = 1, ..., N$ then the recurrence plot RP is an array of points where a nonzero element with coordinates (i, j) corresponds to the case when the distance between x_j and x_i less ε:

$$RP_{i,j} = \Theta(\varepsilon - ||x_i - x_j||), \quad x_i, x_J \in R^m, \quad i, j = 1, ...N,$$

where ε is the neighborhood size of the point x_i, $\|x_i - x_j\|$ is distance between points, $\Theta(\cdot)$ is Heaviside function.

An important step in the construction of the recurrence plot is the choice of the distance metric. The most popular is Euclidean metric, where the shape of the neighborhood is a circle of radius ε and the maximum norm, where the shape of the neighborhood is a square with a side ε. In many cases, the choice of norm is not fundamental, but for each specific task it makes sense to experiment. The obvious fact is that for homogeneous series, the Euclidean norm will be suitable, and in the case of heterogeneous, sharply changing series, the maximum norm for which the neighborhood has a large area is more appropriate.

In this work, when constructing recurrence plots, we used a one-dimensional phase space $m = 1$, which allows us to significantly reduce the constructing time and the Euclidean metric.

3   Convolutional Neural Network

Convolutional neural network (CNN) is a special architecture of artificial neural networks, aimed at efficient pattern recognition [18, 19]. It is a prototype of the visual cortex. The visual cortex has the so-called simple cells that respond to straight lines at different angles, and complex cells, the reaction of which is associated with the activation of a specific set of simple cells. For example, some neurons are activated when they perceive vertical border, and some are horizontal or diagonal. All these neurons together form a visual perception. The idea that specialized components solve specific problems (like cells of the visual cortex that look for specific characteristics) is used in machine learning.

Thus, the idea of convolutional neural networks is to alternate convolutional layers and sub-sampling layers. The network structure is unidirectional (without feedbacks), fundamentally multilayer. For training, standard methods are used, most often the back propagation method of error. The function of activation of neurons can be different, according to the task. The architecture of the network got its name because of the convolution operation, the essence of which is that each image fragment is multiplied by the matrix (core) of the convolution element by element, and the result is summed and written to the same position in the output image.

The network works as follows. An image passes through a series of convolutional, nonlinear layers, union layers, and fully connected layers, and output is generated. The conclusion may be the class or probability of the classes that best describe the image.

The first layer in the CNN is always convolutional. It is a set of feature cards (these are ordinary matrices), each card has a synaptic core (scanning core or filter). The size of all cards of a particular convolutional layer is the same.

The core is a filter or window that slides over the entire area of the previous map and finds certain signs of objects. For example, if the network was trained on faces, then one of the cores during the learning process would give the greatest signal in the area of the eye, mouth, eyebrow or nose, the other core could reveal other signs. The size of the core is usually taken in the range from 3×3 to 7×7. If the size of the nucleus is small, then it will not be able to highlight any signs; if it is too large, the number of connections between neurons increases. Also, the kernel size is chosen so that the size of the convolutional layer cards is even, this allows you to not lose information when reducing the dimension in the subsample layer, described below.

When a picture passes through one convolutional layer, the output of the first layer becomes the input value of the 2nd layer. After applying a set of filters after the first layer, filters that represent higher level properties will be activated. The types of these properties can be half rings (a combination of a straight border with a bend) or squares (a combination of several straight edges). The more convolutional layers an image goes through and the further it moves across the network, the more complex the characteristics are displayed in the feature maps.

After convolutional layers, a pooling layer follows. It is also referred to as a down-sampling layer. In this category, there are also several layer options, with maxpooling being the most popular. This basically takes a filter (normally of size 2 × 22) and a stride of the same length. It then applies it to the input volume and outputs the maximum number in every subregion that the filter convolves around. The last type of layer is the layer of an ordinary multilayer perceptron. The purpose of the layer is classification, it models a complex nonlinear function, optimizing which improves the quality of recognition. The output layer is connected to all neurons of the previous layer. The number of neurons corresponds to the number of recognized classes.

Now we are ready to describe the overall architecture of our CNN. As depicted in Fig. 1, the net contains eight layers with weights; the first five are convolutional and the remaining three are fully-connected.

The output of the last fully-connected layer is fed to a 2-way softmax which produces a distribution over the 2 class labels. The neurons in the fully-connected layers are connected to all neurons in the previous layer. Max-pooling layers, follow second and fourth convolutional layer. The ReLU non-linearity is applied to the output of every convolutional and fully-connected layer.

The first convolutional layer filters the 256 × 256 × 1 input image with 8 kernels of size 5 × 5. The second convolutional layer takes as input the output of the first convolutional layer and filters it with 16 kernels of size 4 × 4. The third convolutional layer has 32 kernels of size 3 × 3 connected to the outputs of the second convolutional layer. The fourth convolutional layer has 64 kernels of size 3 × 3. The fully-connected layers have 1024 neurons each. For training the network was used Adam is an adaptive learning rate optimization algorithm.

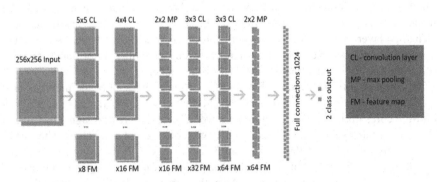

Fig. 1. Architecture of our convolutional neural network

4   Description of the Experiment and Results

As input time series in the work, we selected sinusoid time realizations with different periods of oscillation and different degrees of noise. Such series are typical models of real processes. We can present the time realization as the sum of a sinusoid component and a noise one: $X(t) = Y(t) + z(t)$, where Y(t) is time series, z(t) – additive noise. As a value characterizing the ratio of signal to noise, the coefficient Snr was used $Snr = S[Y(t)]/S[z(t)]$, where S is standard deviation. By changing the coefficient Snr we specify a different degree of noise in the time series.

To carry out the classification, the input time series were split into two classes. The first class consisted of sinusoids, for which the frequencies varied in the range $f2 \pm fR$, for the second class the frequency range was $f2 \pm fR$. The frequency choice to the sine wave from the ranges $f1 \pm fR$ and $f2 \pm fR$ was carried out randomly. The values $f1, f2$, fR, and $Fdist = |f1 - f2|$ varied during the experiment.

Figure 2 shows plots of noisy sinusoids with different frequencies and different noise degree. In this case, the length of the time series is 256 values. At the top of the Fig. 2, sinusoids from the lower frequencies class with parameter Snr values $= 1, 0.7$ and 0.4 are presented. The bottom of Fig. 2 shows examples of sine waves from the second class with the same values Snr.

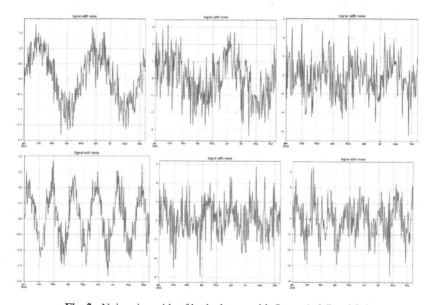

Fig. 2. Noisy sinusoids of both classes with $Snr = 1, 0.7$ and 0.4

Figure 3 shows the recurrence plots corresponding to the time series of both classes. On the left recurrence plots for time series without noise are shown, and on the right ones with noise at $Snr = 1$ are presented. When classifying, the training sample consisted of 200 time series of two classes (100 for one class and 100 for another), each of length 256 values. The test sample also included 200 time series. Such values were chosen in order to get the experimental conditions closer to typical real datasets.

Previously, recurrence plots of each time serie were obtained for input to the neural network. Thus, we have moved from time series to images that a neural network should recognize. A numerical experiment was conducted for different values of the parameters $f1, f2, fR$, $Fdist$ and Snr. Reseach have shown that without noise, the classes are

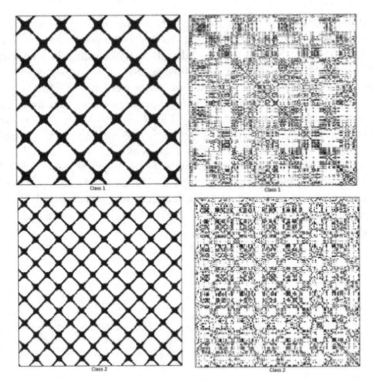

Fig. 3. Recurrence plots of time series without noise and with noise

distinguishable with an accuracy of 100% even when frequency ranges had a common boundary at the value $Fdist = 0$.

The main attention during the experiment was paid to increasing the noise level of the time series, i.e. reduction ratio Snr. The classification results showed very good accuracy at noise level $Snr > 0.6$. It should be noted that when decreasing Snr, the training time of the neural network (the number of epochs) increased from about 10 to 30. It is easily explained by the complexity of recognition at low values Snr.

Figure 4 presents a part of the test of recurrence plot sample that were fed to the input of the classifier with noise level $Snr = 0.7$. This sample is already classified by the neural network. At the top there are recurrence plots from the class with lower frequencies, and at the bottom there are ones from the second class.

Table 1 presents the classification accuracy and the number of epochs depending on the noise level Snr. It is worth noting that with an increase in size of the training sample to 400 values, the classification accuracy at ratio $= 0.4$ Snr increases to 0.811.

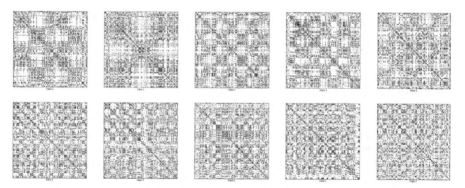

Fig. 4. Classified recurrence plots of time series of both classes at $Snr = 0.7$

Table 1. Classification accuracy and number of epochs

Noise level Snr	Accuracy	Number of epochs
1	0.992	10
0.7	0.967	14
0.6	0.945	17
0.5	0.778	24
0.4	0.66	29

5   Conclusion

In the work, a method for classifying time series based on the construction of recurrence plots using the simple architecture of a convolutional neural network have been investigated. A comparative analysis of the classification of noisy time series was carried out. The dependences of the classification accuracy on the noise level were obtained. The results showed that the considered method has a fairly high classification accuracy even with a large degree of noise. The results of the work can be used for the classification of time series of stochastic type by machine learning methods. In our future research we intend to concentrate on classifying real time series from known datasets.

References

1. Esling, P., Agon, C.: Time series data mining. ACM Comput. Surv. **46**(1), 1–34 (2012)
2. Ben, D: Feature-based time-series analysis. https://arxiv.org/abs/1709.08055. Accessed 07 Aug 2020
3. Bagnall, A., Lines, J., Bostrom, A., Large, J., Keogh, E.: The great time series classification bake off: a review and experimental evaluation of recent algorithmic advances. Data Min. Knowl. Discov. **31**(3), 606–660 (2017). https://doi.org/10.1007/s10618-016-0483-9

4. Fawaz, H., Forestier, G., Weber, J., Idoumghar, L., Muller, Pierre-Alain.: Deep learning for time series classification: a review. Data Min. Knowl. Discov. **33**(4), 917–963 (2019). https://doi.org/10.1007/s10618-019-00619-1

5. Buza, K.: Time series classification and its applications. https://doi.org/10.1145/3227609.322 7690. Accessed 07 Aug 2020

6. Eckmann, J.P., Kamphorst, S.O., Ruelle, D.: Recurrence plots of dynamical systems. EPL (Europhys. Lett.) **4**(9), 973–977 (1987)

7. Marwan, N., Wessel, N., Meyerfeldt, U., Schirdewan, A., Kurths, J.: Recurrence-plots-based measures of complexity and application to heart-rate-variability data. Phys. Rev. E, **66**(2), 026702-1–026702-6 (2002)

8. Marwan, N., Romano, M., Thiel, M., Kurths, J.: Recurrence plots for the analysis of complex system. Phys. Rep. **438**(5–6), 237–329 (2007)

9. Zbilut, J.P., Zaldivar-Comenges, J.M., Strozzi, F.: Recurrence quantification based Liapunov exponent for monitoring divergence in experimental data. Phys. Lett. A **297**(3–4), 173–181 (2002)

10. Ngamga, E.J., Nandi, A., Ramaswamy, R., Romano, M.C., Thiel, M., Kurths, J.: Recurrence analysis of strange nonchaotic dynamics. Phys. Rev. E **75**(3), 036222 (2007). https://doi.org/10.1103/PhysRevE.75.036222

11. Kirichenko, L.O., Kobitskaya, Y., Habacheva, A.: Comparative analysis of the complexity of chaotic and stochastic time series. Radioelectr. Inform. Manag. **2**(31), 126–134 (2014)

12. Kirichenko, L., Radivilova, T., Bulakh, V.: Classification of fractal time series using recurrence plots. In: 2018 International Scientific-Practical Conference Problems of Infocommunications. Science and Technology (PIC S&T), Kharkiv, Ukraine, pp. 719–724 (2018). https://doi.org/10.1109/INFOCOMMST.2018.8632010

13. Michael, T., Spiegel, S., Albayrak, S.: Time series classification using compressed recurrence plots. https://www.dai-labor.de/fileadmin/Files/Publikationen/Buchdatei/Publis hed.pdf. Accessed https://doi.org/10.1145/3227609.3227690

14. Hatami, N., Gavet, Y., Debayle, J.: Bag of recurrence patterns representation for time-series classification https://arxiv.org/abs/1803.11111v1. Accessed 07 Aug 2020

15. Hatami, N., Gavet, Y., Debayle, J.: Classification of time-series images using deep convolutional neural networks https://arxiv.org/abs/1710.00886. Accessed 07 Aug 2020

16. Takens, F.: Detecting strange attractors in turbulence. In: Rand, D., Young, L.-S. (eds.) Dynamical Systems and Turbulence, Warwick 1980. LNM, vol. 898, pp. 366–381. Springer, Heidelberg (1981). https://doi.org/10.1007/BFb0091924

17. Iwanski, J.S., Bredley, E.: Recurrence plots of experimental data: to embed or not to embed? Chaos **8**(4), 861–871 (1998)

18. LeCun, Y., Bengio, Y.: Convolutional networks for images, speech, and time-series. In: Arbib, M.A. (ed.) The Handbook of Brain Theory and Neural Networks. MIT Press, Cambridge (1995)

19. Ciresan, D., Meier, U., Masci, J., Gambardella, L.M., Schmidhuber, J.: Flexible, high performance convolutional neural networks for image classification. In: Proceedings of the Twenty-Second International Joint Conference on Artificial Intelligence, vol. 2, pp. 1237–124. (2013). https://people.idsia.ch/~juergen/ijcai2011.pdf. Accessed 07 Aug 2020

Relation Between Test Coverage and Timed Automata Model Structure

Lukáš Krejčí$^{(\boxtimes)}$ ⓘ, Jan Sobotka$^{(\boxtimes)}$ ⓘ, and Jiří Novák ⓘ

Czech Technical University in Prague, Faculty of Electrical Engineering, Technická 2,
166 27 Prague, Czech Republic
{krejclu6,sobotja2,jnovak}@fel.cvut.cz

Abstract. This paper deals with problematics of structure of Timed Automata models suitable for Model-Based Testing of automotive systems. Previous experiments, primarily focused on the environmental models, have shown that their structure does not significantly affect the coverage speed of testing process. However, similar questions regarding the observer part of the system model remained open. This paper analyzes those remaining questions and focuses on uncovering possible relation between an observer model structure and the quality of generated test sequences according to multiple criteria. Goal of presented experiments is to compare multiple modeling approaches and discover which one is most suitable for automotive systems.

Keywords: Timed Automata · Model-Based · Testing · Structure · Coverage · Automotive · Hardware-in-the-Loop · HiL

1 Introduction

In latest decades, requirements for testing of automotive electronics systems during their development are continually rising. Because of increasing complexity of a typical System-under-Test (SUT) and time restrictions induced by limited resources, the testing process itself poses a substantial challenge [1]. As manual design of test cases and test specifications traditionally used in industry practice might lead to various subjective errors, the employment of Model-Based Testing (MBT) methods into this process is an asset.

The MBT is a technique of utilization of system and environmental models [2] in order to automatically generate test cases and test suites. This process can be driven by various criteria, characteristically related to the coverage of the SUT state space [3] or to the SUT safety. In order to apply the principles of MBT on the area of integration testing of automotive electronic systems, testing tool Taster [4] was introduced. The modelling language used by Taster is based on Timed Automata network (defined by UPPAAL team [5]) virtually divided into an environment and observer part. The environment part is responsible for providing input stimuli to the SUT, and the observer part monitors the SUT behavior and verifies its correctness.

© Springer Nature Switzerland AG 2021
A. Kalenkova et al. (Eds.): TMPA 2019, CCIS 1288, pp. 109–120, 2021.
https://doi.org/10.1007/978-3-030-71472-7_9

Nevertheless, introduction of the MBT brings forth new issue – since creating a model of an SUT requires investment of time and effort, it's necessary to create the system model in most appropriate way. Currently, different approaches of modeling of both parts exist. Both the system environment and the SUT itself can be modeled in many ways – from fully permissive models similar to the random generation of test stimuli to entirely restrictive version allowing only specific test cases based on behavioral modeling [6]. Experiments presented in paper [6] have shown that both simple and complex modeling approaches for modeling of SUT environment are comparable in terms of achieved state space coverage. However, the experiments were focused only on coverage criteria and didn't cover the modelling of the observer part. In this paper, four different approaches of environment and observer modelling of real automotive systems are compared and evaluated with respect to multiple criteria.

2 Background

Experiments presented in this paper are based on the same case study used in previous experiments presented in [6], focused on the application of MBT applied on the Hardware-in-the-Loop (HiL) integration testing of the control unit of car trunk doors. The first part of the case study is the SUT model based on the system specification extended by the model of the control unit of car keyless locking system for purpose of experiments presented in this paper. In the second part of the case study, the Taster tool was used for generating and executing test cases on the HiL testing platform, based on the NI VeriStand and NI PXIe and abstracted away by the EXAM testing system. The workflow diagram of the process is shown in Fig. 1. This paper deals with the model part and the question of what the best modelling methodology is for both environment and observer parts.

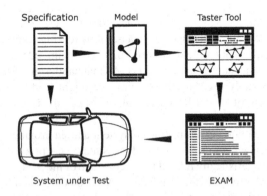

Fig. 1. Diagram of the MBT process using the Taster tool

The case study is focused on two cooperating car subsystems – the trunk doors control unit responsible for operating the automatic trunk doors and keyless locking system control unit responsible for correct function of car's locks. Typical operations performed on the locking system are unlocking and locking the car using the remote control or door handle interaction with remote control in proximity. In the case of the trunk control system, the typical performed operations are opening and closing of automatic trunk and interrupting those operations using one of four trunk control buttons (remote control, dashboard, internal and handle). Inputs of the SUT therefore consist of remote controller position, the door handles, three remote control buttons, one dashboard button and two trunk doors buttons (handle and internal).

During the evaluation of this case study, several questions regarding the modeling techniques has been raised. Questions regarding the environment part of the system models were covered by previous experiments presented in [6]. However, during the experiments, new questions concerning observer part of the model were raised.

Original case study and previous experiments were using a SUT containing only model of the trunk doors control unit. The observer part of the model was created according to the specification of correct behavior of the trunk system and it was fixed for all experiments. While this was sufficient for the purposes of original case study and experiments, it was necessary to find suitable modeling principles for observer part too, once the case study was to be extended with model of the keyless locking system. Similarly to previous situation with environment modeling, multiple approaches for the observer modelling existed and it was not clear, which modeling approach is the best. Consequently, a new set of experiments had to be run.

The experiments presented in this paper are based on the same models as previously. In addition to the two original sets of environment models, two different sets of observer models were created. The first set consists of a single compound observer model and represents the restrictive modelling approach. In the second set, both tested subsystems (the trunk doors control unit and the keyless locking system) have separate synchronized observer models. Both environment models were evaluated with respect to two sets of environment models (restrictive and permissive) used in previous experiments on the HiL testing platform. Test cases were generated by random strategy (selection of next edge randomly from a pool of enabled transitions) and systematic strategy (targeting least taken nodes and edges) in online way. The online approach generates test steps directly during runtime as opposed to the offline approach, where test cases are generated in advance.

3   Related Work

Analysis of MBT approaches, as well measurement of testing efficiency in general, is not straightforward task with standardized methodology. One of possibilities is experimental comparison using some selected criterion or set of criteria. In the field of the MBT, the coverage criteria of a system model are essential parameters [7]. Intuitively, they describe how comprehensively the SUT was tested. Naturally, one of the goals of the MBT [2] is to achieve the best possible model coverage in the minimal time, steps, or similar quantitative measure. Regrettably, there is an infinite number of existing coverage criteria [8, 9]. This work is based on subset called Structural Model Coverage Criteria [7]. Specifically, coverage of all nodes, all edge, and all pairs of edges (i.e. paths of length of two) are being used in the experiment. Authors of [10] demonstrate, how the structural coverage criteria can be used for test generation using a model checker. The paper [11] reveals that utilization of the structural coverage criteria for supplementary guidance of testing strategies can have a positive impact on the fault detection capability in black-box testing. Additionally, if an SUT model is used in the context of Model-Driven Development, i.e. when the model serves for generation of both SUT source codes and test cases, the paper [12] shows a correlation between coverage of the model structure and coverage of generated code achieved by the generated test cases. Consequently, that shows importance of chosen criteria.

This paper works with the progress of coverage over time, just like previous experiments presented in [6]. This progress is influenced by exploration algorithm and by a model structure. In case of Taster, the model is explored by graph search techniques [13]. Model is divided into environment and observer part, as it was mentioned in the Background section. Observer part is concerned immutable, since it describes system correct behavior. Similarly to works [14, 15], the experimental approach was chosen to compare the impact of environment model structure to observer coverage progress. None of the related papers contain results directly comparable with the results presented in this paper.

4   Modeling Language

As mentioned in Introduction, the developed testing tool is designated for testing of automotive electronics system. Those systems are real-time and reactive, so it was necessary to use modeling language fitting systems with those properties. Hence, the used modeling language is based on the theory of timed automata, developed by UPPAAL team [5], allowing to describe the modeled system as a network of Timed Safety Automata (TSA) bound by a set of variables.

The original theory of Timed Automata (TA), described in [16], was extended by UPPAAL team into the TSA (described [5]) by introduction of local invariant conditions that ensure progress of each automaton in the system. A single TSA can be formally defined followingly (described in [17]):

- A timed safety automaton A is a tuple $A = (N, l_0, E, I)$, where:

  - N is a finite set of locations (i.e. nodes),
  - $l_0 \in N$ is initial location,
  - $E \in N \times B(C) \times \Sigma \times 2^C \times N$ is the set of edges and
  - $I: N \rightarrow B(C)$ assigns invariants to locations.

- We shall write $l \rightarrow g, a, r, l'$, when $(l, g, a, r, l') \in E$.
- A local invariant is a constraint $x < n, x \leq n$, where $n \in \mathbb{N}$.

Informally, TSA is an oriented graph containing states (one of them is initial) and transitions between them. Transitions are labeled by guard condition enabling its execution and priorities affecting the probability of their execution.

A single TSA in an SUT model typically represents a separate model of a specific SUT subsystem and is referred to as a template. An SUT model can contain one or more instances of each template that represent one exact instance of tested subsystem. Because the MBT principles require a model of the SUT environment, multiple TSA are typically used for this purpose, providing input stimuli for the SUT. Interoperation of individual automata within model can be synchronized using system of variables and synchronization channels introduced by the UPPAAL team.

5 Models

In order to find most suitable modeling approach, two different model variants were created for both SUT and its environment. Those model variants represent two main modeling paradigms. First approach, referred to as simple, prefers division of the model into multiple simple interoperating automata. Second approach, referred to as complex, prefers utilization of only one, complex automaton. Both of those approaches were applied to modeling of the SUT (car trunk doors and locking systems) and its environment (driver).

5.1 Observer

The observer part of the model describes the correct behavior of the SUT according to the specification and its purpose is to ensure correctness of a tested system. Typically, no input stimuli for the SUT are provided by the observer part. In order to verify correctness of the SUT, observer part contains so called invariant conditions checks. In the used modeling language, those invariant conditions are encoded in nodes and are always verified when an automaton enters given state.

Because observer part can cover multiple subsystems of the SUT, the difference between simple and complex approaches primarily lies in separation of individual subsystem. Both observer model variants are described in following subsections.

Simple Approach. In the simple observer approach, referred to as Obs_S, each subsystem is modeled by separate automaton. In the case study used in the experiments, this means that there are two observer models – one for the locking system and one for the trunk control system. The locking system model is shown on Fig. 2.

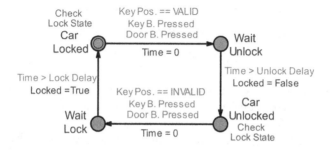

Fig. 2. The locking system observer model.

The trunk control system model is similar to the common observer model used in previous experiments presented in [6] and is shown on Fig. 3.

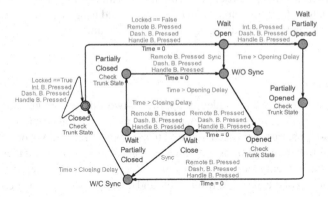

Fig. 3. The trunk system observer model.

Clearly, advantage of this approach lies in its clarity, as it allows to logically divide the SUT model into separate subsystem. Moreover, it allows to capture the parallel nature of a typical SUT. However, it creates additional requirements for synchronization between models of individual subsystems.

Complex Approach. In the complex observer approach, referred to as Ob_C, both subsystems are modeled by a single automaton template. Therefore, both models presented in previous section are merged into one describing complex behavior of combined system. The complex observer model is shown of Fig. 4.

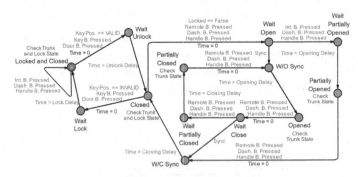

Fig. 4. The complex observer model.

Advantage of complex observer model is the centralization. Unlike in the case of the simple approach, the correct behavior of the SUT is exhaustively described by a single automaton template. Moreover, there is no need for additional synchronization. This approach, however, introduces significant requirements on modeling and bad scalability with increasing number of subsystems. Additionally, this modeling approach fails to capture the parallel nature of the SUT, where multiple subsystems are operated separately.

5.2 Environment

In addition to two variants of observer model, two versions of environment models were utilized in the presented experiment. The environmental part of the SUT model represents manipulation with the SUT inputs, i.e. locking and trunk control buttons.

The key difference between both modeling approaches lies within separation of models of individual inputs. Both variants presented in following sections are based on the environment models used in the previous experiments (described in [6]).

Simple Approach. The simple environment model, referred to as Env_S, introduces a separate automaton instance for each input (i.e. control buttons and remote controller position). Therefore, the full environment model, composed of multiple timed automata instances, represents the set of control inputs. Example of one of the automaton instances is shown in Fig. 5.

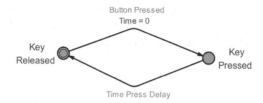

Fig. 5. Example of a button model in the simple environment model.

Depending on chosen test run strategy (see section Experiment for overview of used strategies), the simple environment model behaves as a car user, who is pressing buttons randomly, systematically or with specific pattern, but always with defined timing.

Undoubtedly, the major advantage of the simple model is its simplicity. Modeling the SUT environment in such way is not overly time consuming and might reduce time required for creating an exhaustive SUT model. Disadvantage of this approach might be creation of high number of unrealistic test cases.

Complex Approach. Just like in the case of the complex observer model, the complex environment model, referred to as Env_C, consists only from a single automaton instance representing a sensible car user. That means a user, who uses inputs (i.e. pushes buttons and changes position of remote controller) correctly within the given context.

As this automaton represents a car user, it has ability of manipulate with the SUT inputs encoded in the structure of the automaton itself. That additionally allows to add timing information the SUT operations and make the test runs more realistic. The complex environment model is shown in Fig. 6.

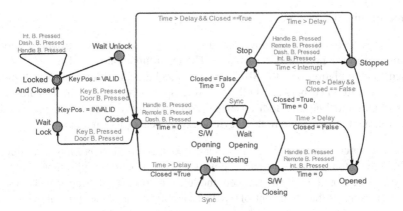

Fig. 6. The complex environment model.

Another advantage of the complex model is ability to utilize Model-Based Statistical Testing (MBST). The MBST is a form of MBT, which additionally uses statistical environment models [18]. Utilization of MBST could potentially provide even more realistic test cases.

6 Experiment

The aim of the presented experiments was to compare all combinations of modeling approaches of both observer and environment parts of the SUT model and find the most suitable combination. Because of the varying model structure of individual model variants, the structural model coverage was chosen as the primary comparison criteria. Therefore, every modeling variant (i.e. element from the space defined as $\{Ob_S, Ob_C\} \times \{Env_S, Env_C\}$) was evaluated on the progress of coverage of nodes (C_N), edges (C_E) and pairs of edges (C_{EP}) over discrete time (i.e. number of executed test steps).

The experimental test runs were executed using the Taster tool. During their execution, the structural coverage data was progressively collected (i.e. C_N, C_E and C_{EP} for each discrete time point). The tests runs were driven by following strategies:

- Random strategy that choses executed transition randomly,
- Systematic strategy that always choses transition to least visited node, and
- Heuristic strategy that choses the least taken transitions with highest priority.

Results for each modeling variant and each testing strategy were obtained from individual test runs, which duration was limited to one hour. This duration is sufficient, as the length of simulation step in the Taster tool was set to 250 ms, which provides up to 14400 test steps within a single test run.

7 Results

First evaluated criterion was the node coverage. While the node coverage is just an elementary criterion, it's still essential since the invariant checks are encoded in states of individual automata. Graphs depicting the progress of node coverage for all model variants and all three strategies is shown in Fig. 7.

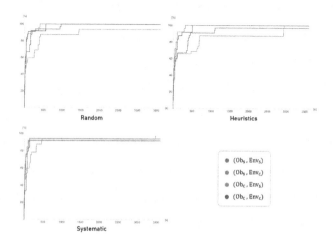

Fig. 7. The node coverage progress.

The evaluated criterion was the edge coverage. Because all actions physically executed with the SUT are bound to the edges in the system model, this criterion is vital. Graph depicting the progress of edge coverage for all model variants and all three strategies is shown in Fig. 8.

Last criterion analyzed in the experiment was the coverage of edge pairs, i.e. coverage of paths of length of two. Since occurrence of some types of faults in the SUT is conditioned by execution of operations in exact order, this criterion can be useful of uncovering of such faults. Graphs depicting progress of the coverage of pairs of edges for all model variants and all three strategies is shown in Fig. 9.

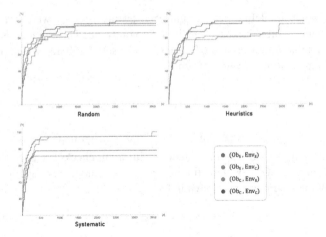

Fig. 8. The edge coverage progress.

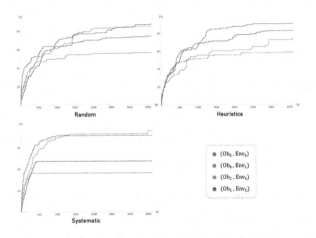

Fig. 9. The edge pairs coverage progress.

All criteria used in above graphs were always obtained from a single test run with given strategy and model variant.

8 Conclusions and Future Work

In this paper, experiment comparing different modeling approaches was presented. The modelling approaches, created as combinations of simple and complex models of both observer (Ob_S, Ob_C) and environment (Env_S, Env_C) parts of the SUT, are described in details in section Models. The experiment and used SUT models were based on the real automotive system (trunk doors system and locking system). All SUT model variants were compared according to the progress of the structural coverage criteria (node, edge and edge pair coverage) using three different test generation strategies (random, heuristic and systematic).

The acquired data, presented in previous section, show that the combination of Obs_S and Env_S provides most stable results among all criteria and used strategies. The noticeably worse performance of variants with Env_C in the edge-based criteria is, however, expected, as it is caused by the restrictive nature of the model – realistically modelled driver cannot perform as many operations (and their combination) with the SUT as the permissive model (Env_S). Additionally, the results suggest that fully complex model variant (using Ob_C and Env_C) provides good results as well, with exception of edge-based criteria and the systematic strategy. That is expected, because the Ob_C was made with real usage of the SUT in mind. Worse results of this variant for edge-based criteria are again caused by restrictive nature of the Env_C. The collected data also suggest that the coverage of the observer model depends on the environment model structure, which refutes the hypothesis suggested in [6].

The results show that the most permissive variant (i.e. combination of Env_S and Ob_S) provides consistently good results among all used testing strategies and coverage criteria. This implies optimistic conclusion – it is more beneficial to create simpler, divided models, which are significantly easier to create and maintain. The results also suggest that if more realistic test cases are required, the fully restrictive model set (i.e. combination of Env_C and Ob_C) should be utilized instead. However, the maintenance of two sets of models is problematic and, as explained before, the worse performance of combination of Env_C and Ob_S in edge-based criteria is expected. Consequently, more suitable variant is to maintain one simple observer model accompanied by one simple environment model (for test cases with higher coverage) and one driver model (for realistic test cases).

In first part of future research, presented results will be utilized to further expand used case study with additional car subsystems and inputs, such as window control subsystem, propulsion systems status, or intrusion detection. This continually growing case study can be created thanks to the cooperation with our industrial partner. Later, more accurate, behavioral model of car user will be obtained for utilization in the final phase of testing process.

Second part of future research will be primarily focused on the Taster tool and its further development. Presented experiments only utilized three basic strategies. Therefore, it would be desirable to add support of other testing strategies. For example, there is an ongoing research of testing strategy using machine perception and learning. All new testing strategies will be experimentally evaluated on the extended case study.

Acknowledgement. This work was supported by the Grant Agency of the Czech Technical University in Prague, projects Optimization methods for Model-Based Testing of automotive systems (grant No. SGS18/144/OHK3/2T/13) and Utilization of machine learning and biologically inspired algorithms in Model-Based Testing of automotive systems (SGS19/071/OHK3/1T/13). This support is gratefully acknowledged.

References

1. Abelein, U., Lochner, H., Hahn, D., Straube, S.: Complexity, quality and robustness - the challenges of tomorrow's automotive electronics. In: 2012 Design, Automation Test in Europe Conference Exhibition (DATE), pp. 870–871 (2012).
2. Peleska, J.: Industrial-strength model-based testing – state of the art and current challenges. In: Petrenko, A.K., Schlingloff, H. (eds.) Proceedings Eighth Workshop on Model-Based Testing, Rome, Italy, 17th March 2013, Electronic Proceedings in Theoretical Computer Science, vol. 111, pp. 3–28 (2013)
3. Groote, J.F., Kouters, T.W.D.M., Osaiweran, A.: Specification guidelines to avoid the state space explosion problem (2015). https://doi.org/10.1002/stvr.1536
4. Sobotka, J., Novák, J.: Testing automotive reactive systems using timed automata. In: Proceedings of the 2017 IEEE 9th International Conference on Intelligent Data Acquisition and Advanced Computing Systems: Technology and Application (IDAACS), pp. 510–513. Ternopil National Economic University, Ternopil (2017)
5. UPPAAL Team, and others: UPPAAL 4.0: Small tutorial, November 2009. https://www.it.uu.se/research/group/darts/uppaal/small_tutorial.pdf. Accessed June 2018
6. Sobotka, J., Krejčí, L.: Testing of automotive systems - complex vs. simple environment models. In: 2018 16th Biennial Baltic Electronics Conference (BEC). IEEE Computer Society, (2018). ISSN 1736-3705. ISBN 978-1-5386-7312-6
7. Utting, M. (eds.): San Francisco: Chapter 4 - Selecting your tests. In: Practical Model-Based Testing, pp. 107–137 (2007)
8. Utting, M., Pretschner, A., Legeard, B.: A taxonomy of modelbased testing approaches. Softw. Test. Verif. Reliab. 22(5), 297–312 (2012)
9. Weißleder, S.: Simulated satisfaction of coverage criteria on UML state machines. In: 2010 Third International Conference on Software Testing, Verification and Validation. IEEE (2010)
10. Rayadurgam, S., Heimdahl, M.P.E.: Coverage based test-case generation using model checkers. In: Eighth Annual IEEE International Conference and Workshop on the Engineering of Computer-Based Systems-ECBS 2001. IEEE (2001)
11. Gay, G., Staats, M., Whalen, M., Heimdahl, M.P.E.: The risks of coverage-directed test case generation. IEEE Trans. Softw. Eng. 41(8), 803–819 (2015)
12. Barasel, A., Conrad, M., Sadeghipour, S., Wegener, J.: The interplay between model coverage and code coverage (2003)
13. Aichernig, B.K., Brandl, H., Jöbstl, E., Krenn, W., Schlick, R., Tiran, S.: Killing strategies for model-based mutation testing. Softw. Test. Verif. Reliab. 25, 716–748 (2015)
14. Gay, G., Rajan, A., Staats, M., Whalen, M., Heimdahl, M.P.E.: The effect of program and model structure on the effectiveness of MC/DC test adequacy coverage. ACM Trans. Softw. Eng. Methodol. 25, 25:1–25:34 (2016)
15. Belli, F., Beyazit, M.: Event-based mutation testing vs. state-based mutation testing – an experimental comparison. In: 2011 IEEE 35th Annual Computer Software and Applications Conference, pp. 650–655 (2011)
16. Alur, R., Dill, D.: Automata for modeling real-time systems. In: Paterson, M.S. (ed.) ICALP 1990. LNCS, vol. 443, pp. 322–335. Springer, Heidelberg (1990). https://doi.org/10.1007/BFb0032042
17. Bengtsson, J., Yi, W.: Timed automata: semantics, algorithms and tools. In: Desel, Jörg., Reisig, Wolfgang, Rozenberg, Grzegorz (eds.) ACPN 2003. LNCS, vol. 3098, pp. 87–124. Springer, Heidelberg (2004). https://doi.org/10.1007/978-3-540-27755-2_3
18. Böhr, F.: Model based statistical testing of embedded systems. In: Proceedings of 2011 IEEE Fourth International Conference Software Testing, Verification and Validation Workshops, pp. 18–25 (2011)

Random Graph Model for Structural Analysis of Online Communications

Ivan Sukharev[ID] and Maria Ivanova[(✉)][ID]

National Research University Higher School of Economics, Moscow, Russia
ivan@sukharev.me, meivanova@outlook.com

Abstract. In this paper, we have explored the problem of social networks analysis using the theory of random graphs. The practical task was to present a communication model that corresponds to the Habrahabr users' actions. We took comments under 61746 publications and described the process of downloading them. Further, we used that information to construct the new random graph model.

Keywords: Random graph theory · Social network · Social graph

1 Introduction

Social networking services collect information about their users. The potential for scientific researches consists in the general profile information, connections between users (friendship, belonging to a certain group, etc.), and the involvement in open discussions. Data of this kind makes it possible to build a model of social network growth, predict users' needs, and even draw up their psychological portraits [1].

A graph is the most convenient form of presenting the data in these cases. Nodes are usually profiles, articles, or comments. Edges indicate connections between them. This type of construction is called a social graph.

However, the use of social networking data has some disadvantages. Firstly, a social graph articles can make the research objects' personal information public. Secondly, the growth of data arrays entails an increase in the processing costs. Thirdly, the limited number of social graphs calls into question the statistical reliability of the studies. Under such conditions, creating random graph models and tools for their generation is a task that is gaining popularity [2].

The creation of synthetic data is being actively implemented; the relevance of its use is still under consideration, though. Alessandra et al. [3] joined the discussion by examining the successful results of generating random graphs compared to a real data. Real graphs were selected in a size range from 30 thousand to 3 million edges based on the *Facebook* network. Only one of the six models considered is suitable for the work. The result of the study showed the ability of random graphs to depict a real information picture.

© Springer Nature Switzerland AG 2021
A. Kalenkova et al. (Eds.): TMPA 2019, CCIS 1288, pp. 121–129, 2021.
https://doi.org/10.1007/978-3-030-71472-7_10

2   Related Works

First let us introduce some notation. Let us define a social graph as a mathematical object. Let $V_n = \{1, ..., n\}$ be a set of graph vertices. Then a set of graph edges for the set of vertices V_n is as follows.

$$E_n = \{(i, j) \mid i, j \in V_n, i \neq j\} \tag{1}$$

A graph is an ordered pair $G := (V_n, E)$, where a set of edges is a subset of the set of all edges $E \subset E_n$.

2.1   Erdos–Renyi Model

One of the most famous random graphs models was proposed by Erdos and Renyi [4]. The graph generation process consists in constructing a set of edges E for a given set of vertices V_n. The edge $e_{ij} \in E_n$ is in the set of edges E of a random graph with probability $p \in [0, 1]$. In their further article, Erdos and Renyi [5] generalized the model. The constant probability p of the appearance of an edge in a random graph was replaced by a function $p \in [0, 1]$, which depends on n. This type of a random graph is extensively applicable; that is why it is popular.

2.2   Barabasi–Albert Growth Model

The advent of the Internet has given impetus to the development of graph theory. Scientists Barabasi and Albert [6,7] were among the first to work with the new network. They proposed a concept of *scale-free networks*, which is a basis of a random graph growth model for the Internet. Subsequently, the model found application in natural and social sciences (social, biological, transportation [14]).

A *scale-free network* is a graph where the degree distribution of the vertices is described by a power-law, at least asymptotically.

Therefore, the probability of a vertex having k edges at large values of k is proportional to $k^{-\gamma}$:

$$P(k) \sim k^{-\gamma} \tag{2}$$

Note that it is necessary to supplement the definition of the graph to describe the model. A *web graph* is a graph where vertices are sites. We call links between sites the edges. Barabasi and Albert [6] also presented the preferential attachment method. According to its idea, new network members are more likely to provide links to popular resources, with many attached edges, rather than less-known ones.

The next model of a random graph [14] is the simplest implementation of this idea. Initially moment, there is a connected graph on n vertices $v_i \in V_n$. Then a new vertex v_{n+1} is added. Then, with probability p_i, there is an edge between the new and the i-th vertices, where p_i is calculated by the following formula:

$$p_i = \frac{\deg(v_i)}{\sum_{j=1}^{n} \deg(v_j)} \tag{3}$$

Almost always a graph constructed according to such model has a small diameter. It is approximately equal to:

$$\operatorname{diam} G_n \sim \frac{\ln n}{\ln \ln n} \tag{4}$$

In 1999 the size of the Internet equaled to 10^7 [8]. According to the formula given, this is equal to the diameter of an approximately 6 edges' graph.

2.3   Nearest Neighbor Model

Another popular model—called the Nearest Neighbor algorithm—was presented by Alessandra et al. [3]. It is based on the fact that two people who have a common friend are likely to become friends too. A graph begins with one vertex and the empty set of edges, gradually growing by the following rules:

1) With probability $(1 - p)$, a new vertex joins a random vertex of the graph and forms a new edge.
2) With probability p, a pair of vertices is selected. The nodes do not have a common edge but are connected through a vertex adjacent to both. This pair is joined by a new edge.

A graph constructed by such rules will be a scale-free network [3].

Vazquez [9] researched dependence of the power-law exponent γ on a parameter $p \in [0, 1]$ and proved that $\gamma \in [2, \infty)$. The model does not allow us to obtain a graph with a power-law exponent $\gamma < 2$.

According to [10,11], large social networks have a power-law degree distribution exponent of a social graph vertices in the range of $1.5 < \gamma < 1.75$. Therefore, there is a modified model [3] for the analysis of social networks. There is one vertex and the empty set of edges. But we add a parameter k, which changes the rules for the following:

1) With probability $(1 - p)$, a new vertex joins a random vertex of the graph and forms a new edge. In addition, two random vertices are selected k times and connected by an edge, if there was not one before.
2) With probability p, a pair of vertices is selected. The nodes do not have a common edge but are connected through a vertex adjacent to the both. This pair is joined by a new edge.
   The power-law degree distribution exponent γ can be smaller with an addition of a new parameter [3].

3   Adaptation of the Barabasi–Albert Growth Model

Now let us find a random graph model that matches our data. We consider models of random graphs with a degree distribution similar to that studied in the models. Note that the graphs under consideration are trees: they do not have cycles and loops. Therefore, the popular models will not work for us in the original wording.

We propose a modified model of the Barabasi–Albert random graph, in which we remove the possibility of cycles occurrence. At every moment, a new vertex is added. It is connected by an edge with one random node. The probability of choosing the node is directly proportional to the number of edges attached to it. We add some parameter k to a root node degree, thereby increasing the likelihood of joining it rather than a comment.

This modification is the simplest interpretation of the appearance of new comments; therefore, it has a noticeable drawback. We noted that trees are characterized by a long chain of nodes with the degree equal to 2 on the initial data set. In this model, branch vertices rarely occur as there is no encouragement for that. Our model encourages large vertices degrees. We come to a conclusion that the closest to the real data values are those obtained for $k = 3$.

We should note that the resulting model has a degree distribution coefficient $\gamma \approx 2$. This is far from being the reality. We correct this inadequacy (shortcoming) in one of the following chapters (see Sect. 5 below).

4   Habrahabr Comments

The professional blog *Habrahabr*[1] is mainly a platform for the news and articles on IT topics. Each registered user can publish new articles in various topics (hereinafter "hubs") and comment on them. An article can be simultaneously in different hubs to cover several topics at once. All open communication of a blog members takes place in comments to articles; therefore, they will be the subject of the research.

Our task was to take comments under 61746 publications. Unfortunately, the service administration could not give us a key token, since this technology did not function correctly at that time. We used the *python* programming language and the *anaconda* computer analysis package for downloading. To reduce the amount of data uploaded, we considered a mobile version of the site. After the first test, an overload protection system was discovered. Access to the resource was closed for a long time after a thousand requests.

Requests library was used to resolve this problem. It imitates the behavior of a real user when accessing the site pages via HTTP requests. Also, it allows managing request headings, which we need to delete a body of cookies. Displayed on the network, the IP address of the computer was changed with a help of the *Tor* proxy servers [13]. The *exit node* [12] was changed with the help of the *Stem* library after the limit of requests had been reached.

It is necessary to save small files with each other. A set of them will take up more disk space than their actual total size. That is why our information was stored in the *SQLite* database. Thus, the amount of the data downloaded was 10 GB, and the size of the database with comment graphs was 120 MB.

---

[1] https://habr.com/.

Out of 61746 articles, we obtained 56003 of those with comments, that is, 90% of the users' activity. The total amount of Habrahabr comments is 2116285. Each article has 38 comments.

We construct the comment graph for each article. The root of the graph is an article. We assume that a comment can be either a response to an article or a response to someone else's comment. Depending on this, we attach it(the comment) either to the tree root or to the comment to which it refers. There does not exist a possibility to delete a comment; therefore, such graph will always be a connected tree. The graph scheme can be seen in Fig. 1.

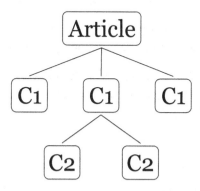

Fig. 1. Comments tree

The path from the root to the node cannot be longer than ten edges in our graph. This is a limitation based on the design of the service. New comments are attached to the last previous node as soon as the limit is reached. Because of that, we obtained a branched subtree that starting from the 9th node and has a unit leaf lengths.

Approximately 24% of comments are attached to the article itself. 60% of them have replies. That is 10% higher compared to all comments.

Let us determine the relevant random graphs models. A degree distribution is a significant feature. In most social random graphs articles it is a power-law degree distribution and our is not an exception. We use *powerlaw* library to find a power-law exponent. The value of this parameter is $\gamma \approx 3.31$.

5   New Random Graph Model

5.1   Algorithm Definition

Let us consider the shortcomings of the previous models (see Sect. 3 above) and make the random graph closer to the real data. Firstly, let us show the philosophy behind the model. With a certain probability p, a user will have a question while reading an article and leave a comment under the news. Otherwise, with probability $1-p$, a comment will go in response to something already left earlier. A user often happens to leave simple messages that no one answers. But sometimes quite the opposite occurs. In our model, we will take this into account by random assigning a "weight" to each new comment. Successful comments appear quite rarely, which should be reflected in the distribution of this random variable by using the function ϕ.

Since a comment already has an answer, the probability of the question being closed or transferred to the next level is quite high. Then we will give the weight λ of the comment to a new answer under it. The model turns out to be a rather natural interpretation of the commentator's logic. Now let us show the exact growth algorithm:

1. With probability p, a new vertex joins the root of the tree, that is, the article itself. Its weight is recorded by the function ϕ, that is an indicator of interest to this message among other users.
2. With probability of $1-p$, a new vertex joins any vertex at random, except for the root of the tree. The probability of joining each of them is proportional to their weights. A new vertex takes up λ from the weight of the vertex to which it is attached.

5.2   Model Fitting

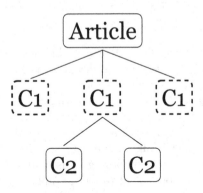

Fig. 2. Parameter p estimation

The value of the first parameter p was calculated: 23.7% of all the vertices are neighbors to the article (Fig. 2).

To find a second parameter, we show how its value affects a leaf type (Fig. 3). When $\lambda = 1$, an entire weight of the vertex will go to the next level in the case of joining an edge. This indicates appearance of long leaves without branching. When $\lambda = 0$, a leaf will not go down beyond the second level and the nodes degrees in the first level will quickly grow. The number vertices in different branches of one leaf will directly depend on the value of this parameter, since

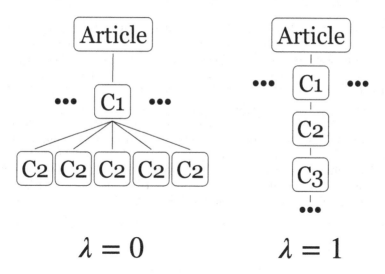

Fig. 3. Parameter λ explanation

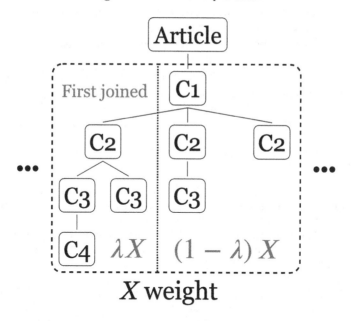

Fig. 4. The nodes weight distribution scheme

the vertices that attached not to the tree root do not initially have weight, and take λ from the value of the previous vertex.

As shown in Fig. 4, the vertex that first joins the first-level comment takes up λ of its weight. Further addition of new nodes will share this weight, but the total amount will not change in any way. The probability of a new vertex joining a certain subtree is directly proportional to its total weight. Therefore, the subtree weight is proportional to the number of comments at the end of the discussion. As a result, the ratio of the first joined C2-subtree comments number to the C1-subtree comments number is proportional to λ. The value of this parameter is $\lambda = 0.7629$.

The distribution of the random variable ϕ could be found from the subtree comments number. We use *scipy* library for statistical testing. We find that the random variable ϕ has an exponential distribution with the parameter equal to 0.53. This software tool also allows generating random numbers with a given distribution, which opens an opportunity to build random graphs using our model of any size. Note that this model produces trees with the power-law degree distribution exponent $\gamma \approx 3.5$, which turns out to be close to the real data.

6 Conclusion

We have considered the most popular random graphs models in the analysis of social networks. We have built a new model based on the Habrahabr blog's data. The highest quality among all the known algorithms was implemented, since the model was built based on the characteristics required. This topic is relevant and is gaining popularity along with the open media development. Future research may be directed towards an identifying of the discussion theme. For example, by the type of comments distinguish whether the discussion is about politics or on more common topics. Yet the issues of random graphs modeling of different in structure social communities and creating more sensitive metrics on them are still open.

References

1. Yoram, B., Michal, K., Thore, G., Pushmeet, K., David, S.: Personality and patterns of Facebook usage. In: Proceedings of the 3rd Annual ACM Web Science Conference, WebSci 2012, pp. 24–32. ACM, New York (2012)
2. Korshunov, A., et al.: Analysis of social networks: methods and applications. In: Proceedings of the Institute for System Programming RAS, vol. 1, p. 26 (2014). (in Russian)
3. Sala, A., Cao, L., Wilson, C., Zablit, R., Zheng, H., Zhao, B.Y.: Measurement-calibrated graph models for social network experiments. In: Proceedings of the 19th International Conference on World Wide Web. Raleigh, North Carolina, USA, pp. 861–870. Association for Computing Machinery, New York (2010). https://doi.org/10.1145/1772690.1772778
4. Erdos, P., Renyi, A.: On random graphs I. Publ. Math. Debrecen. **6**, 290–297 (1959)
5. Erdos, P., Renyi, A.: On the evolution of random graphs. A Matematika Kutato Intezet Kozlemenyei, V.A/1-2 (1960)
6. Barabasi, L., Albert, R.: Emergence of scaling in random networks. Science **286**, 509–512 (1999)
7. Barabasi, L., Albert, R., Jeong, H.: Scale-free characteristics of random networks: the topology of the world-wide web. Physica **A281**, 69–77 (2000)

8. Albert, R., Jeong, H., Barabasi, L.: Diameter of the world-wide web. Nature **401**, 130–131 (1999)
9. Vazquez, A.: Growing network with local rules: preferential attachment, clustering hierarchy, and degree correlations. Phys. Rev. **67**, 056104 (2003)
10. Mislove, A., Marcon, M., Gummadi, K.P., Druschel, P., Bhattacharjee, B.: Measurement and analysis of online social networks. Max Planck Institute for Software Systems, Rice University, University of Maryland (2007)
11. Wilson, C., Boe, B., Sala, A., Puttaswamy, K.P.N., Zhao, B.Y.: User interactions in social networks and their implications. Computer Science Department, University of California at Santa Barbara (2009)
12. Dingledine, R., Mathewson, N., Syverson: Tor: the second generation onion router. In: SSYM 2004 Proceedings of the 13th Conference on USENIX Security Symposium, San Diego, CA, 09–13 August, vol. 13, p. 21 (2004)
13. Shapiro, M.: Structure and encapsulation in distributed systems: the proxy principle. In: International Conference on Distributed Computing Systems (ICDCS), pp. 198–204. IEEE, Cambridge (1986)
14. Raigorodskii, A.: Models of random graphs and their applications to the web-graph analysis. In: Braslavski, P., et al. (eds.) RuSSIR 2015. CCIS, vol. 573, pp. 101–118. Springer, Cham (2016). https://doi.org/10.1007/978-3-319-41718-9_5

The Influence of Self-organizing Teams on the Structure of the Social Graph

Ilya Samonenko(iD) and Tamara Voznesenskaya$^{(\boxtimes)}$(iD)

National Research University Higher School of Economics, Moscow, Russia
{isamonenko,tvoznesenskaya}@hse.ru

Abstract. In this paper, we study the evolution of a social graph structure under the leverage of various projects performed by self-organizing teams. Suppose we have a group of specialists with different skills. Some of the team members are acquainted with each other, which is expressed by a social graph. We assume that each project requires a variety of skills, therefore the group members form teams in order to have at least one specialist with each skill required for the project. As a result of work on the project, all team members get acquainted with each other, which changes the social graph. In this paper, a model is proposed for this process. Properties and characteristics of the model have been studied analytically and via computer simulation.

Keywords: Social graph · Self-organizing teams · Evolving graphs · Saturated graphs

1 Introduction

The study of social networks is one of the key areas at the intersection of sociology and computer science. The aim of our work is to study the changes in social relations under the influence of self-organizing teams.

Suppose we have various specialists with different skills, some of which are familiar with each other. We will describe acquaintances with an undirected graph $G = (V, E)$, where the set of vertices V denotes specialists, and the edges E denote acquaintance (friendship) between them.

Specialists are going to carry out projects, and each project requires a variety of skills. One specialist cannot complete a project because his/her skills are not enough for the whole project. Therefore, they need to invite each other and team up so that the team has at least one specialist with each skill required for the project. As a result of work on the project, all team members get acquainted with each other, which changes the social graph.

Each specialist can participate only in one team at the same time. After completion of the project, he can take part in the work of a new team. Gradually, new connections appear in the social graph, and the graph can become saturated (a strict definition is given below).

© Springer Nature Switzerland AG 2021
A. Kalenkova et al. (Eds.): TMPA 2019, CCIS 1288, pp. 130–141, 2021.
https://doi.org/10.1007/978-3-030-71472-7_11

We investigate the number of such iterations necessary to make the graph saturated on average and in the best case scenario. If specialists form the same teams every time (worst case scenario), new connections will not appear.

There are quite a lot of researchers, who work at the social graphs and team-building area.

In [5] the problem of efficient shortest-path query evaluation on evolving social graphs is studied. The authors proposed "temporal" shortest-path queries: they can refer to any time-point or time-interval in the graph's evolution, and corresponding valid answers should be returned. To efficiently support this type of temporal query, the authors extend the traditional Dijkstra's algorithm to compute shortest-path distance(s) for a time-point or a time-interval.

Evolving graphs were introduced in [4]. The evolving graphs are a simple model which aims at harnessing the complexity of an evolving setting as yielded by dynamic communication networks. The authors exemplify its use through the computation of shortest paths under different hypotheses in fixed-schedule dynamic networks. Later this concept has been studied in other papers [1].

The problem of efficient query processing on an evolving graph sequence and a solution framework called FVF were presented in [10]. Through extensive experiments on both real and synthetic datasets, it was shown that our FVF framework is highly efficient in evolving graph sequence query processing.

In [6] the strongly connected components (SCC) in evolving graphs with geometric properties were studied. It was shown that SCC is NP-hard in case the nodes are placed on a grid and two points are connected if the Euclidean distance is equal or less than 2. On the other hand, it was proved that if the underlying graph is a tree this problem can be solved in polynomial time.

A new algorithm based on clique percolation was developed in [8]. This algorithm allows to investigate the time dependence of overlapping communities on a large scale and as such, to uncover basic relationships characterising community evolution. The authors focused on networks capturing the collaboration between scientists and the calls between mobile phone users. They find that large groups persist longer if they are capable of dynamically altering their membership, suggesting that an ability to change the composition results in better adaptability. The behaviour of small groups displays the opposite tendency, the condition for stability being that their composition remains unchanged.

The study of the social graph structure of active Facebook users was carried out in [11]. The authors compute numerous figures of the graph including the number of users and friendships, the degree distribution, path lengths, clustering, and mixing patterns. The results centre around three main observations. First, a characterization of the global graph structure, determining that the social network is nearly fully connected, with 99.91% of individuals belonging to a single large connected component, and the confirmation of the 'six degrees of separation' phenomenon on a global scale. Second, a studying the average local clustering coefficient and degeneracy of graph neighborhoods. It was shown that while the Facebook graph as a whole is clearly sparse, the graph neighborhoods of users contain a surprisingly dense structure. Third, a characterization of the assortativity patterns present in the graph by studying the basic demographic and network properties of users.

A rumour spreading in random evolving graphs was studied in [2]. The aim of this paper is to analyze the Push protocol in dynamic networks. The authors consider the edge-Markovian evolving graph model which captures natural between the structure of the network at time t, and the one at time t+1. Precisely, a non-edge appears temporal dependencies bet with probability p, while an existing edge dies with probability q. In order to fit with real-world traces, the authors mostly concentrate they study on the case where $p = \Omega(\frac{1}{n})$ and q is constant. They that, in this realistic scenario, the Push protocol does perform well, completing information spreading in O(log n) time steps with high probability.

In [9] take a close, empirical look at the degree-degree correlation structure of social bipartite collaboration networks. The authors arise three questions in this context. First, what is the structure of the bipartite network? Second, what can be stated in general of the one-mode projection graph and its correlations? Third, comparison of growing of a bipartite network model and a team assembly model.

In [7] the authors investigate the origins of homophily in a large university community, using network data in which interactions, attributes, and affiliations are all recorded over time. The analysis indicates that highly similar pairs do show greater than average propensity to form new ties; however, it also finds that tie formation is heavily biased by triadic closure and focal closure, which effectively constrain the opportunities among which individuals may select.

The research [3] examines the problem of team formation in social networks. Agents, each possessing certain skills, are given tasks that require particular combinations of skills, and they must form teams to complete the tasks and receive payoffs. However, agents can only join teams to which they have direct connections in the social network. The authors found a simple, locally-rational team formation strategy can form team configurations with near-optimal earnings, though this greedy hill-climbing search does converge to suboptimal local maxima.

2   Model Description

Suppose we have n specialists $V = \{v_1, \ldots, v_n\}$, some of whom are in acquaintance with each other. The acquaintance is described by an undirected graph $G = (V, E)$, so that the specialists v_i and v_j are acquaintance if and only if the edge $\{v_i, v_j\} \in E$. Subset $T \subseteq V$ that are vertexes of connected subgraph of G will be called **team**.

In addition, there is a series of similar projects, and each project requires the same set of skills. The set of skills is described by the vector $\alpha = (a_1, \ldots, a_k)$, where $a_i \in \mathbb{N}$. Each a_i describes the total skill with the number i needed to complete the project. Hereinafter, a project and a set of skills required for this project we will be denoted by a single letter α.

Each specialist also has some skills. This is described by the function:

$$\pi : V \rightarrow \mathbb{Z}_{\geq 0}^{k},$$

where $\mathbb{Z}_{\geq 0}$ – denotes a set of non-negative integers. For the team $T \subseteq V$, their common skill is defined as:

$$\pi(T) = \sum_{v \in T} \pi(v)$$

We introduce a partial order on the set $\mathbb{Z}_{\geq 0}^{k} \preceq$ as follows:

$$(a_1, \ldots, a_k) \preceq (b_1, \ldots, b_k) \Leftrightarrow a_i \leq b_i, \ i = 1, \ldots, k.$$

Denote by $|\alpha|$ the weight of the vector α:

$$|\alpha| = |(a_1, \ldots, a_k)| = a_1 + \cdots + a_k$$

A team $T \subseteq V$ **can execute** project α if:

$$\alpha \preceq \pi(T).$$

Such a team will be called **complete**.

Any specialist v (initiator) can form a new team $T = \{v\}$ and start inviting other specialists to this team. Any team member $v \in T$ may invite to the team T specialist $u \in V \setminus T$ if:

1. they are acquaintance, i.e. $\{u, v\} \in E$;
2. specialist u not busy in any other team;
3. specialist u increases the skills required to complete a project: let $\alpha = (a_1, \ldots, a_k)$, $\pi(T) = (b_1, \ldots, b_k)$, $\pi(u) = (d_1, \ldots, d_k)$, if $\exists i : a_i > b_i$ and $d_i > 0$.

In addition, if a specialist is invited to the team, he/she necessarily agrees. As a result of this process is either formed completed team T, such that $\alpha \preceq \pi(T)$, is either not formed and the team disbanded. The team initiator no longer attempts to create a new team, but he can be invited to other teams. This process is non-deterministic and it varies the sequence of initiators and invitations. A set of completed teams $Q = \{T_1, \ldots, T_q\}$ is formed as a result of a single run of this model.

Further in this paper we fix set of specialists V, the skills function π and the project α.

The following is pseudocode of a random function $GetTeams(G)$, which returns one of the possible sets of completed teams for the graph G, the given skill function π and the project α. This function has several random operations that can give different values for different function calls.

Description of variables and functions:

Initiators – a set of vertices that have not yet been initiators of any team.
NotInTeams – a set of vertices that do not belong to any one team.

$Teams$ – a set of competed teams.

$AllNeighbors(x)$ – a set of vertices adjacent to the vertex x.

$X.randomPop()$ – returns a uniformly distributed random element from the set X and removes this element from the set X.

$CreateRandomQueue(X)$ – equiprobable shuffles elements X and create a queue of them.

$Q.randomPush(X)$ – equiprobable shuffles elements X and adds them to the queue Q.

$Q.pop()$ – returns the first item in the queue Q and removes it from the queue.

$isComplete(T)$ – checks if the team T is complete. This function depends on the skill function π and the project α. But the values of π and α are fixed, so for brevity we will not specify π and α as arguments of the functions $GetTeams$ and $isComplete$.

```
function GETTEAMS(G)
    Initiators = V
    NotInTeams = V
    Teams = ∅
    while Initiators ≠ ∅ do
        x = Initiators.randomPop()
        CurrentTeam = {x}
        Queue = CreateRandomQueue(AllNeighbors(x) ∩ NotInTeams)
        while (Queue ≠ ∅) OR (NOT Complete(CurrentTeam)) do
            y = Queue.pop()
            if π(y) \ π(CurrentTeam) ≠ ∅ then
                Queue.randomPush(AllNeighbors(y) ∩ NotInTeams)
                CurrentTeam = CurrentTeam ∪ {y}
            end if
        end while
        if isComplete(CurrentTeam) then
            Teams = Teams ∪ {CurrentTeam}
            NotInTeams = NotInTeams \ CurrentTeam
        end if
    end while
    Return Teams
end function
```

There are many random choices when the function $GetTeams(G)$ is calling. Denote by $Runs(G)$ all possible scenarios of model runs for the graph G. For each specific model run $r \in Runs(G)$ we get a specific result of the function $GetTeams(G)$ – a set (possibly empty) of completed teams $Q = \{T_1, \ldots, T_q\}$. Denote by $GetTeams_r(G)$ the result of the function $GetTeams(G)$ for a specific model run $r \in Ruins(G)$.

3 Evolution of the Social Graph Structure

As a result of the project completed by team $T = \{v_1, \ldots, v_r\}$ all team members acquainted to each other. Consequently, new edges $\{v_i, v_j\}$, $1 \le i < j \le r$ appeared in the graph G. When the model starts again, it will work with the changed graph.

For the graph $G = (V, E)$ and the set of teams $Q = \{T_1, \ldots, T_q\}$ graph $\hat{G} = (V, \hat{E})$ we be called the **extension** of G by Q, where:

$$\hat{E} = E \cup \{\{u, v\} | u, v \in T_i, \ u \ne v, \ i = 1, \ldots, q\}.$$

We denote the extension G by Q through $Extension(G, Q)$. We call an extension **nontrivial** if $Extension(G, Q) \ne G$.

The **triviality** of the $Extension(G, Q) = G$ means that all teams $T \in Q$ are cliques, i.e. all team members were acquainted with each other before the team was created.

We call a graph G **saturated** if for any $r \in Runs(G)$ we have:

$$Extension(G, GetTeams_r(G)) = G.$$

In other words, a graph is called **saturated** if its extension by any set of its teams is trivial. Otherwise, we call the graph **unsaturated**.

The main results of this paper are the study of how the sequential extensions of an unsaturated graph G make it's saturated (Fig. 1).

4 Examples

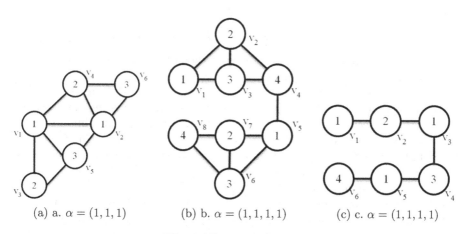

(a) a. $\alpha = (1, 1, 1)$ (b) b. $\alpha = (1, 1, 1, 1)$ (c) c. $\alpha = (1, 1, 1, 1)$

Fig. 1. Three social graph

Consider the examples of the model. For all the examples in the vertices indicate the number of the skill that the vertex has. That is, if the label at the vertex v is i, then $\pi(v) = e_i$, where e_i is a vector of zeros with 1 at position i.

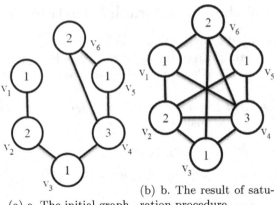

(a) a. The initial graph

(b) b. The result of saturation procedure

Fig. 2. Graph saturation. $\alpha = (1, 1, 1)$

For the graph in Fig. 2a there are four different sets of completed teams:

$$Q_1 = \{\{v_1, v_4, v_5\}\}, Q_2 = \{\{v_2, v_4, v_5\}\},$$

$$Q_3 = \{\{v_1, v_4, v_5\}, \{v_4, v_2, v_6\}\} \text{ and } Q_4 = \{\{v_1, v_4, v_6\}, \{v_3, v_5, v_2\}\}.$$

For example, a single team of Q_1 can be created if the initiator of v_1 invites v_4 and v_5. However, no other team can be created.

For the graph in Fig. 2b there are three different sets of completed teams:

$$Q_1 = \{\{v_1, v_2, v_3, v_4\}, \{v_5, v_6, v_7, v_8\}\},$$

$$Q_2 = \{\{v_4, v_3, v_2, v_5\}\} \text{ and } Q_3 = \{\{v_5, v_4, v_6, v_7\}.$$

For example, a single team of Q_2 is created if the initiator v_4 invokes v_2, v_3, and v_5. However, no other team can be created.

Moreover, for a given graph, the set $L = \{v_3, v_4, v_5, v_7\}$ formally satisfies the skill requirement: $\pi(L) = \alpha$. However, the set L cannot be the result of $GetTeams(G)$ because any initiator at first invites its free neighbours. This example shows that the considered problem differs from the problem of enumeration of all connected subgraphs whose vertices cover a given set of values.

In Fig. 2c here is an example of a graph without completed teams.

The initial graph presented at Fig. 2a, and Fig. 2b shows the result of its saturation procedure. For this graph, all sets of competed teams consist only of one team, because we have only one specialist v_3 with e_3 skill. Consider the saturation procedure: $Q_1 = \{\{v_2, v_3, v_4\}\}$ (the initiator v_3) adds the edge $\{v_2, v_4\}$, $Q_2 = \{\{v_2, v_1, v_4\}\}$ (the initiator v_2) adds the edge $\{v_1, v_4\}$ and $Q_3 = \{\{v_4, v_2, v_5\}\}$ (the initiator v_4) adds the edge $\{v_2, v_5\}$, $Q_4 = \{\{v_1, v_4, v_6\}\}$ (the initiator v_4) adds the edge $\{v_1, v_6\}$, $Q_4 = \{\{v_3, v_4, v_6\}\}$ (the initiator v_4) adds the edge $\{v_3, v_6\}$.

5 Results

Further results are obtained under the following assumptions:

– Each specialist has exactly one skill:

$$\forall v \in V \ |\pi(v)| = 1$$

  In particular, this means that any completed team $T \in GetTeams_r(G)$ consists of $|\alpha|$ specialists.
– At least three specialists are required to complete the project:

$$|\alpha| \geq 3$$

  The case $|\alpha| < 3$ is not interesting in terms of changing the social graph. At $|\alpha| = 2$ any team consists of two specialists who should know each other before form this team. At $|\alpha| = 1$ all projects are done by one specialist without a team.
– Let $\alpha = (a_1, \ldots, a_k)$. A pair of vertices $\{u, v\}$ is called **dummy** if $a_j = 1$, $\pi(u) = \pi(v) = e_j$. The edge between a dummy pair of vertices is also called a dummy. For example, in Fig. 2a the edge $\{v_1, v_2\}$ is dummy. Dummy edges are never used to form teams, so they can be excluded from the graph without affecting the operation of the model.
– The graph G remains connected after removing the dummy edges. For a disconnected graph, the problem is divided into independent problems for each connected component.
– For the graph G there is at least one complete team, i.e.:

$$\exists r \in Runs(G): \ GetReams_r(G) \neq \emptyset$$

Theorem 1. *For any graph $G = (V, E)$, there is a sequence of graphs $G_0, G_1, \ldots, G_s$, $s \leq \frac{|V|(|V|-1)}{2}$ such that:*

1. $G_0 = G$;
2. $G_{i+1} = Extension(G_i, GetTeams_{r_i}(G))$ for some $r_i \in Runs(G_i)$;
3. G_s is saturated.

Proof. If $G_0 = G$ is not saturated, then there is a model run $r \in Ruins(G_0)$ such that $T_j \in GetTeams_r(G_0)$ is not a clique. Let $G_1 = Extension(G, GetTeams_r(G))$ and use similar reasoning to G_1, and so on. Each extension adds at least one edge to the graph. Hence for some $s \leq \frac{|V|(|V|-1)}{2}$ we get that G_s is saturated. □

Theorem 2. *The following statements are equivalent:*

1. Graph G is saturated.
2. Graph G is complete without dummy edges.

Proof. 1. → 2. Let $T_0 = \{u_1, \ldots, u_k\}$ be some completed team for G. The graph G is saturated, hence T_0 is a clique. Let us denote by U the vertices of maximum (by —U—) clique of G (without dummy edges) containing T_0. If there are several such cliques, then choose any. We prove that $U = V$.

Let $V \setminus U \neq \emptyset$. Choose $v_1 \in V \setminus U$ such that there is an edge from v_1 to some vertex $v_2 \in U$. This choice can be made due to the connectivity of the graph. Consider any vertex $v_3 \in U$ such that the pair $\{v_1, v_3\}$ is not dummy and prove that there exists an $\{v_1, v_3\} \in E$.

Without loss of generality, we assume that:

$$\pi(v_1) = \pi(u_1), \ \pi(v_2) = \pi(u_2), \pi(v_3) = \pi(u_3).$$

Then the team $T_1 = \{v_1, v_2, v_3, u_4, \ldots, u_k\}$ is completed and possible constructed as follows. The initiator is v_2 invites sequentially $v_1, v_3, u_4, \ldots, u_k$. The graph G is saturated, hence T_1 is a clique and there is an edge $\{v_1, v_3\} \in E$. We may chose any $v_3 \in U$ and prove than $\{v_1, v_3\} \in E$, hence $v_1 \in U$. Therefore $U = V$, which proves that G is a complete graph without dummy edges.

2. → 1. Any team is a clique, hence G is saturated.   □

The Theorem 2 gives a method to verify that a graph is saturated with complexity $O(n^2)$. Let the function $IsSaturated(G)$ determine whether the graph G is saturated.

Let G be a social graph, we define a random variable $\gamma(G)$, which equals to the number of extensions needed to make the graph saturated:

function SATURATIONTIME(G)
    $Counter = 0$
    while NOT $IsSaturated(G)$ **do**
        $G = Extension(G, GetTeams(G))$
        $Counter = Counter + 1$
    end while
    Return $Counter$
end function

We call $\gamma(G)$ the **saturation time** of the graph G. The value of the function $\gamma(G)$ is indeed a random variable because we randomly chose the set of teams $GetTeams(G)$. Now we prove the correctness of this definition: the probability that the loop **while** will not complete is zero.

Indeed, let loop **while** is not complete, for some unsaturated graph G. This means that after a sequence of nontrivial extensions, the graph G is transformed to an unsaturated G' and all subsequent extensions are trivial (do not changing the graph G'). Consider all runs of the model $Runs(G') = \{r_1, \ldots, r_N\}$. Let p_i be the probability that r_i has been started. Since the graph G' is unsaturated, there are $Q \subset Runs(G')$ for which $G' \neq Extension(G', GetTeams_r(G'))$ and $r \in Q$. Hence the probability that the set of teams $GetTeams(G')$ will yield a trivial extension is:

$$p = P(G' = Extension(G', GetTeams(G'))) = 1 - \sum_{r \in Q} p_r < 1.$$

The probability that the loop **while** will work s times without changing G' equals p^s. Therefore, the probability of the loop **while** is not completed equals

$$\lim_{s \to \infty} p^s = 0.$$

6   Simulation

This section presents the results of a computational estimation of saturation time for some classes of graphs. We will consider random graphs with a given probability of occurrence of an edge. As before, we will assume that for any $v \in V$ $|\pi(v)| = 1$. Will consider only projects of the form $\alpha = (a_1, \ldots, a_k)$, where all $a_i = 1$, i.e. for each project you need exactly k specialists with different skills. In addition, we assume that n is divided by k and for each skill there are exactly $\frac{n}{k}$ specialists with this skill.

Let $p \in [0, 1]$ be fixed. Consider the function $GetRandomGraph(n, p)$, which randomly returns an undirected graph $G = (V, E)$ with:

$$P(\{u, v\} \in E) = p.$$

As noted above, we consider the case in which for any $v \in V$ has $|\pi(v)| = 1$. Therefore, we can present the function π as an array of length $|V|$ with values in the set $\{1, \ldots, k\}$:

$$\pi(v_i) = e_{\pi[i]}.$$

Now we describe the function $GetRandomSocialGraph(n, k, p)$, which will randomly return the skill function π and the undirected graph G, connected after removing all the dummy edges.

The function $ShuffleArray(A)$ – equiprobable shuffles the elements of the array A.

The function $IsSkillConnected(G, \pi)$ – checks is the graph G will be connected after remove all dummy edges.

function GETRANDOMSOCIALGRAPH(n,k,p)
    $r = \frac{n}{k}$
    $\pi = ShuffleArray([\underbrace{1, \ldots, 1}_{r}, \underbrace{2, \ldots, 2}_{r}, \ldots, \underbrace{k, \ldots, k}_{r}])$
    $G = GetRandomGraph(n, p)$
    while NOT $IsSkillConnected(G, \pi)$ **do**
        $G = GetRandomGraph(n, p)$
    end while
    Return G, π
end function

Thus, for fixed n, k, p we can obtain a random variable

$$\gamma(n, k, p) = SaturationTime(GetRandomSocialGraph(n, k, p)),$$

which describes the saturation time of a random graph with n vertices, k skills, and probability of acquaintance equals p.

The Fig. 3 shows the results of computational experiments. We estimate the mean value of $\gamma(n, k, p)$ at $n = 24$, $k = 3, 4, 6, 12$ and the values of p at the interval $[0.1, 1]$ in increments equals 0.025.

Note that there is a random selection of the completed teams set $GetTeams(G)$ in function $Saturation(G)$. The corresponding extension can be trivial (does not change the graph) or nontrivial (changes the graph). Figure 3 shows the average saturation time (all extensions) as well as the number of trivial and nontrivial extensions.

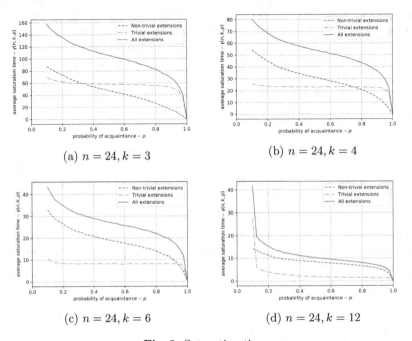

(a) $n = 24, k = 3$

(b) $n = 24, k = 4$

(c) $n = 24, k = 6$

(d) $n = 24, k = 12$

Fig. 3. Saturation time

References

1. Bhadra, S., Ferreira, A.: Complexity of connected components in evolving graphs and the computation of multicast trees in dynamic networks. In: Pierre, S., Barbeau, M., Kranakis, E. (eds.) ADHOC-NOW 2003. LNCS, vol. 2865, pp. 259–270. Springer, Heidelberg (2003). https://doi.org/10.1007/978-3-540-39611-6_23
2. Clementi, A., et al.: Rumor spreading in random evolving graphs. In: Bodlaender, H.L., Italiano, G.F. (eds.) ESA 2013. LNCS, vol. 8125, pp. 325–336. Springer, Heidelberg (2013). https://doi.org/10.1007/978-3-642-40450-4_28
3. Dykhuis, N., Cohen, P., Chang, Y.H.: Simulating team formation in social networks, pp. 244–253, September 2013. https://doi.org/10.1109/SocialCom.2013.42
4. Ferreira, A.: On models and algorithms for dynamic communication networks: the case for evolving graphs. In: Proceedings of the ALGOTEL, January 2002

5. Huo, W., Tsotras, V.: Efficient temporal shortest path queries on evolving social graphs. In: ACM International Conference Proceeding Series, June 2014. https://doi.org/10.1145/2618243.2618282
6. Jarry, A., Lotker, Z.: Connectivity in evolving graph with geometric properties, pp. 24–30, January 2004. https://doi.org/10.1145/1022630.1022635
7. Kossinets, G.: Origins of homophily in an evolving social network. Am. J. Sociol. **115**, 405–450 (2009). https://doi.org/10.1086/599247
8. Palla, G., Barabasi, A.L., Vicsek, T.: Quantifying social group evolution. Nature **446**, 664–667 (2007). https://doi.org/10.1038/nature05670
9. Peltomäki, M., Alava, M.: Correlations in bipartite collaboration networks. J. Stat. Mech. Theory Exp. **2006** (2005). https://doi.org/10.1088/1742-5468/2006/01/P01010
10. Ren, C., Lo, E., Kao, B., Zhu, X., Cheng, R., Cheung, D.W.: Efficient processing of shortest path queries in evolving graph sequences. Inf. Syst. **70**, 18–31 (2017). https://doi.org/10.1016/j.is.2017.05.004. http://www.sciencedirect.com/science/article/pii/S0306437916303374. Advances in databases and Information Systems
11. Ugander, J., Karrer, B., Backstrom, L., Marlow, C.: The anatomy of the Facebook social graph. arXiv preprint 1111.4503, November 2011

Making Bounded Model Checking Interprocedural in (Static Analysis) Style

Daniil Stepanov[1,2]([✉]), Marat Akhin[1,2], and Mikhail Belyaev[1,2]

[1] Saint Petersburg Polytechnic University, St. Petersburg, Russia
{stepanov,akhin,belyaev}@kspt.icc.spbstu.ru
[2] Jetbrains Research, St. Petersburg, Russia

Abstract. Bounded model checking (BMC) is one of the most interesting and practical methods of software quality assurance; it converts the program to a logical formula, which is checked for correctness using SAT or SMT solvers. An inherent problem of BMC is how one does interprocedural analysis, which is usually performed using function inlining. However, inlining greatly increases the size and complexity of the resulting formula, making analysis close to impossible to perform in a reasonable time. In this work we propose a method of interprocedural BMC based on ideas from the related area of program static analysis; it works by creating context-sensitive versions of formulae for interesting safety properties, which are considerably smaller than formulae with full inlining. We have implemented a prototype based on our approach in a BMC tool called Borealis, evaluated it on a number of real-world programs and shown our approach to greatly improve analysis performance and precision.

Keywords: Program analysis · Interprocedural analysis · Bounded model checking · Context sensitivity

1 Introduction

Software development is a very complex and time-consuming process, where software bugs may lead to undesirable and dangerous consequences. To reduce these risks one may use different methods of program analysis, e.g., bounded model checking (BMC). This method is a natural extension of traditional model checking, where the program is translated to a formula in first order logic (FOL), which is then sent to a specialized solver. The results of the formula checking may be lifted back to the original program and used to reason about different safety properties, such as null pointer dereferences or out-of-bounds array accesses.

One of the hardest problems in BMC is interprocedural analysis—how one analyzes function calls inside other functions and represents them as a formula [12]. The de facto standard approach is function inlining, when function bodies are inserted at their corresponding call sites. Unfortunately, inlining often makes BMC infeasible in practice, as it exponentially increases the size of the resulting formula with the respective increase in processing time.

© Springer Nature Switzerland AG 2021
A. Kalenkova et al. (Eds.): TMPA 2019, CCIS 1288, pp. 142–154, 2021.
https://doi.org/10.1007/978-3-030-71472-7_12

An alternative to function inlining, widely used in program static analysis, are *context-sensitive analyses* [17], which handle interactions between different functions by capturing their calling contexts. One may use different approaches to how calling contexts are collected and processed, which typically vary on the types of analysis and safety properties in question.

In this paper we present an approach to interprocedural BMC, which borrows the idea of context sensitivity from classic static analysis and applies it to BMC. By traversing the call graph bottom-up in an adaptive manner, we capture the function calling contexts w.r.t. their call sites, obtaining formulae smaller compared to inlining while retaining much of its precision at the same time. In cases when the behaviour is dependent on a sibling function call, we locally alternate to top-down traversal and capture relevant information from such calls, which is also incorporated in the formulae.

We have implemented a prototype of our approach based on the bounded model checker Borealis [3], but it is general enough to be incorporated with most other BMC tools [9,10,15]. We have also evaluated the prototype on a number of real-world software projects and shown our approach to achieve an efficient balance between the performance and the precision of BMC.

The rest of the paper is organized as follows. We lay the foundation of our work by introducing bounded model checking and its implementation in Borealis in Sect. 2. The core of our approach to interprocedural BMC is explained in Sect. 3. The evaluation and related work are discussed in Sects. 4 and 5 respectively.

2   Bounded Model Checking Overview

As we noted earlier, BMC [7] is an extension of traditional model checking, which tackles the state space explosion problem by limiting the length of possible paths it considers. For programs, this usually means unrolling loops to bounded sequences of iterations and restricting function recursion. After that, the unrolled program p is translated to a FOL formula $\phi(p)$, which is then combined with a *negated* security property $\neg\psi(q)$ (also translated to a FOL formula) and checked for satisfiability by a SAT- or SMT-solver. If $\phi(p) \wedge \neg\psi(q)$ is unsatisfiable, it is impossible to falsify the security property, meaning it always holds and the program is safe w.r.t. the property. Otherwise, we get a satisfying assignment for the program variables, which can be interpreted as a safety-violating counterexample.

Tools implementing such an approach are called bounded model checkers, and they are usually based on some kind of program intermediate representation (IR). For the C programming language LLVM IR [13] is an IR which got a lot of traction in recent years and is widely used in bounded model checkers [3,15]. LLVM IR is based on a typed meta-assembler with inherent support for static single assignment (SSA) form and various program normalization and optimization techniques, which make development of program analyses and analyzers more convenient.

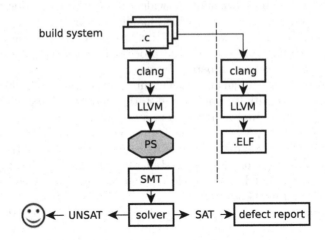

Fig. 1. An overview of Borealis analysis pipeline

⟨*PredicateState*⟩ ::= **Basic** data:⟨*ListOfPredicates*⟩
  | **Choice** choices:⟨*ListOfPredicateStates*⟩
  | **Chain** head:⟨*PredicateState*⟩ tail:⟨*PredicateState*⟩

⟨*Predicate*⟩ ::= **EqualityPredicate** lhv:⟨*Term*⟩ rhv:⟨*Term*⟩
  | **StorePredicate** ptr:⟨*Term*⟩ value:⟨*Term*⟩
  | ...

⟨*Term*⟩ ::= **ArgumentTerm** idx:*UInt32* kind:⟨*ArgumentKind*⟩
  | **BinaryTerm** op:⟨*BinaryOp*⟩ lhv:⟨*Term*⟩ rhv:⟨*Term*⟩
  | ...

Fig. 2. A simplified predicate state definition

We decided to base our work on a bounded model checker called Borealis [3], as it is open source and freely available for research and modification. An overview of how Borealis analyzes a program is shown in Fig. 1. In order to facilitate the support of different SMT solvers, Borealis introduces yet another level in between LLVM IR and SMT formula, called predicate state (PS). As PS is the cornerstone of how Borealis represents a program, let us discuss it in more detail.

A simplified PS definition[1] is shown in Fig. 2; a PS is specialized to represent the program code in a form most suitable for BMC, i.e., fully unrolled and simplified, retaining only essential information about the program. As far as we know, PS also can be efficiently (de)serialized, which is required for incremental-style analyses.

---

[1] This is a reduced version of PS definition from [3].

2.1   Interprocedural Analysis in BMC

In its most basic form BMC is an intraprocedural analysis; everything is done in the scope of a single function, with no consideration for function calls. This significantly lowers the precision of the analysis (i.e., we will encounter a lot of false positives), however, BMC still is complete modulo loops (i.e., we will not skip a possible bug, if all loops are sufficiently unrolled). This combination of features makes basic BMC ill-suited to be used in real-world scenarios, as developers value low false positive rates very highly [8].

To increase precision one needs to make BMC interprocedural; the standard approach is to implement function inlining, when full function bodies are inserted in place of all call sites. Compared to basic BMC, inlining gives us more precise, but also much larger formula; for many programs the resulting formula becomes infeasible to process using existing solvers. An alternative approach would be to introduce *context sensitivity*, when functions are inserted at call sites not concretely, but abstractly, usually as some form of calling contexts—descriptions of how function input influences its output.

Context-sensitive analysis has been used in traditional static analyses for quite some time now; however, its use in the context of BMC has been pretty limited. In this paper we present an approach for interprocedural BMC, based on context sensitivity, when the calling contexts are embedded as parts of the resulting FOL formulae; as these embeddings are much smaller compared to full function bodies, we end up with the overall smaller formula, speeding up the analysis process.

3   Interprocedural BMC

With inlining the analysis would proceed top-down, from the function to its callees, inserting function bodies in the process; as a result, we would end up with an inflated function containing all other function bodies as-is. We propose to do the analysis the other way around—bottom-up, from the points of interest (e.g., possible bug locations) to the callers, collecting information relevant to the safety checks as calling contexts, which are stored in the corresponding PS. The resulting formula is then analyzed using traditional BMC approach. Therefore, our algorithm is naturally divided into 2 phases: collect phase and analysis phase. Let us consider these phases in more detail.

3.1   Collect Phase

The collect phase does the following: given a function F and its safety property Q, it gathers argument-specific information, which is relevant to Q, from all call sites of F. Informally, one can say we are building an *context-sensitive interprocedural slice* of how F is used in different parts of the program (traversing the call graph bottom-up, from the callees to the callers) and how its arguments influence Q. Algorithm 1 outlines how we collect the context-sensitive PS *State* about function call *Call* w.r.t. safety property query *Query*.

First, we check whether we have encountered a recursive call; if we did, we conservatively stop the collect phase and return the result. In this work we did not consider other strategies of dealing with recursion, this is one of the most interesting directions of possible future work.

Second, we slice the function w.r.t. current query [20], removing all irrelevant parts. In many cases, this slice is usable as-is; if it contains nested calls to other functions, however, their behaviour can impact the behaviour of the current function either implicitly or explicitly. An example of such a situation is presented in Listing 1.1. Depending on the result of **get_next_index** function, we may or may not have an out-of-bounds error in line 6.

To accommodate these situations, we peek inside such nested functions and attempt to understand whether or not they impact the safety property, in essence, locally switching to a top down call graph analysis. Once again, there are several approaches to it; we decided to opt for an approach presented in Algorithm 2.

In our peek-inside algorithm we also utilize slicing of the nested function, which in this case is used to retain only parts of this function relevant to its caller and the corresponding query. To do that, we reformulate the query in the context of the nested call and use it to guide the process by slicing w.r.t. its arguments and return value. However, the analysis of a nested function may itself encounter a dependency on this function's nested calls or recursion. Once again, we decided to use a conservative approach, and our peek-inside algorithm always processes only one level of calls; in the future we would like to explore how the different values of call depth influence the analysis performance.

Last, after we have processed all nested calls, we merge their PS into the resulting *State* and continue to traverse the call graph. For every use (caller) of the function, we update the query to include the calling context: parameter-to-argument mappings and how the function's return value is used. The collect phase then analyzes the caller and merges the result to the final *State*.

Listing 1.1. Running program example which needs alternating call graph traversal

```
int get_next_index(int a) {
    return a + 1;
}

void print_element(int* arr, int num) {
    printf("arr=%i\n", arr[num]);
}

void print_next_element(int* arr, int num) {
    int idx = get_next_index(num);
    print_element(arr, idx);
}

int main(int argc, char* argv[]) {
    int a[] = {1, 2, 3};
    print_element(a, 0);
    print_next_element(a, 0);
    return 0;
}
```

Algorithm 1. High-level collect phase algorithm

INPUT: *Call* (function call)
INPUT: *Query* (query)
INPUT: *State* (current state)
OUTPUT: state extended with bottom-up calling context of *Call*

```
 1: function COLLECTCALLINGCONTEXT(Call, Query, State)
 2:     if isRecursive(Call, State) then
 3:         return State
 4:     end if
 5:     Function ⇐ getFunction(Call)
 6:     StateUpdate ⇐ getQuerySlice(Function, Query)
 7:     for all NestedCall from getNestedCalls(StateUpdate) do
 8:         StateUpdate ⇐ peekInto(
 9:             NestedCall, Query, StateUpdate)
10:     end for
11:     State ⇐ mergeChain(State, StateUpdate)
12:     for all Use from getUses(Function) do
13:         UseQuery ⇐ getCallerQuery(Use, Query)
14:         UseState ⇐ collectCallingContext(
15:             Use, State, UseQuery)
16:         State ⇐ mergeChoice(State, UseState)
17:     end for
18:     return State
19: end function
```

Let us zoom in on the following key components of our approach.

- slicing of the target function w.r.t. query (`getQuerySlice`)
- transformation of the query between callers and callees (`getCallerQuery`, `getCalleeQuery`)
- merging of different PS (`mergeChain`, `mergeChoice`)

For the slicing implementation, we utilize the facilities provided by the Borealis BMC tool; it works on PS and supports slicing a given PS w.r.t. another query PS. As far as our knowledge goes, Borealis does advanced backward slicing [20], taking into account pointer aliasing and different interprocedural effects (e.g., changes to a value via a pointer passed to another function); this means such a slice is *safe*, i.e., it is guaranteed to retain all parts of the program relevant to the query PS.

For the alias analysis, Borealis slicing uses implementation based on well-known Steensgaard algorithm [19], but done over the PS instead of the original program. The authors state this approach is safe, as the collected aliases are sound w.r.t. target PS.

To transform the query when moving between different contexts, we employ a simple, but efficient technique: query Q is extended with the calling context, i.e., we add expressions binding function parameters to the call arguments, and function return value to the call assignment (if present). This technique is very

Algorithm 2. Nested function peek-inside algorithm

INPUT: *Call* (function call)
INPUT: *Query* (query)
INPUT: *State* (current state)
OUTPUT: state extended with top-down calling context of *Call*

  1: **function** PEEKINTO(*Call*, *Query*, *State*)
  2:     *Function* ⟸ getFunction(*Call*)
  3:     *CalleeQuery* ⟸ getCalleeQuery(*Call*, *Query*)
  4:     *StateUpdate* ⟸ getQuerySlice(*Function*, *CalleeQuery*)
  5:     *State* ⟸ mergeChain(*State*, *StateUpdate*)
  6:     return *State*
  7: **end function**

---

similar, for example, to how the bddbddb [11] static analyzer handles interprocedural analysis; all calling contexts are encoded as-is, and the reasoning is done via an efficient binary decision diagram (BDD) implementation. In our case, instead of BDDs we build upon SMT solvers, which are well-suited to processing such formulae [4].

Merging information from different PS actively uses their persistent nature and compositability. Both `mergeChain` and `mergeChoice` simplify the resulting PS and remove redundant parts of the formula, e.g., common prefixes present in several alternative expressions are joined into one.

3.2   Analysis Phase

After the collect phase is complete, we end up with a PS representing all calling contexts interesting w.r.t. the safety property Q. This PS corresponds to a formula of the form $P_0 \vee P_1 \vee \ldots \vee P_n$, where P_i represents a particular calling context. An example of such PS for our running example from Listing 1.1 is shown in Listing 1.2.

Listing 1.2. Resulting predicate state for the running example

```
(BEGIN
  <OR>(
    @P free_var=0
  )->(
    main_%0=alloca(3,(3 * 1)),
    @I main_arraydecay=gep[inbounds](main_%0,0+0+0),
    num=0
    arr=main_arraydecay
  )->(
    @I idxprom=cast(+Integer(64), num),
    @I arrayidx=gep(arr,0+idxprom)
  ),
  <OR>(
    @P free_var=1
  )->(
    main_%0=alloca(3,(3 * 1)),
    @I main_arraydecay1=gep[inbounds](main_%0,0+0+0),
    print_next_element_num=0
```

```
  print_next_element_arr=main_arraydecay1
)->(
  @I get_next_index_add=(print_next_element_num + 1),
  print_next_element_call=get_next_index_add
)->(
  num=print_next_element_call
  arr=print_next_element_arr
)->(
  @I idxprom=cast(+Integer(64), num),
  @I arrayidx=gep(arr,0+idxprom)
)
END)
```

In the example, function `print_element` is called in two distinct contexts, and the resulting choice PS contains two alternatives corresponding to these contexts. A synthetic variable `free_var` is used to identify calling contexts; if an SMT solver produces a satisfying assignment for our safety property, the values of `free_var` can be used to find the exact context triggering a bug.

As the resulting formula can be represented as a set of formulae joined by disjunction, there are 2 equivalent ways of processing it via an SMT solver: either check it for satisfiability as one large formula or check each small disjunct separately. However, despite being equivalent from the result point-of-view, they are very different w.r.t. performance. Our experiments show the latter way to be more performant in practice; we speculate this to happen, because the SMT solver needs more time to preprocess the larger formula and additional efforts to infer the disjuncts to be completely independent of each other.

4   Evaluation

We implemented our approach as an extension to the Borealis bounded model checker. For the evaluation benchmark, we selected several small- and medium-sized C language projects, shown in Table 1. We analyzed these projects in three modes: basic intraprocedural BMC (intra), BMC with full inlining (inline) and our interprocedural BMC approach (inter)[2]. The resulting bug reports have been

Table 1. Benchmark projects

Name	SLOC	Description	Github name	Commit
iputils	12k	Set of tools for Linux networking	iputils/iputils	1ef0e4c8
progress	1k	Coreutils progress viewer	xfennec/progress	a52b47c1
reptyr	2k	Tool for "re-ptying" programs	nelhage/reptyr	fe7a276d
mptun	1k	Multi-path tunnel VPN	cloudwu/mptun	78a6a220
pit	3.5k	Cmd project manager	michaeldv/pit	4d205578
linenoise	2k	**readline** replacement	antirez/linenoise	2eb49568
mdp	1.5k	Cmd Markdown presentation tool	visit1985/mdp	d697dc51

---

[2] The test machine had Intel Core i7-4790 3.6 GHz processor, 32 GB of memory, and Intel 535 SSD storage.

summarized into the following reference parameters: number of bugs found and the total analysis time. The results are presented in Table 2.

Table 2. Evaluation results

Project	Time (min:sec)			Bugs		
	Intra	Inter	Inline	Intra	Inter	Inline
`iputils`	0:57	2:29	–	467	369	–
`progress`	0:28	3:50	80:00	85	54	50
`reptyr`	0:03	1:08	105:37	130	63	43
`mptun`	0:02	1:05	1:53	64	11	10
`pit`	0:09	0:51	26:01	313	269	250
`linenoise`	0:02	1:35	–	117	71	–
`mdp`	0:58	25:44	445:39	167	82	80

We can make the following conclusions from the numbers. First, in all cases our interprocedural approach to BMC is more precise than the naive intraprocedural approach and has 100% recall compared to the full inlining; i.e., for three sets of bugs *Intra*, *Inter* and *Inline*, it is true that *Intra* $\supset$ *Inter* $\supset$ *Inline*[3]. Second, the interprocedural mode significantly outperforms the inlining by the analysis time in all cases except for `mptun`[4]. Third, it also manages to successfully analyze all seven projects, whereas inlining fails to terminate in reasonable time on two of the seven projects (`iputils` and `linenoise`).

The results support the practical applicability of our interprocedural approach, which allows one to achieve reasonable analysis time and preserve much of the precision of inlining.

4.1 Causes of Imprecision

One of the more interesting questions is: why does our approach not achieve the same precision as full inlining? Our approach has the following sources of possible imprecision.

The most important reason is our handling of recursion; if we encounter a recursive calling context, we stop the analysis without any attempts to process the recursion. This means in some cases we will not traverse the call graph far enough to collect information needed to prove the safety property. Inlining, on the other hand, starts top down and can iteratively inline recursive functions until we have collected all information needed. Another cause of differences is that our peek-inside algorithm from Sect. 3.1 goes inside only one level, whereas inlining does not have such a limitation.

---

[3] This was confirmed by analyzing the full bug reports, which are omitted for brevity.

[4] It is important to note that for `mptun` interprocedural mode finds exactly the same bugs as inlining, while being faster at the same time.

These two reasons can be summarized as a principled decision to restrict the scope of call graph traversal, to simplify the approach and its implementation, so that we can quickly check its real-world applicability. In our future work we may explore how one may surmount these limitations by traversing the call graph in a more comprehensive and intelligent way.

5   Related Work

5.1   Craig Interpolation

In the context of BMC, there already exists several ways of interprocedural analysis. One of the better known ones is Craig interpolation [16,18]. The main idea of Craig interpolation lies in finding Craig interpolants; for an inconsistent pair of formulas (B, Q) in first-order logic, a Craig interpolant is a formula I such that:

- $B \rightarrow I$
- (I, Q) is also an inconsistent pair of formulae
- I contains only uninterpreted symbols common to B and Q

A Craig interpolant can be built for any inconsistent pair of formulae, and modern SMT solvers can create interpolants as a byproduct of the unsatisfiability proof. An interpolant I of a function B w.r.t. a safety property Q may be considered an approximation of B and used in place of its call sites.

However, Craig interpolation has a number of limitations; the main one is that the pair of formulas (B, Q) must be inconsistent for the interpolant I to exist. In the context of BMC, this means an approximation may be constructed only if the security property always holds for a given function, which makes this approach ill-suited for many practical applications.

5.2   External Specifications

Another approach to interprocedural analysis in BMC is to forgo automatic function approximation and instead rely on external specifications provided by the developer. This fact is one of the main downsides to this approach, as writing specifications for any practical program may be as difficult as writing the program itself [14], which makes this approach very hard to use in most practical cases.

The first approach is based on using annotating comments to describe the behavior of different code fragments, such as functions or loops. A good example of such an approach is the ACSL language [6], which allows to specify additional information about the behavior of whole functions or separate statements.

An alternative to specialized comments is to use an embedded DSL to describe program behaviour. This approach requires less integration with the target language compiler, however, it also has less declarative power (as embedded DSLs are restricted by the host language). An example of such an approach is the Clang analyzer [1], which uses GCC-style attributes and assert calls to enrich the program with additional semantics.

An external DSL is the most powerful approach in the family of external specifications. As the DSL may be custom tailored to the needs of any given analysis, this approach is the most flexible; however, it requires development of said DSL, which may take a lot of additional time and effort. SLIC (Specification Language for the Interface Checking), developed by Microsoft Research [5], is an example of such an external DSL.

5.3   Interprocedural Analysis

As we stated before, our approach may be considered an attempt to apply interprocedural analysis techniques from the field of program static analysis to BMC. The classic paper [21] describes a combination of two approaches to interprocedural analysis—bottom up and top down—and shows how their combination can be used to improve analysis performance and precision. Top-down analyses start from a set of root functions in a program and go down, bottom-up analyses begin from interesting points inside the program and proceed up. Our approach was heavily inspired by this idea; however, as in the BMC case full top-down analyses end up being similar to full inlining, we adopted a localized bottom-up strategy (as described in Sect. 3.1).

Saturn [2] was one of the first static analysis system to support interprocedural analysis. It achieved this via the use of procedure summaries: specifically crafted pieces of information about function behaviour which are used when interprocedural analysis is needed. These summaries may also be attached to specific types, global variables, etc. However, the summaries are not universal: every interesting function behaviour and safety property needs to be extracted by a separate analysis. Our approach adapts to safety properties being analyzed without the need to change existing or create new analyses.

6   Conclusion

In this paper we presented a novel approach to interprocedural analysis in the context of BMC. The approach is based on a combined bottom-up and top-down call graph traversal, which only collects information relevant to the given safety property. This allows us to avoid the excessive growth of the resulting SMT formula common to function inlining, while also achieving good precision.

We implemented the proposed approach in a prototype plugin for Borealis BMC tool and evaluated it on a number of projects. The results showed our approach to have positive impact on both the performance and precision of BMC; however, there are several topics we could explore further in our future work.

References

1. Clang static analyzer. http://clang-analyzer.llvm.org/ (2019). Accessed 20 Feb 2019

2. Aiken, A., Bugrara, S., Dillig, I., Dillig, T., Hackett, B., Hawkins, P.: An overview of the saturn project. In: Proceedings of the 7th ACM SIGPLAN-SIGSOFT Workshop on Program Analysis for Software Tools and Engineering, pp. 43–48. ACM (2007)
3. Akhin, M., Belyaev, M., Itsykson, V.: Borealis bounded model checker: the coming of age story. Present and Ulterior Software Engineering, pp. 119–137. Springer, Cham (2017). https://doi.org/10.1007/978-3-319-67425-4_8
4. Armando, A., Mantovani, J., Platania, L.: Bounded model checking of software using SMT solvers instead of SAT solvers. In: Valmari, A. (ed.) SPIN 2006. LNCS, vol. 3925, pp. 146–162. Springer, Heidelberg (2006). https://doi.org/10.1007/11691617_9
5. Ball, T., Rajamani, S.K., Rajamani, S., Ball, T.: SLIC: a specification language for interface checking (of c). Microsoft Research (2002)
6. Baudin, P., et al.: ACSL: ANSI/ISO C Specification Language. Preliminary Design, version 1.4, 2008, preliminary edn. (2008)
7. Biere, A., Cimatti, A., Clarke, E., Zhu, Y.: Symbolic model checking without BDDs. In: Cleaveland, W.R. (ed.) TACAS 1999. LNCS, vol. 1579, pp. 193–207. Springer, Heidelberg (1999). https://doi.org/10.1007/3-540-49059-0_14
8. Christakis, M., Bird, C.: What developers want and need from program analysis: an empirical study. In: Proceedings of the 31st IEEE/ACM International Conference on Automated Software Engineering, ASE 2016, pp. 332–343. ACM, New York (2016). https://doi.org/10.1145/2970276.2970347. http://doi.acm.org/10.1145/2970276.2970347
9. Ivancic, F., et al.: Model checking C programs using f-soft. In: 2005 IEEE International Conference on Computer Design: VLSI in Computers and Processors, ICCD 2005, Proceedings, pp. 297–308. IEEE (2005)
10. Kroening, D., Tautschnig, M.: CBMC – C bounded model checker. In: Ábrahám, E., Havelund, K. (eds.) TACAS 2014. LNCS, vol. 8413, pp. 389–391. Springer, Heidelberg (2014). https://doi.org/10.1007/978-3-642-54862-8_26
11. Lam, M.S., et al.: Context-sensitive program analysis as database queries. In: Proceedings of the Twenty-fourth ACM SIGMOD-SIGACT-SIGART Symposium on Principles of Database Systems, PODS 2005, pp. 1–12. ACM, New York(2005). https://doi.org/10.1145/1065167.1065169. http://doi.acm.org/10.1145/1065167.1065169
12. Landi, W.: Undecidability of static analysis. LOPLAS 1(4), 323–337 (1992)
13. Lattner, C., Adve, V.: LLVM: a compilation framework for lifelong program analysis & transformation. In: CGO 2004, pp. 75–86 (2004)
14. Leavens, G.T., Clifton, C.: Lessons from the JML project. In: Meyer, B., Woodcock, J. (eds.) VSTTE 2005. LNCS, vol. 4171, pp. 134–143. Springer, Heidelberg (2008). https://doi.org/10.1007/978-3-540-69149-5_15
15. Merz, F., Falke, S., Sinz, C.: LLBMC: bounded model checking of C and C++ programs using a compiler IR. In: Joshi, R., Müller, P., Podelski, A. (eds.) VSTTE 2012. LNCS, vol. 7152, pp. 146–161. Springer, Heidelberg (2012). https://doi.org/10.1007/978-3-642-27705-4_12
16. Sery, O., Fedyukovich, G., Sharygina, N.: Interpolation-based function summaries in bounded model checking. In: Eder, K., Lourenço, J., Shehory, O. (eds.) HVC 2011. LNCS, vol. 7261, pp. 160–175. Springer, Heidelberg (2012). https://doi.org/10.1007/978-3-642-34188-5_15
17. Sharir, M., Pnueli, A., et al.: Two approaches to interprocedural data flow analysis. New York University. Courant Institute of Mathematical Sciences, Computer Science Department (1978)

18. Smullyan, R.R.: First-Order Logic, vol. 43. Springer, Heidelberg (2012)
19. Steensgaard, B.: Points-to analysis in almost linear time. In: Proceedings of the 23rd ACM SIGPLAN-SIGACT Symposium on Principles of Programming Languages, pp. 32–41. ACM (1996)
20. Weiser, M.: Program slicing. In: Proceedings of the 5th International Conference on Software Engineering, pp. 439–449. IEEE Press (1981)
21. Zhang, X., Mangal, R., Naik, M., Yang, H.: Hybrid top-down and bottom-up interprocedural analysis. SIGPLAN Not. **49**(6), 249–258 (2014). https://doi.org/10.1145/2666356.2594328. http://doi.acm.org/10.1145/2666356.2594328

Static Taint Analysis for JavaScript Programs

Nabil Almashfi$^{(\boxtimes)}$ and Lunjin Lu

Computer Science and Engineering Department,
Oakland University, Rochester, MI 48309, USA
{nalmashfi,l2lu}@oakland.edu

Abstract. Web applications have become an essential component of many different fields. As a client-side scripting language, JavaScript is ubiquitous across the web. Malicious JavaScript code can exploit a user's browser, cookies, and security permissions. In this paper, we propose a static taint analysis approach for precise detection of taint-style vulnerabilities, such as DOM-based Cross-site Scripting (XSS), in JavaScript programs. The approach divides sinks into contexts to ensure that untrusted data passed to a certain context has been sufficiently sanitized. We reengineered TAJS resulting in a new analyzer, TAJS$_\text{taint}$, that adopts the new approach and uses finite state automata as its abstract string domain in order to track tainted flows more precisely. We run TAJS$_\text{taint}$ on a set of real Web pages and show that TAJS$_\text{taint}$ can precisely detect taint-style vulnerabilities, especially those that are caused by insufficient input sanitization.

Keywords: JavaScript · Static analysis · Abstract interpretation · Taint analysis

1 Introduction

JavaScript is primarily a scripting language and a top contender in real-world usage. It can effectively be used to write large and complex applications due to its flexibility and power. JavaScript code is written into an HTML page and it gets executed at the client-side. With Web applications moving towards client-side functionality and storage, exploitable JavaScript code exposes the user and even the system on which the program is being executed to significant damage. One of the top JavaScript vulnerabilities is DOM-based Cross-site Scripting (XSS) which purely occurs on the client-side. This vulnerability takes place when a client-side script reads data from a part of the DOM that can be controlled by an attacker and executes it as valid JavaScript code. For example, a script may read some data from the URL which enables the attacker to construct a URL injected with malicious JavaScript code. If the data read from the URL is not sufficiently sanitized, this code can be executed within the user's browser and it can perform various harmful actions. Therefore, sufficient input sanitization is key in preventing this attack and strengthening program integrity.

© Springer Nature Switzerland AG 2021
A. Kalenkova et al. (Eds.): TMPA 2019, CCIS 1288, pp. 155–167, 2021.
https://doi.org/10.1007/978-3-030-71472-7_13

Taint analysis is a type of analysis that detects flows of data that violate program integrity. It is a powerful technique designed to detect security vulnerabilities, such as DOM-based XSS, through data flow analysis. Taint analysis identifies taint sources and follows them into sink locations, looking for a trace from source to sink that does not pass through a sanitizer. Taint sources are program points that can be controlled by a malicious user whereas sinks are program points where rendered data can be interpreted as executable code.

This paper presents $TAJS_{taint}$, a reengineered version of TAJS [10]. $TAJS_{taint}$ is an analyzer that performs static taint analysis for JavaScript programs using data flow analysis. Our taint analysis is context-sensitive and is capable of accurately detecting taint-style vulnerabilities. The main contributions of this paper are the following:

- We propose a static taint analysis approach for precise detection of taint-style vulnerabilities in JavaScript programs. The analysis is based on identifying various rendering contexts in a Web page and it ensures that the data received from tainted sources has been sufficiently sanitized for each context.
- We use an abstract string domain based on finite state automata to handle dynamic property accesses in order to track taint more precisely and reduce the number of false positives.
- Finally, we test $TAJS_{taint}$ on a set of real Web pages and show that $TAJS_{taint}$ is capable of discovering taint-style vulnerabilities that are caused by unsanitized or insufficiently sanitized input.

The structure of this paper is as follows. Section 2 provides a background introduction to TAJS and Web applications. Section 3 gives a motivating example. Section 4 describes our taint analysis approach. Section 5 describes the abstract string domain. Section 6 presents the evaluation results of our taint analysis. Section 7 presents related work and Sect. 8 concludes.

2   Background

2.1   TAJS (Type Analyzer for JavaScript)

TAJS is a context-sensitive analyzer for JavaScript that supports the ECMAScript language and parts of the DOM. It infers type information as well as call graphs. TAJS constructs flow graphs to represent JavaScript program code and performs the analysis on the flow graphs. The analysis is designed to be sound and is based on the monotone framework using a lattice structure. The lattice is based on constant propagation for all the primitive types of JavaScript values. TAJS allows the call graph to be constructed on-the-fly to handle higher-order functions and its heap abstraction is based on allocation sites.

2.2   Web Applications

A Web application is a client-server software that can be accessed via a Web browser. It is often a combination of server-side scripts, written in languages such as PHP and ASP, and client-side scripts, written in languages such as HTML and JavaScript. Server-side scripts run on a Web server and they handle requests from the client such as the storage and retrieval of information. Client-side scripts render this information on a Web browser.

In a typical Web application, a user sends a request to the Web server via a Web browser. The Web server determines the appropriate application to handle the request. The application processes the request and carries out the task which may include the storage or retrieval of information from a database. The application then sends the results to the Web server and the Web server responds back to the user with the results.

In this paper, we focus on the client-side mechanism, particularly, HTML and JavaScript. HTML is the standard markup language that describes the structure of Web pages. It consists of a number of HTML elements that tell the browser how to display the content of the Web page. HTML elements are represented by opening and closing tags. The <html> element is the root element of an HTML page. The <head> element contains meta information about the document. The <title> element specifies a title for the document. The <body> element contains the visible page content. The Document Object Model (DOM) is a programming interface for HTML representing the Web page so it can be manipulated with a scripting language such as JavaScript. JavaScript uses the DOM to access the document and its elements. Finally, JavaScript code is inline in a <script> element.

3   Motivation

Figure 1 is a simple Javascript program that is prone to DOM-based XXS attacks. It illustrates some of the challenges faced by taint analysis when dealing with the dynamic features of JavaScript. Particularly, the program shows the necessity of choosing the right kind of sanitizers for each rendering context. In addition, it demonstrates how imprecise string analysis can negatively affect the precision of taint analysis when dealing with features such as dynamic property accesses and property lookups via the prototype-chain.

The script starts by reading the value of param that is provided in the URL, at lines 4–5. The document object (document) is an object that represents the Web page and it allows JavaScript to access and manipulate the document elements. The location object (location) contains information about the URL and the property href returns the entire URL. The script then defines two constructor functions G, at lines 6–8, and K, at lines 11–13, where each constructor has one property. Constructor functions are used to create objects of the same type. At lines 9 and 15, two object of type G and K are created respectively. At line 10, property g1 of object g is assigned the value of unsafeData which is coming from a tainted source. The value of property g.g1 is assigned to property k1 of constructor K which indicates that each object of K will have its own copy of the value of k1. At line 14, the prototype of constructor K is assigned a link to object g. When a function is created, as well as objects, in JavaScript, JavaScript

```
1   <html><head><title> DOM-based XSS! </title></head>
2   <body><div id="d1"></div><div id="d2"></div>
3   <script>
4   var pos = document.location.href.indexOf("param=") + 6;
5   var unsafeData = document.location.href.substring(pos);
6   function G() {
7       this.g1 = new Object();
8   }
9   var g = new G();
10  g.g1 = unsafeData;
11  function K() {
12      this.k1 = g.g1;
13  }
14  K.prototype = g;
15  var k = new K();
16  var c = k;
17  var d1 = document.getElementById("d1");
18  d1.innerHTML = k.g1; // unsafe
19  document.write("<a id=' " + encodeURI(unsafeData) + " '>Click
        Here</a>"); // unsafe
20  var d2 = document.getElementById("d2");
21  d2.innerHTML = encodeForJS(encodeForHTML(k.k1)); // safe
22  document.write(lookup(c, "g", "1")); // unsafe
23  update(c, "k", "1");
24  document.write(lookup(c, "k", "1")); // safe
25  </script>
26  </body></html>
```

Fig. 1. A JavaScript program

engine creates a prototype property and attach it to that function or object. This
prototype property holds a link to another object which also has a prototype
property that holds a link to another object and so on until we reach an object
with its prototype property set to null. When trying to access a property of
an object, JavaScript engine checks the object, the prototype of the object, the
prototype of the prototype and so on until either the property is found or the
end of the prototype chain is reached. As a consequence, Object k has access to
all properties of object g via its prototype.

The Document method getElementById() at lines 17 and 20 returns an Element object representing the element that has the ID attribute with the specified
value. The innerHTML property at lines 18 and 21 changes the content (inner
HTML) of an HTML element. The assignment of property k.g1 to sink field
d1.innerHTML at line 18 is clearly not safe because property g1 has not been
sanitized. However, the assignment at line 21 is safe because property g1 is sufficiently sanitized by using encodeJS and encodeHTML following the prevention
rules in [1], further explained in Sect. 4.1.

```
1  function lookup(o, s, p) {
2      while(p.length < N)
3          p = s + p;
4      return o[p];
5  }
```

```
1  function update(o, s, p) {
2      while(p.length < N)
3          p = s + p;
4      o[p] = "";
5  }
```

Fig. 2. Two functions that read and update properties of obj o

The function document.write(), at line 19, is a sink function that writes to the document stream. It writes the HTML element a to the document and initializes its ID property from a tainted source. The sanitizer function $encodeURI()$ encodes a Uniform Resource Identifier (URI). However, this function does not encode the single quotation mark nor the equality sign which makes it possible for a malicious user to insert the closing delimiter, in this case the single quotation mark, and add more attributes to the a element. The following string can pass the sanitizer and add a new attribute

```
9' href='http://www.site.com
```

To make clear how update() and lookup() work, we briefly introduce dynamic property access. Property names in JavaScript can be accessed using either dot notation or bracket notation. A property p of an object o, for instance, can be accessed as o.p or o["p"]. The property name must be a valid identifier when using dot notation whereas it can be a variable, or an expression using bracket notation.

The functions update() and lookup() in Fig. 2 dynamically constructs a property name. The function update() updates the specified property whereas lookup() returns the property value. The value of N is an integer and is unknown at compile time. A sound but imprecise analysis can safely approximate p at line 3 in both functions to be any string and property p would point to all properties of object o including properties in the prototype hierarchy. In our analysis, we use finite state automata to track all possible strings a variable might hold during execution. Therefore, the analysis can determine that property p is represented by g^n1, excluding all other properties, when the call to lookup() is made at line 22 making it unsafe. The call to update() at line 23 will update property k1 to an empty string making the call at line 24 safe.

4 Taint Analysis

Static taint analysis is used to test for security vulnerabilities in programs. It tracks data coming from untrusted sources that could cause security vulnerabilities and follows them into sinks ensuring that all data are sufficiently sanitized. In this section, we describe our approach to precisely detect taint-style vulnerabilities.

4.1   Rendering Contexts

There are many contexts in a Web page that can be reached and set via JavaScript execution context. A malicious user may try to attack these contexts from within JavaScript context and insert malicious code that can cause serious damage such as stealing user information or simply break the application display of data. User input can be inserted into several contexts in a Web page. As a consequence, putting untrusted data safely into each context requires following specific rules. Some characters that may be innocuous in one context can be significant in another context and thus it is important to determine where the user input ends up. The most common contexts in a Web page are JavaScript Context ($\mathcal{JSC}$), HTML Element Context ($\mathcal{HEC}$), HTML Attribute Context ($\mathcal{HAC}$), HTML Event-handler Attribute Context ($\mathcal{HHC}$), HTML URL Attribute Context ($\mathcal{HUC}$), and CSS attribute Context ($\mathcal{HCC}$). Any context where data is inserted into an HTML element, such as a div element, is a $\mathcal{HEC}$ context. $\mathcal{HAC}$ context includes all locations where data are inserted into HTML attributes except event-handler and URL attributes. Event-handler attributes trigger actions in a browser when an event occurs. For example, onclick attribute triggers some action specified by the developer when an HTML element is clicked. A URL attribute sets a URL inside an HTML element and CSS attributes set the presentation of an element. The following lines of code illustrates all fives contexts:

```
1   <SCRIPT>𝒥𝒮𝒞</SCRIPT>
2   <div id="ℋ𝒜𝒞" style="ℋ𝒞𝒞" onclick="ℋℋ𝒞">ℋℰ𝒞</div>
3   <a id="a1" href="ℋ𝒰𝒞"></a>
```

All these contexts can be accesses via JavaScript context using a number of DOM methods.

There are certain characters that need to be encoded for each context to ensure that the attacker can not insert the closing delimiter for that context and inject malicious code. For instance, in order to sanitize the data inserted into a $\mathcal{HAC}$ context, the characters (&, <, ", ') have to be encoded to prevent the exit out of the HTML attribute and attempt to add additional attributes. In a context such as $\mathcal{HEC}$, we first need to HTML encode then JavaScript encode all characters before inserting untrusted data into the context.

4.2   Analysis Rules

TAJS$_{\text{taint}}$ defines a set of *rules* that are used to check whether the application being tested is vulnerable. Let $\$_1$ be the set of *sources*, $\$_2$ be the set of *sanitizers*, and $\$_3$ be the set of *sinks*. Each *rule* is of the form (S_1, S_2, S_3) where $S_1 \in \$_1$, $S_2 \in \mathcal{P}(\$_2)$, and $S_3 \in \$_3$. *Sources* are either functions or object properties that can be controlled by the attacker. For instance, the property location.hash, which returns the anchor part of a URL, is a *source*. *Sinks* are functions or object properties where data are rendered and can be executed. For instance, the function document.write(), which writes some text directly to the HTML document stream, is a *sink*. Sinks are classified by TAJS$_{\text{taint}}$ according to their

Table 1. Encoding mechanisms required for each context

	$\mathcal{JE}$	$\mathcal{HE}$	$\mathcal{UE}$
$\mathcal{JSC}$	–	–	–
$\mathcal{HEC}$	✓	✓	–
$\mathcal{HAC}$	–	✓	–
$\mathcal{HHC}$	–	–	–
$\mathcal{HUC}$	–	✓	✓
$\mathcal{HCC}$	–	✓	✓

contexts. A context $\mathcal{C} \subseteq \{\mathcal{HEC}, \mathcal{HAC}, \mathcal{HHC}, \mathcal{HUC}, \mathcal{HCC}\}$. *Sanitizers* are functions that transform data as innocuous data by encoding harmful characters so they can be safely passed to sinks. There are a number of encoding mechanisms that sanitizers implement.

TAJS$_{\text{taint}}$ expects each sanitizer R to implement one or more out of the following three encoding mechanisms E: JavaScript encoding ($\mathcal{JE}$), HTML encoding ($\mathcal{HE}$), and URL encoding ($\mathcal{UE}$). Formally, $R \in \mathcal{P}(E = \{\mathcal{JE}, \mathcal{HE}, \mathcal{UE}\})$. JavaScript built-in sanitizers are recognized by TAJS$_{\text{taint}}$. However, sanitizers that are from an external encoding library can be easily added to the default specification as a set of pairs (X, Y) where X is the function name and $Y \subseteq E$. In general, JavaScript encoding serves to stop malicious Javascript code from being executed. HTML encoding serves to castrate HTML tags which are placed in $\mathcal{HEC}$ and $\mathcal{HAC}$ contexts whereas URL encoding performs percent-encoding for a component of a Uniform Resource Identifier to ensure that special characters in the component do not get interpreted as part of another component.

Based on the defined rules, TAJS$_{\text{taint}}$ tracks flows of data from sources to sinks to ensure that the data has been intercepted by a set of sanitizers in the same rule. The rules defined in TAJS$_{\text{taint}}$ follows the rules specified by [1], which is summarized in Table 1, in order to determine the kind of sanitizing needed for each sink. For the $\mathcal{JSC}$ and $\mathcal{HHC}$ contexts, the primary recommendation by [1] is to avoid inserting untrusted data into them because encodings might not mitigate against DOM-based XSS. Therefore, we consider all flows of untrusted data to these contexts to be invalid.

Example: The following is an example of the way rules are defined in TAJS$_{\text{taint}}$.

$S_1 = \{document.URL,\ location.href\}$
$S_2 = \{\{encodeForJS(),\ encodeForHTML()\}\}$
$S_3 = \{document.write()\}$

This rule states that *document.URL* and *location.href* are two sources of taint and that the data flowing from these sources to sink *document.write()* need to by intercepted by the two sanitizers *encodeForJS()* and *encodeForHTML()*.

Abstract Domain For Taint. Tainted values may go through a number of sanitizers that implement different encoding rules. We design a new abstract domain in order to determine the kinds of encodings a tainted value has gone through. Let $T = \{\mathsf{HTML\text{-}encoded}, \mathsf{JavaScript\text{-}encoded}, \mathsf{URL\text{-}encoded}\}$. The abstract element $\mathsf{HTML\text{-}encoded}$ indicates that the value has been HTML-encoded, $\mathsf{JavaScript\text{-}encoded}}$ indicates that the value has been JavaScript-encoded, and $\mathsf{URL\text{-}encoded}$ indicates that the value has been URL-encoded. The abstract domain for taint analysis is $\mathcal{P}(T)$ ordered by $\supseteq$. Note that the least-upper-bound operation is $\cap$ and the greatest-lower-bound operation is $\cup$. Let String be the set of all possible strings. Define

$$\gamma_T(\mathsf{HTML\text{-}encoded}) = \{\mathcal{HE}(s) \mid s \in \mathsf{String}\}$$
$$\gamma_T(\mathsf{JavaScript\text{-}encoded}) = \{\mathcal{JS}(s) \mid s \in \mathsf{String}\}$$
$$\gamma_T(\mathsf{URL\text{-}encoded}) = \{\mathcal{HU}(s) \mid s \in \mathsf{String}\}$$

Define $\gamma : \mathcal{P}(T) \to \mathcal{P}(\mathsf{String})$ is defined as follows:

$$\gamma(\mathcal{T}) = \cap\,\{\,\gamma_T(t) \mid t \in \mathcal{T}\,\}$$

It can be shown that (α, γ) is a Galois connection where $\alpha : \mathcal{P}(\mathsf{String}) \to \mathcal{P}(T)$ is defined

$$\alpha(S) = \{\,t \mid t \in T \wedge S \subseteq \gamma_T(t)\,\}$$

5   Handling Dynamic Property Access

The constant propagation domain used in TAJS and other related work is very imprecise in dealing with dynamic property access. It is common that object properties in JavaScript hold data coming from a tainted source. Furthermore, object properties can also store function that can manipulate data in a way that results in tainted information being stored or read from untrusted sources. As discussed in Sect. 3, imprecise analysis can safely approximate p in Fig. 2 to be any string and property p would point to all properties of object o including properties in the prototype hierarchy. However, this broad approximation will increase the number of false positives. To overcome the loss in precision, $\mathsf{TAJS_{taint}}$ uses a precise abstract string domain in order to precisely abstract property names.

Abstract String Domain. $\mathsf{TAJS_{taint}}$ associates every string variable with a deterministic finite automaton that denotes the set of string values the variable can have at runtime along with a widening operator [4].

Let M_1 and M_2 be two finite state automata. We can define the partial order as the following:

$$M_1 \leq M_2 \overset{\text{def}}{=} L(M_1) \subseteq L(M_2)$$

where $\leq$ is a preorder. This induces an equivalent relation $\equiv$

$$M_1 \equiv M_2 \quad \overset{\text{def}}{=} \quad L(M_1) \leq L(M_2) \land L(M_2) \leq L(M_1)$$
$$\sqsubseteq \quad \overset{\text{def}}{=} \quad \leq_{/\equiv} \quad \text{that is}$$
$$[M_1]_\equiv \sqsubseteq [M_2]_\equiv \quad \text{iff} \quad L(M_1) \leq L(M_2)$$

We use a member of an equivalent class of $\equiv$ as its representative and will not distinguish between $[M]$ and M.

The abstract string domain is defined by $(DFAs_{/\equiv}, \bot, \top, \sqcup, \sqcap)$. $DFAs_{/\equiv}$ is a set of equivalent classes. The bottom element $\bot$ is the empty set $\emptyset$. The top element $\top$ is the set of all strings String. The least upper bound $\sqcup$ of M_1 and M_2 is the union of the languages $L(M_1)$ and $L(M_2)$. The greatest lower bound $\sqcap$ of M_1 and M_2 is the intersection of the languages $L(M_1)$ and $L(M_2)$. The concretization function $\gamma : DFA \rightarrow \mathcal{P}(\text{String})$ is defined as follows:

$$\gamma(M) = L(M)$$

The abstraction function $\alpha : \mathcal{P}(\text{String}) \rightarrow DFA$ is defined as follows:

$$\alpha(s) = \sqcap\{s \subseteq L(M)\}$$

6   Evaluation

In order to test TAJS$_{\text{taint}}$ and our approach to detect taint-style vulnerabilities, we chose two sets of benchmarks on which we run the analysis. The first set is a test suite designed by the authors of [8] which consists of over 140 micro benchmarks. These micro benchmarks includes a combination of basic and complex tests. The basic tests are made simple whereas complex tests are made more advanced in that they include tainting lexically scoped variables, tainting variables that are interproceduraly aliased, overwriting sanitizers, accessing variables through the arguments array, and accessing tainted data through the prototype chain. The second set of benchmarks comprises 50 real Web sites chosen from Alexa [2]. Typically, each Web site consists of a number of pages. We randomly choose one page from each Web site and test for vulnerabilities.

As for the first set of benchmarks, TAJS$_{\text{taint}}$ was able to discover all exploits in these tests. Table 2 shows the results of running the analysis on some of the benchmarks in the second set. The second column contains the total number of the true positives that were found in each Web page. The third column contains the number of true positives that were caused by insufficient sanitization for the context. As the results show, there is a number of true positives in some Web pages that were introduced because of the wrong choice of sanitizers. Many of these true positives were the cause of using the function encodeURI() in the wrong context. Although it is recommended that developers use a security-focused encoding library to properly implement prevention rules, many developers rely on the built-in JavaScript encoding functions to sanitize user input and they seem unaware of the internal implementation of each function. Figure 3 shows the analysis time needed to complete the tests for each Web page which is still considered within practical limits.

7   Related Work

In this section, we present the work related to static taint analysis for JavaScript programs.

Table 2. True positives found by TAJS$_{taint}$

Web page	True positives	Insufficient sanitization
A	4	0
B	4	4
C	4	1
D	3	2
E	3	3
F	2	2
G	1	1
H	1	1
I	1	1
J	1	1
K	1	0
L	1	0

Modern browsers have taken measures to prevent cross-site scripting (XSS) attacks. They implement a strong *Content-Security-Policy (CSP)* that disables the use of inline JavaScript. CSP is an added layer of security that allows server administrators to control resources the user agent is allowed to load for a given page. As a developer, you can specify the CSP through a HTTP response header called *Content-Security-Policy*. In the case where the site doesn't offer the CSP header, browsers use the standard same-origin policy. Although, using CSP helps detect and mitigate Cross Site Scripting (XSS), security is about defense in depth. CSP is one layer of security and preventing Cross-site Scripting Attacks vulnerabilities requires the sanitization performed on input. In addition, server administrators still have the ability to disable CSP, causing the site to be vulnerable to attacks.

Guarnieri et al. presented ACTARUS [8], a static taint analysis for JavaScript. ACTARUS builds a static representation of the program, consisting of a call graph and a pointer analysis and perform a taint analysis of JavaScript Web applications. ACTARUS also uses a storeless view of the heap and the data-flow analysis carried out by ACTARUS is based on the notion of an "access path". The abstract string domain in ACTARUS is a constant propagation domain that tracks a single concrete string resulting in loss of precision especially when dealing with dynamic property access feature. In addition, ACTARUS does not differentiate between different rendering contexts.

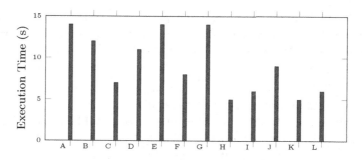

Fig. 3. Analysis time (seconds) in TAJS$_{taint}$

Guarnieri and Livshits proposed Gatekeeper [7], a mostly static approach to enforce security and reliability policies in JavaScript programs. These policies are expressed in the form of succinct declarative Datalog queries. Gatekeeper implements points-to analysis for program understanding, and uses the analysis to detect dangerous behavior. TAJS$_{taint}$ is also based on a points-to analysis and contains advanced rules to handle different contexts.

Wei and Ryder presented blended taint analysis [19] that combines static and dynamic analysis approach. In the Dynamic Phase, a web tester interacts with the target website and the *Execution Collector* collects traces of each Web page. These traces contains some information that is not statically known such as recorded method calls, types of created objects, etc. Finally, a subset of traces representing the program is selected. In the Static Phase, the JavaScript code executed is identified and a call graph is created from the recorded calls. Next, a static taint analysis is run on the program. Finally, solutions from different page traces are combined into a single solution for that webpage. TAJS$_{taint}$ is purely based on static analysis.

8   Conclusion

The dynamic nature of JavaScript makes it prone to errors and security vulnerabilities that can be challenging to find. The widespread popularity of javascript requires analysis tools to be precise and effective in helping developers secure their code. In this paper, we introduced a new approach to analyze JavaScript programs for the detection of DOM-based XSS vulnerability. Our analysis can detect DOM-based XSS vulnerability more precisely. Results show that what some developers think enough sanitization may not always be the case.

References

1. https://cheatsheetseries.owasp.org/cheatsheets/DOM_based_XSS_Prevention_Cheat_Sheet.html
2. https://www.alexa.com/topsites

3. Almashfi, N., Lu, L., Picker, K., Maldonado, C.: Precise string analysis for JavaScript programs using automata. In: Proceedings of the 2019 8th International Conference on Software and Computer Applications, ICSCA 2019, pp. 159–166. ACM, New York (2019)

4. Bartzis, C., Bultan, T.: Widening arithmetic automata. In: Alur, R., Peled, D.A. (eds.) CAV 2004. LNCS, vol. 3114, pp. 321–333. Springer, Heidelberg (2004). https://doi.org/10.1007/978-3-540-27813-9_25

5. Cousot, P., Cousot, R.: Abstract interpretation: a unified lattice model for static analysis of programs by construction or approximation of fixpoints. In: Proceedings of the 4th ACM SIGACT-SIGPLAN Symposium on Principles of Programming Languages, pp. 238–252. ACM (1977)

6. Goguen, J., Meseguer, J.: Security policies and security models. In: Proceedings of the IEEE Symposium on Security and Privacy (July), pp. 11–20, July 2012

7. Guarnieri, S., Livshits, B.: Gatekeeper: mostly static enforcement of security and reliability policies for JavaScript code, pp. 151–168, January 2009

8. Guarnieri, S., Pistoia, M., Tripp, O., Dolby, J., Teilhet, S., Berg, R.: Saving the world wide web from vulnerable JavaScript. In: Proceedings of the 2011 International Symposium on Software Testing and Analysis, ISSTA 2011, pp. 177–187. ACM, New York (2011)

9. Guha, A., Krishnamurthi, S., Jim, T.: Using static analysis for ajax intrusion detection. In: Proceedings of the 18th International Conference on World Wide Web, WWW 2009, pp. 561–570. ACM, New York (2009)

10. Jensen, S.H., Møller, A., Thiemann, P.: Type analysis for JavaScript. In: Palsberg, J., Su, Z. (eds.) SAS 2009. LNCS, vol. 5673, pp. 238–255. Springer, Heidelberg (2009). https://doi.org/10.1007/978-3-642-03237-0_17

11. Jensen, S.H., Madsen, M., Møller, A.: Modeling the HTML DOM and browser API in static analysis of JavaScript web applications. In: Proceedings of the 8th Joint Meeting of the European Software Engineering Conference and the ACM SIGSOFT Symposium on the Foundations of Software Engineering (ESEC/FSE), September 2011

12. Livshits, V.B., Lam, M.S.: Finding security vulnerabilities in Java applications with static analysis. In: Proceedings of the 14th Conference on USENIX Security Symposium, SSYM 2005, vol. 14, p. 18. USENIX Association, Berkeley (2005)

13. Madsen, M., Andreasen, E.: String analysis for dynamic field access. In: Cohen, A. (ed.) CC 2014. LNCS, vol. 8409, pp. 197–217. Springer, Heidelberg (2014). https://doi.org/10.1007/978-3-642-54807-9_12

14. Sridharan, M., Dolby, J., Chandra, S., Schäfer, M., Tip, F.: Correlation tracking for points-to analysis of JavaScript. In: Noble, J. (ed.) ECOOP 2012. LNCS, vol. 7313, pp. 435–458. Springer, Heidelberg (2012). https://doi.org/10.1007/978-3-642-31057-7_20

15. Tripp, O., Pistoia, M., Fink, S.J., Sridharan, M., Weisman, O.: Taj: effective taint analysis of web applications. In: Proceedings of the 30th ACM SIGPLAN Conference on Programming Language Design and Implementation, PLDI 2009, pp. 87–97. ACM, New York (2009)

16. Vogt, P., Nentwich, F., Jovanovic, N., Kirda, E., Krügel, C., Vigna, G.: Cross site scripting prevention with dynamic data tainting and static analysis. In: NDSS (2007)

17. Wassermann, G., Su, Z.: Static detection of cross-site scripting vulnerabilities. In: 2008 ACM/IEEE 30th International Conference on Software Engineering, ICSE 2008. IEEE Computer Society, Los Alamitos, May 2008

18. Wassermann, G., Su, Z.: Sound and precise analysis of web applications for injection vulnerabilities. In: Proceedings of the 28th ACM SIGPLAN Conference on Programming Language Design and Implementation, PLDI 2007, pp. 32–41. ACM, New York (2007)
19. Wei, S., Ryder, B.G.: Practical blended taint analysis for JavaScript. In: Proceedings of the 2013 International Symposium on Software Testing and Analysis, ISSTA 2013, pp. 336–346. ACM, New York (2013)
20. Yu, F., Bultan, T., Cova, M., Ibarra, O.H.: Symbolic string verification: an automata-based approach. In: Havelund, K., Majumdar, R., Palsberg, J. (eds.) SPIN 2008. LNCS, vol. 5156, pp. 306–324. Springer, Heidelberg (2008). https://doi.org/10.1007/978-3-540-85114-1_21

Generation of Testing Metrics by Using Cluster Analysis of Bug Reports

Anna Gromova[1(✉)], Iosif Itkin[2(✉)], and Sergey Pavlov[1(✉)]

[1] Exactpro Systems, 2nd Yuzhnoportovy Projezd 20A Str. 4, Moscow 115088, Russia
{anna.gromova,sergey.pavlov}@exactprosystems.com
[2] Exactpro Systems, Suite 3.02, St Clements House, 27 Clements Lane,
London EC4N 7AE, UK
iosif.itkin@exactprosystems.com
https://exactpro.com

Abstract. One of the most significant challenges of defect reporting is how to compute and predict the testing metrics. Any software development project needs certain suitable testing metrics. Cluster analysis can be used to generate them. The interpretation of the received clusters helps to determine explicit and implicit characteristics of software testing and development.

This paper describes several software solutions for clustering bug reports. We have extracted bug reports related to three open-source JBOSS projects and experimented using that data. Our experiments demonstrate that effective results can be achieved in the area of defect clustering. We provide the results achieved by using two clustering algorithms: k-means and EM. Our research shows that the usage of the EM algorithm generates more detailed information about the specifics of the project than the usage of the k-means algorithm. So, EM gives a possibility to create more diverse testing metrics suitable for project needs.

Keywords: Defect management · Bug report · Cluster analysis · Testing metrics

1 Introduction

According to a review of research conducted in the area of software defect reporting [31], predicting the testing metrics is currently one of the key problems in the field. In this work, testing metrics are different from the test coverage metrics. A group of testing metrics can be used to build a dashboard that project managers or analysts review on a regular basis to maintain quality assessments, expert opinions, and development and testing strategies. Testing metrics are the standard of measurement of the defect management process. There are many kinds of metrics for testing: time to fix, which defects get reopened, which defects get rejected, which defects get fixed, etc. The reviewed research has been mainly aimed at predicting them. The ability to predict certain testing metrics should

© Springer Nature Switzerland AG 2021
A. Kalenkova et al. (Eds.): TMPA 2019, CCIS 1288, pp. 168–181, 2021.
https://doi.org/10.1007/978-3-030-71472-7_14

result in getting a clearer picture of the risks associated with software defects, which is something the project managers strive for. However, such metrics should be generated according to project specifics. Such specifics occur due to the characteristics of the software development cycle, the proprietary and the domain aspects of the project.

This challenge can be resolved by conducting defect analysis because, on the one hand, software weaknesses manifest themselves through defects while, on the other hand, discovered and missed defects attest to the quality of testing. However, it is not enough to evaluate only the statistical data such as priority, resolution distribution or the number of reopened bugs, etc. This is due to the fact that certain project characteristics can have some implicit dependencies. For example, software defects found in some area of functionality under test can require longer time to resolve, and it can affect the release policy, the testing strategy, etc.

Cluster analysis helps to resolve this problem. A separate analysis of each cluster helps to discover certain software development and testing problems or some atypical situations. Testing metrics should allow tracking such problems and/or situations to solve and/or prevent them.

This work extends our previous work on defect report clustering, in which we only experimented with the k-means clustering algorithm and the Silhouette and the Davies-Bouldin indexes [8]. In that work, we didn't create any recommendations about testing metrics, but only worked on cluster interpretation. In contrast to our previous work, we have used the EM clustering algorithm in this paper. We have substantiated the number of clusters by calculating Akaike and Bayes information criteria. We have processed new projects, corrected the list of attributes and ways to preprocess them. Our experimental data consists of 6,308 defect reports derived from three open-source projects related to JBOSS software. In addition, this time we have not obfuscated the real values for all bug attributes, so the results of our work presented in this paper are more understandable and meaningful. This work also presents the testing metrics that can be helpful in testing and project management.

We claim the following contribution in this work:

- The approach to generation of testing metrics via clustering of defect reports.
- Enhancement of a set of attributes of defect reports.
- Empirical comparison of different clustering algorithms for the considered task.

The remainder of this paper is organized as follows: in Sect. 2, we present an overview of the related work; in Sect. 3, we describe the structure of a defect report; in Sect. 4, we outline the process of clustering. Further, in Sect. 5, we present the results of experimental evaluations of this technique; Sect. 6 discusses threats to validity, and Sect. 7 comprises our conclusions.

2   Related Work

There are many researchers who deal with testing metrics predictions. This topic is important for open-source projects due to the fact that such projects use bug tracking systems (BTS) where bug reports can be posted by anyone. Effectively, triaging bug reports is key to saving the time spent on addressing the defects. Zimmerman et al. propose to predict defect reopening [34]. They analyse comments, description, time to fix and the components describing the defects. Weiss et al., Giger et al. and Marks et al. try to predict time to resolve [6,16,32]. They consider a set of various attributes in order to evaluate significant factors. Guo et al. investigate the particulars affecting which defects get fixed [10]. Yang et al. propose to predict high-impact bugs which appear at an unexpected time or location and cause more unexpected effects or break some pre-existing functionalities and destroy the user experience [33]. Due to the fact that only a small proportion of defects are high-impact ones, the researchers use imbalanced data learning strategies. In order to resolve this task, they use two combinations: the synthetic minority over-sampling technique + K-nearest neighbours and random under-sampling + naive Bayes. Sabor et al. propose to predict bug severity [28]. They used stack-trace data in order to identify the severity level.

Defect clustering is described in a variety of academic papers. It is a popular method for defining duplicates of defect reports [18], because clustering can help to determine text characteristics [27]. Clustering the defects according to a calculated bug duration can help to plan the testing workload [19]. Cluster analysis also helps to triage and fix defects via aggregation of bug-reports [5,15]. Hammad et al. propose to use agglomerative hierarchical clustering in order to identify the related bugs [1]. The researchers analysed such text attributes as summary and description. The majority of them retrieve text data from bug reports and miss other important boolean, numeric and categorical attributes of software defects. As in the case of predicting the testing metrics, the tasks of clustering are aimed at triage improvement.

A review of the related work demonstrates the importance of the task of metrics prediction. The aforementioned researchers have analysed different attributes of defect reports and have evaluated how they can influence the metrics. However, it is not yet obvious which testing metrics are more suitable for which software development projects. When dealing with thousands of bugs, this task is not easy as it requires discovering the necessary non-trivial indicators which can characterize the project from a new perspective. In our previous work, we proposed using cluster analysis in order to determine the project peculiarities. In this work, we are considering how these discovered dependencies calculated by different clustering algorithms based on an improved set of attributes can help generate the testing metrics.

3   Background

Each bug report can be presented as a set of attributes. Bug reports were downloaded as XML files from the JIRA bug-tracking system. The defect dataset is presented as follows: $D = \{d_1, d_2, \ldots d_j, \ldots d_n\}$, where d_j is a defect, n is the number of defects in the project.

For resolving a given task, each defect was described by the following attributes: $d_j = \{Priority, Resolution, was\_reopened, Time\ To\ Resolve, Count\ Of\ Attachments, Count\ Of\ Comments, Area_1, \ldots Area_k\}$, where k is the number of defined areas of testing. We propose to use only closed and resolved defects because only such bugs have the values of *Resolution, Time to resolve, Count of attachments, Count of comments*, etc., known for a fact. For defects that have not been closed or resolved, the values of these attributes are indefinite.

The improved list of attributes with their descriptions is presented below.

"Priority" attribute has an ordinal data type, and it is an absolute classification [14]. It includes such values as "Blocker", "Critical", "Major", "Minor", "Optional", "Trivial". This data should be mapped to integer values [14]. The "Resolution" attribute is a categorical variable. Its values are "Cannot Reproduce", "Done", "Duplicate Issue", "Explained", "Migrated to another ITS", "Out of Date", "Rejected", "Resolved at Apache", "Unresolved", "Won't Fix". The "Resolution" values should be converted to indicator variables [22]. "Was_reopened" is a boolean attribute and is an indicator of how thoroughly the bug is described [30]. If a defect was reopened once, the attribute equals 1.

Time to resolve (TTR), count of comments and count of attachments are numeric attributes. All of them should be normalized via the zero-mean normalization (standardization) in order to resolve the problem of attributes having a variance that is orders of magnitude larger than others, which might dominate the objective function and distort results. This method standardizes the features so that they are centered around 0 with a standard deviation of 1. The samples are calculated as follows: $z = (x - \mu)/\sigma$, where μ is the mean, and σ is the standard deviation from the mean. These attributes are important indicators [12]. Time to resolve is an indicator of how expensive a bug report is. Plenty of comments is an indicator of insufficient defect description.

Area of testing is a boolean attribute, and it's a group of software components. If a defect belongs to this area, then attribute is equal to 1. Area of testing can be calculated via text fields classification, like *Summary* and *Components* [7], or via using regular expressions.

4 Approach

4.1 Objects

We extracted 6,308 bug reports of JBOSS projects from the JIRA BTS [26]. These projects are Application Server 7 [23] (AS7), JBoss Enterprise SOA Platform [25] (SOA) and JBoss Enterprise Application Platform 6 [24] (AP6). JBOSS is a popular instrument for building software applications. It is developing dynamically and includes a lot of useful components. JBOSS is an open-source project community, so defect reports extracted from JBOSS are available to anybody, which helps to reproduce the results of the approach. Some brief information about these projects is presented in Table 1.

Table 1. Projects information

	AS7	SOA	AP6
Number of defects	2944	2298	1066
Number of areas of testing	15	10	15
Number of reopened defects	253	510	408
Time to resolve: min/max/mean	0/1792/39.535	0/1354/118.827	0/609/112.282
Count of attachments: min/max/mean	0/15/0.215	0/13/0.327	0/17/0.280
Count of comments: min/max/mean	0/83/2.909	0/34/4.535	0/126/7.280

The distribution of defect reports of projects is presented in Figs. 1, 2.

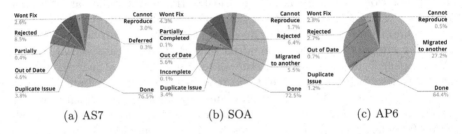

(a) AS7   (b) SOA   (c) AP6

Fig. 1. Distribution of defect reports by the "resolution" attribute

As can be seen from Fig. 1, defects with some resolutions are really rare, and new dummy features for these values will be useless. So, after one hot encoding, we need to create new variables which include rare values. For example, for project SOA, we create a new variable "Resolution_Out of Date_new" that includes values "Resolution_Out of Date", "Resolution_Deferred", "Resolution_Partially Completed" and a new variable "Resolution_Won't Fix_new" that includes values "Resolution_Won't Fix", "Resolution_Cannot Reproduce", and "Resolution_Incomplete Description". Similar transformations were made for projects AS7 (new variables "Resolution_Won't Fix_new" and "Resolution_Out of Date_new") and AP6 (new variables "Resolution_Won't Fix_new" and "Resolution_Migrated_new").

According to Fig. 2, each bar chart includes an "Other" value. This value corresponds to the defects that have rare components or an unfilled field.

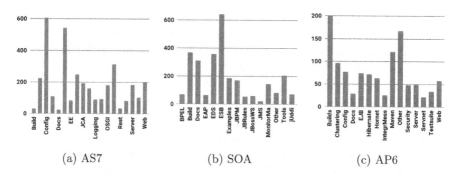

(a) AS7   (b) SOA   (c) AP6

Fig. 2. Distribution of defect reports by the "area of testing" attribute

4.2   Clustering

Clustering task is to construct the set $C = \{c_1, c_2, \ldots c_k, \ldots c_g\}$ where c_k is the cluster that contains similar objects from dataset D. For clustering, we used k-means and EM algorithms. Therefore we compared the results received from applying both algorithms for the three projects.

K-means helps to divide the points into clusters, so that the distances between the different points in each cluster are minimized. The number of clusters in this method should be predefined in advance. This helps the algorithm to build the clusters' centroids. The algorithm starts by selecting random centroids, then it calculates distances between these centroids and the other points. After that, the points are assigned to clusters according to the calculated distances. Then, the algorithm recalculates the centroids and the distances. This procedure repeats until all the data points end up in the same clusters as in the previous iteration. The K-means algorithm has its advantages. It is faster than other algorithms (for example, hierarchical clustering), especially if there is large number of variables. In addition, it is conceptually simple and can be used in a broad number of different scenarios [11].

The EM algorithm consists of two steps: an expectation (E) step and a maximization (M) step. The E step calculates an expectation of the likelihood by including the latent variables as if they were observed, and the maximization (M) step calculates the maximum likelihood estimates of the parameters by maximizing the expected likelihood found at the last E step. The parameters found at the M step are then used to begin another E step, and the process is repeated until convergence. We used EM because cluster assignment is much more flexible in this algorithm than in k-means [3].

Also, we substantiated the number of clusters. We used the following criteria: the silhouette method for k-means, Akaike and Bayes information criteria for EM.

The Silhouette index allows to estimate the count of received groups (clusters) [4]. The optimal number of clusters in this method is proved to be the maximum value of the calculated indexes. Silhouette index is calculated for each point according to its membership in any cluster:

$$SI_i = \frac{b_i - a_i}{max(b_i, a_i)} \tag{1}$$

Where a_i is the average distance between point i and all other points in its own cluster, b_i is the minimum of the average dissimilarities between i and points in other clusters. For Cluster C_k the mean silhouette is calculated as follows:

$$S_k = \frac{1}{n} \sum_{i \in I} SI_i \tag{2}$$

where n is the total number of points in cluster. The global silhouette index is calculated as follows:

$$C = \frac{1}{K} \sum_{k=1}^{K} S_k \tag{3}$$

where K is the count of clusters.

Increasing the number of clusters in the EM model results in an increase in the dimensionality of the model, causing a monotonous increase in its likelihood. In order to avoid a situation when every data point is the sole member of its own cluster, an Information Criterion is used for selection among models with different number of parameters. It seeks to balance the increase in likelihood due to additional parameters by introducing a penalty term for each parameter. Akaike's Information Criterion (AIC) [2] and Bayesian Information Criterion (BIC) [29] are widely used for this.

The results of the validity criteria for k-means and EM are presented in Figs. 3, 4.

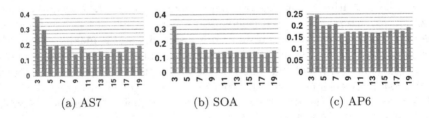

(a) AS7   (b) SOA   (c) AP6

Fig. 3. Results of the validity criteria for k-means

According to the received results, the optimal count for clustering of this data from project AS7 is 3 and 15, from project SOA is 3 and 11, and from project AP6 is 4 and 11.

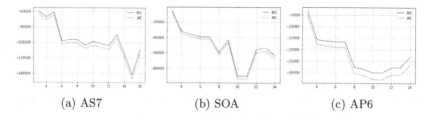

(a) AS7   (b) SOA   (c) AP6

Fig. 4. Results of the validity criteria for EM

All calculations including data extracting, data preprocessing and data clustering were made with Python and its libraries such as pandas [17], scikit-learn [21], numpy [20] and scipy [13].

5   Results

5.1   The Received Clusters

We calculated the centroids of clusters for k-means and the mean values of clusters for EM for the three projects. All materials including the datasets, the source code and the received clusters are hosted on Github [9].

According to zero-mean normalization, any value that is lower than 0 is lower than the mean value; any value that is higher than 0 is higher than the mean value. Therefore, the defects that have the "Time to resolve", the count of attachments and the count of comments lower than 0 can be called "inexpensive-to-resolve", since they don't require a lot of human input or investment of time. At the same time, if the "Time to resolve", the count of attachments and the count of comments are higher than 0, then we can consider these defects "expensive-to-resolve" because the process of their fixing is resource-heavy.

Generally, k-means identifies three main clusters of bugs for the projects under consideration. The first cluster is "inexpensive-to-resolve" defects. The majority of defects belonging to this cluster has a "Major" priority and a "Done" resolution. This cluster is the largest. The second cluster contains the "longest-to-resolve" defects. The majority of defects belonging to this cluster has a "Minor" priority and an "Out of Date" or a "Migrated to another IS" resolution. The last and smallest cluster contains the bugs with a large number of collateral comments and attachments. The priority of these defects is "Major" or "Blocker", and their time to resolve is longer than the mean. The resolution of this cluster may vary and includes such values as "Rejected", "Migrated to another IS", "Won't Fix". K-means clusters don't have a definite area of testing. The algorithm helps to determine the potentially problematic bugs, i.e. the defects that require human and time resources. But K-means clusters are too large and don't produce a "fingerprint".

In contrast to K-means, the EM algorithm identifies more clusters, and they are more detailed. We revealed the following types of bugs:

- "inexpensive-to-resolve",
- "longest-to-resolve",
- "expensive-to-resolve",
- "invalid",
- "underestimated".

Below, we consider the essence of each cluster type in order to demonstrate what outputs can be made, based on clustering.

Half of the calculated clusters are "inexpensive-to-resolve" defects. The difference between defects that belong to these clusters is in the area of testing. The majority of such bugs belonging to this cluster has a "Major" priority and a "Done" resolution. Just like with K-means, these clusters are the largest.

A quarter of the received clusters is made up of "expensive-to-resolve" defects. These clusters are small. They have a high value of "Time to resolve" and a large number of collateral comments and/or attachments.

Similar to K-means, the EM algorithm has identified clusters of "longest-to-resolve" defects as well. In case of, these clusters are characterized by such resolutions as "Out of date" or "Migrated to another IS". According to the clustering results, an extremely high value of "Time to resolve" can be a consequence of irrelevant or outdated defects.

There are few clusters of "underestimated" defects. They have a "Done" resolution, but they have been reopened before. It is important to mention that reopened bugs can be rare, or the reasons for their reopening can be more trivial than the problem of the defect fixing process. But the "Time to resolve" value is high for this cluster, which means that they have not been reopened suddenly or accidentally. The "underestimated" bugs belonging to this cluster have a "Major", "Critical" and "Blocker" priority.

Finally, there are few clusters of "invalid" bugs. They have a low value of "Time to resolve", a small number of collateral comments and attachments and such resolutions as "Won't Fix", "Rejected" and "Duplicate". So these defects can be considered "invalid" from the point of view of bug fixing. The resolution on them is taken instantly and without additional discussions between developer(s) and QA engineer(s).

It is important to mention that each cluster corresponds to a certain area of testing. For example, "invalid" bugs are connected to documentation and configuration. Such defects occur because of misinterpretation of specifications or incorrect environment settings on the part of QA engineers.

5.2   Generating Metrics via Cluster Interpretation

Through knowledge of the clusters' "fingerprints", the project managers and QA team leads can generate new testing metrics. Based on the received EM clusters, we distinguished the following testing metrics that are most essential for designing the testing and the development strategies:

1. **The number of underestimated defects.** Underestimated defects are important because they can lead to a situation when a Critical or a Blocker

bug can persist in the system for a long time and undermine software quality. It is quite important to discover potential root causes of such situations.

2. **The number of expensive-to-resolve/inexpensive-to-resolve defects.** The Project Manager can change the release decision when he or she knows that a bug could be fixed within a certain time period. Knowing that, they can either include this software feature into the next version of the software or exclude it from the next version. This decision can be made due to the knowledge of the number of expensive-to-resolve and inexpensive-to-resolve defects.

3. **The number of "invalid" defects.** A high number of invalid defects can help to evaluate the quality of testing. It can be useful to discover the areas of testing where such defects can occur, in order to create recommendations for QA engineers.

We excluded the "outdated" (aka "longest-to-resolve") defects, because it is quite difficult to predict possible software components which will become irrelevant for the current development tasks. We also excluded the "accidentally reopened" defects because it is problematic to forecast the potential human element in the testing process.

We investigated the characteristics of each cluster and built a scheme that explains how metrics can be generated based on cluster specifics. The scheme is presented in Fig. 5.

6   Threats to Validity

Threats to External Validity. While our experiments were designed to demonstrate the usefulness of our approach of clustering defect reports produced by different bug tracking systems, our results may not generalize to practice. For example, our approach may not generalize to all BTS defect reports because we have only considered JIRA projects. In order to mitigate this threat, we selected defect attributes that are commonly used across many BTSs. They are not specific or belong to custom settings.

Threats to Internal Validity. These threats concern the changeability of values of defect attributes. The chief threat here concerns the quality of the data. The values, as submitted into the bug database, are not tracked during the issue. In order to mitigate this threat, we selected only closed and/or resolved defect reports because their values are set and are less likely to be changed. So, we analyse the "final" statement of defect reports. But in our future work, we are also planning to investigate the problem of defect report changes during the bug life cycle.

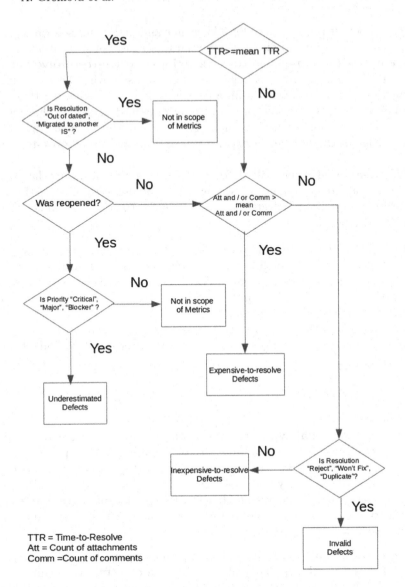

Fig. 5. Generation of testing metrics

7   Conclusion

This paper is devoted to the clustering of software defects.

We propose to use cluster analysis of defects before predicting the testing metrics. Cluster analysis helps to understand the nature of software defects and determine new testing metrics or improve the existing ones. Our proposal is proven by the experiment conducted with three JBOSS projects. Clustering of the defects extracted from these projects allows seeing new possibilities in the generation of testing metrics. Project managers and QA team leads can use the metrics that are most suitable for any particular characteristics of their projects, which make up the calculated cluster's "fingerprints". It can be more useful than using any of the default metrics. Calculation and prediction of these metrics can influence the release policy and the testing strategy. Thus, project participants can change the release composition or the library composition for regression testing.

We have used two clustering algorithms. The K-means allows conducting a brief review of the project, while the EM allows getting a detailed picture. We have also substantiated the number of clusters. For clustering, we improved the set of defect attributes. Using the enhanced attribute set helps to consider the clusters in-depth.

In the nearest future, we plan to analyse not only snapshot data, but also data in the context of dynamic changes. It will allow us to discover more complex dependencies.

References

1. Ahmed, A., Ghazali, R.: An improved self-organizing map for bugs data clustering. In: 2016 IEEE International Conference on Automatic Control and Intelligent Systems (I2CACIS), pp. 135–140. IEEE (2016)
2. Akaike, H.: Information theory and an extension of the maximum likelihood principle. In: Parzen, E., Tanabe, K., Kitagawa, G. (eds.) Selected Papers of Hirotugu Akaike. Springer Series in Statistics (Perspectives in Statistics), pp. 199–213. Springer, New York (1998). https://doi.org/10.1007/978-1-4612-1694-0_15
3. Dempster, A.P., Laird, N.M., Rubin, D.B.: Maximum likelihood from incomplete data via the EM algorithm. J. R. Stat. Soc. Ser. B (Methodol.) **39**(1), 1–22 (1977)
4. Desgraupes, B.: Clustering indices. Univ. Paris Ouest-Lab Modal'X **1**, 34 (2013)
5. Fry, Z.P., Weimer, W.: Clustering static analysis defect reports to reduce maintenance costs. In: 2013 20th Working Conference on Reverse Engineering (WCRE), pp. 282–291. IEEE (2013)
6. Giger, E., Pinzger, M., Gall, H.: Predicting the fix time of bugs. In: Proceedings of the 2nd International Workshop on Recommendation Systems for Software Engineering, pp. 52–56 (2010)
7. Gromova, A.: Defect report classification in accordance with areas of testing. In: Itsykson, V., Scedrov, A., Zakharov, V. (eds.) TMPA 2017. CCIS, vol. 779, pp. 38–50. Springer, Cham (2018). https://doi.org/10.1007/978-3-319-71734-0_4
8. Gromova, A.: Using cluster analysis for characteristics detection in software defect reports. In: van der Aalst, W.M.P., et al. (eds.) AIST 2017. LNCS, vol. 10716, pp. 152–163. Springer, Cham (2018). https://doi.org/10.1007/978-3-319-73013-4_14
9. Gromova, A.: Defect clustering. Github repository (2019). https://github.com/AnkaGromova/DefectClustering/. Accessed August 2019
10. Guo, P.J., Zimmermann, T., Nagappan, N., Murphy, B.: Characterizing and predicting which bugs get fixed: an empirical study of Microsoft windows. In: Proceedings of the 32nd ACM/IEEE International Conference on Software Engineering, vol. 1, pp. 495–504 (2010)

11. Hartigan, J.A., Wong, M.A.: A k-means clustering algorithm. JSTOR Appl. Stat. **28**(1), 100–108 (1979)

12. Hooimeijer, P., Weimer, W.: Modeling bug report quality. In: Proceedings of the Twenty-Second IEEE/ACM International Conference on Automated Software Engineering, pp. 34–43 (2007)

13. Jones, E., Oliphant, T., Peterson, P., et al.: SciPy: open source scientific tools for Python (2001). http://www.scipy.org/

14. Lamkanfi, A., Demeyer, S., Soetens, Q.D., Verdonck, T.: Comparing mining algorithms for predicting the severity of a reported bug. In: 2011 15th European Conference on Software Maintenance and Reengineering, pp. 249–258. IEEE (2011)

15. Limsettho, N., Hata, H., Monden, A., Matsumoto, K.: Automatic unsupervised bug report categorization. In: 2014 6th International Workshop on Empirical Software Engineering in Practice, pp. 7–12. IEEE (2014)

16. Marks, L., Zou, Y., Hassan, A.E.: Studying the fix-time for bugs in large open source projects. In: Proceedings of the 7th International Conference on Predictive Models in Software Engineering, pp. 1–8 (2011)

17. McKinney, W., et al.: Data structures for statistical computing in Python. In: Proceedings of the 9th Python in Science Conference, Austin, TX, vol. 445, pp. 51–56 (2010)

18. Minh, P.N.: An approach to detecting duplicate bug reports using n-gram features and cluster chrinkage technique. Int. J. Sci. Res. Publ. (IJSRP) **4**(5), 89–100 (2014)

19. Nagwani, N.K., Bhansali, A.: A data mining model to predict software bug complexity using bug estimation and clustering. In: 2010 International Conference on Recent Trends in Information, Telecommunication and Computing, pp. 13–17. IEEE (2010)

20. Oliphant, T.E.: A Guide to NumPy, vol. 1. Trelgol Publishing USA, Austin (2006)

21. Pedregosa, F., et al.: Scikit-learn: machine learning in Python. J. Mach. Learn. Res. **12**, 2825–2830 (2011)

22. Raschka, S.: Python Machine Learning. Packt Publishing Ltd., Birmingham (2015)

23. Red Hat: Application Server 7 getting started guide. https://docs.jboss.org/author/display/AS7. Accessed 21 Aug 2019

24. Red Hat: Product Documentation for JBoss Enterprise Application Platform 6. https://access.redhat.com/documentation/en-us/red_hat_jboss_enterprise_application_platform/6/. Accessed 21 Aug 2019

25. Red Hat: Product Documentation for JBoss Enterprise SOA Platform 5. https://access.redhat.com/documentation/en-us/jboss_enterprise_soa_platform/5/. Accessed 21 Aug 2019

26. Red Hat: System Dashboard. https://issues.jboss.org/secure/Dashboard.jspa. Accessed 21 Aug 2019

27. Rus, V., Nan, X., Shiva, S.G., Chen, Y.: Clustering of defect reports using graph partitioning algorithms. In: SEKE, pp. 442–445 (2009)

28. Sabor, K.K., Hamdaqa, M., Hamou-Lhadj, A.: Automatic prediction of the severity of bugs using stack traces. In: Proceedings of the 26th Annual International Conference on Computer Science and Software Engineering, pp. 96–105 (2016)

29. Schwarz, G., et al.: Estimating the dimension of a model. Ann. Stat. **6**(2), 461–464 (1978)

30. Shihab, E., et al.: Predicting re-opened bugs: a case study on the eclipse project. In: 2010 17th Working Conference on Reverse Engineering, pp. 249–258. IEEE (2010)

31. Strate, J.D., Laplante, P.A.: A literature review of research in software defect reporting. IEEE Trans. Reliab. **62**(2), 444–454 (2013)

32. Weiss, C., Premraj, R., Zimmermann, T., Zeller, A.: How long will it take to fix this bug? In: Fourth International Workshop on Mining Software Repositories (MSR 2007: ICSE Workshops 2007), p. 1. IEEE (2007)
33. Yang, X.L., Lo, D., Xia, X., Huang, Q., Sun, J.L.: High-impact bug report identification with imbalanced learning strategies. J. Comput. Sci. Technol. **32**(1), 181–198 (2017)
34. Zimmermann, T., Nagappan, N., Guo, P.J., Murphy, B.: Characterizing and predicting which bugs get reopened. In: 2012 34th International Conference on Software Engineering (ICSE), pp. 1074–1083. IEEE (2012)

Building an Adaptive Logs Classification System: Industrial Report

Kirill Rudakov[1], Andrey Novikov[2(✉)], Anton Sitnikov[3], Eugeny Tsymbalov[4], and Alexey Zverev[5]

[1] Faculty of Computer Science, High School of Economics, 20 Myasnitskaya str., 101000 Moscow, Russia
[2] SynData.io, 30a Leninskiy Avenue, 119334 Moscow, Russia
andreyn@syndata.io
[3] Exactpro Systems, 71 Vazha Pshavela Avenue, Block 8, floor 4, Office 27, 0186 Tbilisi, Georgia
[4] Skolkovo Institute of Science and Technology, 3, Nobelya str., 121205 Moscow, Russia
[5] Exactpro Systems, St Clements House 27, Clements Lane, London EC4N 7AE, UK

Abstract. This article outlines experience of instrumental log analysis performed by industry QA company aimed at discovery of system abnormal behaviour by early traces in its logs. Addressed issues include dealing with massive logs, log line polymorphism, choosing appropriate cluster size, stability of clusters while adding new logs, linking machine-generated clusters to human understanding of "same type" and keeping the system output clearly understandable.

1 Introduction

Testing high-load Fintech systems is a complex task, taking into attention frequent code modification, parallel and concurrent execution, and massiveness of traces produced. However, the financial and reputational impact of risks associated with undiscovered errors motivates for using every opportunity for effective QA.

One of the majorly used approaches is Passive testing, where natural system behavior (in production load or test environment) is observed by its traces, which are analyzed 1) to check compliance with expectations and 2) to get a human understanding of what is happening in the system.

In the area of code error discovery, a promising technique is to observe the error (STDERR or alike) output produced by the system, as intuitively it should contain traces of a considerable percentage of errors, including those not yet known to users or testers. This is especially true for new errors, previously never appeared and therefore immune to regression testing.

Challenges here are all around logs massiveness - typically up to millions of log lines per working day. Still, a human QA engineer would argue that not all of these logs may be of interest, and many of log lines represent essentially same

A. Kalenkova et al. (Eds.): TMPA 2019, CCIS 1288, pp. 182–194, 2021.
https://doi.org/10.1007/978-3-030-71472-7_15

information, though looking different and not easily associated by an analyzing algorithm.

In this paper, we discuss the experience gained and decisions taken while designing an industrial error log analysis system used to analyze logs produced by multiple Fintech high-load distributed applications (clearing and settlement). We address the above-mentioned challenges and describe the final system design as it is used after a lengthy try-and-adapt process.

2 Literature Overview

Modern large-scale systems describe their current state, the errors and warnings within the log that arise from the various parts of the system pipeline [1,2]. The amount and quality of generated logs vary depending on the application, and so the means of processing and analysis differ.

Most of the log processing pipelines start with a pre-processing, with a goal of preparing the raw data for further analysis by cleansing, filtering and unifying the internal representation for the other parts of the pipeline [2,3]. If the further problem in hand allows for a thorough *offline* analysis, one can use the template extraction [4–6] and various NLP (natural language processing) techniques, such as in [7], where the task of separating a template from variables is considered as sequential data labeling. Various embedding techniques, such as word2vec [8] and its variations [9] may also be applied [10].

In a large-scale application, *online* approaches are used to provide shallow analysis, e.g., to detect anomalies, extract source or classify the logs. The algorithm called "Spell"proposed in [11] is one of the streaming-type algorithms that utilize the longest common subsequence approach. Another streaming algorithm based on Fixed Depth Tree for online log processing is proposed in [12,13]. It uses directed acyclic graphs to divide massive logs to disjoint log groups.

There are several approaches focused on log data enrichment, starting from the semi-supervised approach [14] with a language model and topic modeling as the tools for rapid processing, up to suggestions to log message improvement in the code [15,16], as this affects the quality of analysis significantly [17].

A thorough analysis of existing solutions for parsing logs can be round in review [18], where research and production tools were analyzed. According to the report, many algorithms successfully cope with the presentation of unstructured logs in a structured manner, provided that the message structure is simple. However, as the complexity of the log structure increases, the quality of separating template parts of the messages from the parameters drops significantly, which means that the universal algorithm able to adapt to an arbitrary message structure is yet far from reality. Moreover, the authors note that the most significant bottleneck in log analysis systems is slow performance of parsing algorithms.

Typical applications of logs analysis include the error analysis [19], system behavior understanding [20], diagnostics of failures [15], and detection of anomalies [21].

For anomalies search, there are three categories of methods generally used: PCA-based approaches [22], invariant mining-based methods [23,24], and workflow-based methods [25]. A comprehensive review of the existing methods of searching for anomalies based on log analysis may be found in [26], where an attempt to formalize the process of searching for anomalies starting with parsing of raw logs received from the system was made.

Recently, the methods based on deep learning have been actively used for log analysis [9,21,27]. Neural networks here emerge as a promising tool for fast and efficient anomaly prediction and log classification.

This paper describes a practical attempt to analyze massive amounts of logs for QA purposes and build a framework which is simple yet robust enough to provide test engineers with understanding of system states, behaviour and changes, as well as to provide insights on what components and modules require deeper testing and investigation at the moment.

We describe a number of approaches tried - from the naive approach of classifying raw log to three-layered data processing with parameters adjustment to make clustering "good" from QA engineer point of view and compact enough to make it observable.

This work aims at providing practical insight into what worked and what did not, in application to the particular task of discovering new record types and having informed control of the system behavior.

3   Business Context and Task

Our target user is a QA engineer/manager responsible for the correct operation of a financial transactions system (trade, post-trade, or both) or its part. The user reviews the logs during routine work on bug investigation and understands the nature of most of the messages. However, due to the massiveness of logs, it would be impossible to review the logs as a whole to get insight on what is happening in the system.

To facilitate human understanding of logs, we introduce a notion of "error class". An error class is a set of log lines meaning essentially the same in human understanding. Specific lines in class may differ by timestamps, IP addresses, and other parameters. Sometimes a difference of messages within an error class is substantial:

- Developers may change error output between versions
- Error descriptions produced by same code may come with different number of parameters
- Some parameters are hard to universally tokenize, such as IDs that may look much like IP addresses, or words. or number or a mixture.
- Sometimes absolutely different log lines mean the same for the QA engineer, as they are traces of one situation.

If error classes are perfectly distilled, an engineer will mark some (usually most) of them as "not interesting" as they normally appear, for example, on system start. Others will be well known to him, and others will be new.

A minimally viable product should allow answering the following questions:

- What new error classes (not known before) appeared today?
- What is the general picture of the day - what error classes appeared and how many instances of each?
- What is the story of a particular error class - first appearance, basic appearance statistics over time?

In the following parts of this article, we describe means and decisions to grasp the error class through clusterization as close to human understanding of error classes as possible.

As the primary result, we come to clusterization providing clusters that are:

- Stable over time. When we add logs from next days and update clusters, we need to be sure that Cluster X today is the same error as Cluster X two weeks ago.
- Big enough to make engineer work doable, even with million log lines per day.
- Close to human understanding of error classes. An error class may span across several machine-generated clusters, but not vice versa.

In the closing part of this article, we describe the functioning of a resultant clustering-based tool used by QA engineers to explore the error logs.

4 Data Structure

In this chapter, we describe the log structure from both applications that our tool is working with.

For experiments, we retrieved two datasets of logs, one (further referenced as A) from November 2018 to January 2019 inclusive, and the second (B) with logs dated July 2019. The A data set contains 7.2M messages with length up to 15,000 characters (including error trace stacks). B data set contains 0.37M messages with mean message length about 9 words (no error trace stacks). Log messages are accompanied by supplementary information on the system with up to 42 fields in each message.

The information comprising each message (see Fig. 1) may be discerned into three main categories:

- Timeline information. For every log message, this includes a timestamp; however, on the timeline such logs may form various structures based on periodicity or event triggering. In some cases, statistical estimates of log appearing time may be derived.
- Log text itself. It may include a stack trace, some of the system details, error codes, or even some information on the error in executables, modules or lines of code. This subject to further detailed analysis by templates or text mining techniques.

- Supplementary information. This may include out-of-log information such as instance details, application details, and output type. Each of these properties is naturally presented as a categorical variable. The pattern, in this case, may be represented as a subset of the categories set. While most of aforementioned works are focused on log text analysis, we would like to note that thorough processing of supplementary data may help in classification and labeling on the training stage; time-series analysis, on the other hand, may assist in the task of anomaly prediction and system load estimation.

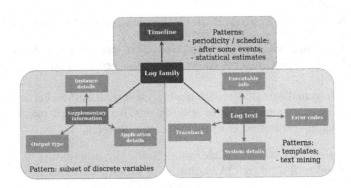

Fig. 1. Various kinds of log data.

We provide a general overview of the analyzed data to highlight some of its properties.

First we analyzed the A dataset as described in the previous section. The amount of information each message contains is related to its length, thus we provide a cumulative number of logs with the length not exceeding a certain value at Fig. 2a. 84% of all the log messages are as short as 600 characters; 92 % of the logs have the length of under 6,000 characters, which allows us to focus on the short messages first.

While every log message contains a text of warning, error or similar event, the availability of supplementary information varies, see Fig. 2b. The typical supplementary fields are stream (STDOUT, STDERR), host, application, and some others. Approximately one-third of the fields are mandatory for each message, while another third of features are unavailable for most messages. The occurrence of the rare features may indicate an anomaly in the system or data.

The available features have different label distribution (see Fig. 2c), which encourages labels-based analysis to be performed. The message classification procedure can benefit from discrete pattern mining on both training and inference stages. However, our preliminary analysis is focused on the text, which is always available compared to supplementary information.

Another type of information we consistently have is timestamp. While time-series analytics is an essential part of every tracking system, and the load peaks must be forecast and responded to promptly, one would expect to have some daily or weekly patterns in it. However, we would like to illustrate (see Fig. 2d) the fact that high load peaks may occur in different time windows during the day or may not occur at all, due to stochastic nature of the log data.

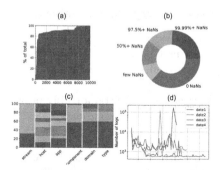

Fig. 2. General overview of the data. a) Cumulative number of logs with length not exceeding N. b) Data availability plot. c) Data diversity bar plot. d) Number of logs grouped in 15-min intervals as a function of time for a few trading days.

The most important insight from the data we want to highlight is that while log messages are dissimilar in time occurrences, label availability, and classes, most of them (up to 84%) are short, with the length not exceeding 600 characters. This encourages us to use in our analysis the more robust and straightforward techniques for data processing based on string comparison algorithms. In this way, for further experiments only text messages were used from B data set.

5   Raw Log Clustering

As the first step, we tried rather straightforward approach to get the visible and usable result as fast as possible. On the one hand, this would deliver business benefit fast. On the other, this was a foundation for establishing an evidence-based dialogue with users necessary before trying more sophisticated methods.

We implemented K-means on raw (non-tokenized) strings with the number of clusters around 100, which seemed to be reasonable from an expert point of view. The daily launched algorithm would learn on previous three days and report on any log line distant enough from any of existing cluster.

Although this approach led to fast results and, it showed the following limitations:

- Clustering did not allow user assessments. Because of large size (hundreds thousands of records each day), there was no means for a human to judge on the quality of clustering and how it related to human understanding of an "error class".

– There was no link between clusters calculated in different days. Although clusterizations could be compared, there was no direct inheritance of clusters, and certain patterns moved from cluster to cluster.
– The technique did not allow to make the whole log volume something tangible for a QA manager.

The decisions taken after the first experiment were:

– Tokenize;
– Allow for the addition of new data to set of clusters;
– Make clusters compact enough so that one cluster represents only one error class
– Make a hierarchy so that a user could comfortably browse clusters, mark some of them as unimportant and others as important.

Tokenization led to a notion of "signature" (called by analogy with antivirus software that catches viruses that have common DNA but are polymorphic). A signature is represented by a string like "DATETIME — fatal error in aspx.py in line NUM NUM IPADDR". At this stage, we learned that in the UI, a signature should always be accompanied with one example string implementing it, so that a QA engineer understands it without a learning curve.

A search for suitable clustering led to trying several methods and comparing their results. In the next chapter, we focus on two different approaches we used for clustering.

6   Clustering Comparisons

In this chapter, we compare two different approaches for clustering on signatures: template-based one and NLP-based pipeline on A data set.

The log data we observe contains a lot of user-sensitive information, such as IDs and IP addresses with instance names, as well as time labels mixed in a number of ways. Our basic pre-processing is focused on bleaching the messages from this information.

6.1   Template-Based Approach

Here, we focus on short logs (with less than 600 characters), which make up the majority of all messages. This approach, which is similar to an intermediate step between log-hashing approach [28] and regular expressions is based on a brute-force string comparison for all the logs. We consider two messages belonging to two different templates if they differ by at least 20% of their content (in the sense of total length of common non-intersecting substrings larger that three characters). The log message which is different from its predecessors forms a new template. This results in a greedy approach that runs through all the messages and compares them with the templates that were already found.

While being time-consuming for the large data sets yet simple, this approach results in a set of templates, which can be rapidly compared with each new message using the aforementioned string comparison or regular expressions. However, we found 109 templates for a short messages, see Fig. 3 for visualization.

Fig. 3. Dendrogram for the templates found. The distance metric used here is a weighted length of common non-intersecting substrings larger that 3 characters.

6.2   NLP-Based Approach

While the previous approach is focused more on the short messages, here we do not get rid of long log messages, investigating a broader set of data. The approach is based on text vectorization with linear dimensionality reduction and further clustering. This is a baseline model that will continue to improve.

As the first step, we pre-processed a random yet evenly sampled subset consisting of 70K initial logs messages and tokenized them into a list of tokens with only alphabet chars for each entity. At the second step, we trained the TF-IDF model on the entire data set. During the training, we ignored the terms with the document frequency less than 3. Also, we visualized the most frequent keywords on a graph combining the TF-IDF model and horizontal visibility graphs (HVG) [29]. These words are candidates to be significant features as they determine the properties of clusters; also, they are intended to be used as visual tags by human operators while drilling down into large sets of logs. (The graph visualization is not included here to avoid disclosure of the customer sensitive information.)

After that, we applied our TF-IDF model and transformed the tokenized data to a document-term sparse matrix, i.e., each textual member was converted to 6,776-dimensional vector representation where each component is a TF-IDF vocabulary term.

At the third step, we truncated the dimensionality from 6,776 into 25 with the cumulative sum of explained variance ratio greater than 0.99 using the truncated singular value decomposition (SVD) method. In other words, we applied the technique inherent to latent semantic analysis (LSA) [30].

At the last step, we applied the K-Means clustering and assessed the resultant cluster sets by the mean Silhouette Coefficient [31]. For the number of clusters greater than 50, the silhouette coefficient value does not grow sharply. It can be explained by large clusters splitting into more specific ones. We can see such separation on Fig. 4a and Fig. 4b. Moreover, we can notice that the composition changed slightly with increasing number of clusters, there are a few clusters which contain more than a half members.

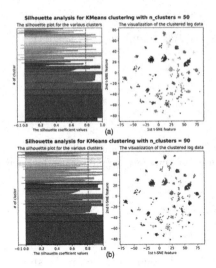

Fig. 4. Visualization of obtained clusters using t-SNE [32] (right-side) and silhouette score over their amount (left-side). a) 50 clusters. b) 90 clusters.

6.3   Approaches Comparison

Both approaches result in approximately 100 clusters in the data. Both clustering algorithms are in good correspondence with each other, with an adjusted Rand index [33] of 0.896 for 90 NLP-based clusters and 0.904 for 50 NLP-based clusters.

This outcome allows for the intuition that there are actually around 100 substantially different message types in human understanding. Further, this result ensures that practically "good enough" classification is obtained for the initial human understanding on the content of the logs. That understanding is to be rectified on further steps of the methodology development.

7   Greedy Clustering with Cutoff by Jaccard Index

In this chapter, we outline the final clustering algorithm we implemented for this tool. It addresses all the challenges, including cluster stability and correlation to human understanding of an error. The aim was to develop an algorithm that will allow retraining on new data without changing old clusters if there is no user's suggestion (to unite or divide the clusters).

The approach is the same for both log series and based on kind of greedy clustering algorithm with the Jaccard coefficient as the metric. The Jaccard coefficient was chosen because a log message structure is often not like natural language. We decided to use a set of 1, 2, 3-g for each message and compare Jaccard index for them.

At the first step, a data set should be split into training (historical) and test (new day). Also, each message of a data set should be tokenized and transformed into a set of 1,2,3-grams. Next, at the historical set the pairwise similarity matrix is calculated using Jaccard index and according to the indicated threshold messages (sets) are collected in clusters. If there are messages that cannot be attributed to the cluster (there are no pairs with similarity at least the threshold) the message should be referred to "lonely rangers". The density inside the cluster cannot fall below the threshold. At the end of this step, nested list with cluster members is received. At the new day set the same steps should be happen; statistics on active and new clusters is also added. Prior "lonely rangers" can form new clusters. Figure 5 outlines the working loop. The difference between the number of clusters and "lonely rangers" for full *A* data set and its split data sets into one historical data set and batches of a new day are presented on Fig. 6. According to the results, the proposed algorithm does not significantly reduce the number of clusters and crucially increase the number of "lonely rangers" at additional learning.

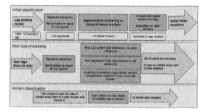

Fig. 5. Data analysis loop.

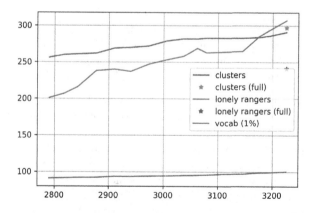

Fig. 6. Warm start learning of the model.

Compared to template-based and NLP-based approaches this algorithm generates more clusters including lonely rangers if the high threshold is set, but changing the threshold utilizes the algorithm as an agglomerative clustering, so that parent (larger) clusters can be generated. Moreover, the approach allows unite or divide clusters easier and assign ambiguous signatures to the appropriate group.

The algorithm was implemented and deployed at lightweight WSGI web application framework Flask with access for respective QA team. The appearance of a developed tool is presented on Fig. 7 (to avoid disclosing client confidential information some fields are blurred).

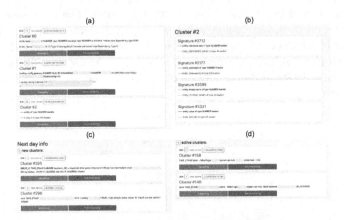

Fig. 7. Appearance of the developed tool. a) Historical clusters list. b) Detailed content of the cluster. c) New clusters at a new day. d) Active clusters at a new day.

8 Conclusion

Log analysis for industrial-scale distributed financial software is an important yet difficult part of the quality control process. Over a process of try-and-update work, we have applied different data analysis methods to the project of testing clearing and settlement systems. The main results are as follows:

- Logs unify massive amounts of records produced by many modules. Modules and configurations evolve and impact the output, making the log files a changing system useful but difficult to analyze.
- The naive approach of clustering raw log data produces clusters with unclear quality that cannot be assessed by a human. Moreover, these clusters tend to move when new logs are added over time. So signature extraction and clustering to dense and stable clusters is a crucial part of the analysis process.
- Clustering parameters should be adjusted in a way to make sure that a single error class may span across several clusters, but all errors in a cluster represent the same error. This is accomplished through close interaction with the system users.
- For large systems, the number of so defined "good" clusters can be large. In this case, they may be grouped to larger sets ("user clusters") to make them understandable. Part of user clusters will be then probably moved out of attention as not interesting.

The project is in its active phase. Our future plans include extending the functionality of the log analysis framework as well as developing a consolidated user interface, which will result in a stand-alone tool for user-assisted quality control of distributed applications from different domains.

References

1. Haibo, M., Huaimin, W., Yangfan, Z., Lyu, M.R., Hua, C.: Toward fine-grained, unsupervised, scalable performance diagnosis for production cloud computing systems. IEEE Trans. Parallel Distrib. Syst. **26**(6), 1245–1255 (2013)
2. Yuan, D., Park, S., Zhou, Y.: Characterizing logging practices in open-source software. In: Proceedings of the 34th International Conference on Software Engineering, pp. 102–112 (2012)
3. Zhu, J., He, P., Fu, Q., Zhang, H., Lyu, M.R., Zhang, D.: Learning to log: helping developers make informed logging decisions. In: Proceedings of the 37th International Conference on Software Engineering-Volume 1, pp. 415–425 (2015)
4. Messaoudi, S., Panichella, A., Bianculli, D., Briand, L., Sasnauskas, R.: A search-based approach for accurate identification of log message formats. In: Proceedings of the 26th IEEE/ACM International Conference on Program Comprehension (ICPC 2018) (2018)
5. Li, Y., Wang, Y., Zhang, Z., Wang, Y., Ma, D., Huang, J.: A novel fast and memory efficient parallel MLCS algorithm for long and large-scale sequences alignments. In: 2016 IEEE 32nd International Conference on Data Engineering (ICDE), pp. 1170–1181 (2016)
6. Makanju, A., Zincir-Heywood, A.N., Milios, E.E.: A lightweight algorithm for message type extraction in system application logs. IEEE Trans. Knowl. Data Eng. **24**(11), 1921–1936 (2012)
7. Kobayashi, S., Fukuda, K., Esaki, H.: Towards an NLP-based log template generation algorithm for system log analysis. In: Proceedings of The Ninth International Conference on Future Internet Technologies, p. 11. ACM (2014)
8. Mikolov, T., Sutskever, I., Chen, K., Corrado, G.S., Dean, J.: Distributed representations of words and phrases and their compositionality. In: Advances in Neural Information Processing Systems, pp. 3111–3119 (2013)
9. Zhu, Y., et al.: LogAnomaly: unsupervised detection of sequential and quantitative anomalies in unstructured logs. In: Proceedings of the Twenty-Eighth International Joint Conference on Artificial Intelligence, pp. 4739–4745 (2019)
10. Bertero, C., Roy, M., Sauvanaud, C., Trédan, G.: Experience report: log mining using natural language processing and application to anomaly detection. In: 2017 IEEE 28th International Symposium on Software Reliability Engineering (ISSRE), pp. 351–360. IEEE (2017)
11. Du, M., Li, F.: Spell: streaming parsing of system event logs. In: 2016 IEEE 16th International Conference on Data Mining (ICDM), pp. 859–864. IEEE (2016)
12. He, P., Zhu, J., Zheng, Z., Lyu, M.R.: Drain: an online log parsing approach with fixed depth tree. In: 2017 IEEE International Conference on Web Services (ICWS), pp. 33–40. IEEE (2017)
13. He, P., Zhu, J., Xu, P., Zheng, Z., Lyu, M.R.: A directed acyclic graph approach to online log parsing, arXiv preprint arXiv:1806.04356 (2018)
14. Li, G., Zhu, P., Chen, Z.: Accelerating system log processing by semi-supervised learning: a technical report, arXiv preprint arXiv:1811.01833 (2018)

15. Yuan, D., et al.: Be conservative: enhancing failure diagnosis with proactive logging. In: OSDI 2012, pp. 293–306 (2012)

16. Fu, Q., et al.: Where do developers log? An empirical study on logging practices in industry. In: Companion Proceedings of the 36th International Conference on Software Engineering, pp. 24–33. ACM (2014)

17. Yuan, D., Zheng, J., Park, S., Zhou, Y., Savage, S.: Improving software diagnosability via log enhancement. ACM Trans. Comput. Syst. (TOCS) **30**(1), 4 (2012)

18. Zhu, J., et al.: Tools and benchmarks for automated log parsing, arXiv preprint arXiv:1811.03509 (2018)

19. Nagaraj, K., Killian, C., Neville, J.: Structured comparative analysis of systems logs to diagnose performance problems. In: Proceedings of the 9th USENIX Conference on Networked Systems Design and Implementation, p. 26. USENIX Association (2012)

20. Glerum, K., et al.: Debugging in the (very) large: ten years of implementation and experience. In: Proceedings of the ACM SIGOPS 22nd Symposium on Operating Systems Principles, pp. 103–116. ACM (2009)

21. Du, M., Li, F., Zheng, G., Srikumar, V.: Deeplog: anomaly detection and diagnosis from system logs through deep learning. In: Proceedings of the 2017 ACM SIGSAC Conference on Computer and Communications Security, pp. 1285–1298 (2017)

22. Xu, W., Huang, L., Fox, A., Patterson, D., Jordan, M.I.: Detecting large-scale system problems by mining console logs. In: Proceedings of the ACM SIGOPS 22nd Symposium on Operating Systems Principles, pp. 117–132. ACM (2009)

23. Lou, J.-G., Fu, Q., Yang, S., Li, J., Wu, B.: Mining program workflow from interleaved traces. In: Proceedings of the 16th ACM SIGKDD International Conference on Knowledge Discovery and Data Mining, pp. 613–622. ACM (2010)

24. Lou, J.-G., Fu, Q., Yang, S., Xu, Y., Li, J.: Mining invariants from console logs for system problem detection. In: USENIX Annual Technical Conference, pp. 23–25 (2010)

25. Yu, X., Joshi, P., Xu, J., Jin, G., Zhang, H., Jiang, G.: CloudSeer: workflow monitoring of cloud infrastructures via interleaved logs. In: ACM SIGPLAN Notices, vol. 51, no. 4, pp. 489–502. ACM (2016)

26. He, S., Zhu, J., He, P., Lyu, M.R.: Experience report: system log analysis for anomaly detection. In: 2016 IEEE 27th International Symposium on Software Reliability Engineering (ISSRE), pp. 207–218. IEEE (2016)

27. Brown, A., Tuor, A., Hutchinson, B., Nichols, N.: Recurrent neural network attention mechanisms for interpretable system log anomaly detection. In: ACM HPDC (First Workshop On Machine Learning for Computer Systems) (2018)

28. Fu, Q., Lou, J.-G., Wang, Y., Li, J.: Execution anomaly detection in distributed systems through unstructured log analysis. In: 2009 Ninth IEEE International Conference on Data Mining: ICDM 2009, pp. 149–158. IEEE (2009)

29. Luque, B., Lacasa, L., Ballesteros, F., Luque, J.: Horizontal visibility graphs: exact results for random time series. Phys. Rev. E **80**(4), 046103 (2009)

30. Deerwester, S., Dumais, S.T., Furnas, G.W., Landauer, T.K., Harshman, R.: Indexing by latent semantic analysis. J. Am. Soc. Inf. Sci. **41**(6), 391–407 (1990)

31. Rousseeuw, P.J.: Silhouettes: a graphical aid to the interpretation and validation of cluster analysis. J. Comput. Appl. Math. **20**, 53–65 (1987)

32. van der Maaten, L., Hinton, G.: Visualizing data using t-SNE. J. Mach. Learn. Res. **9**(Nov), 2579–2605 (2008)

33. Hubert, L., Arabie, P.: Comparing partitions. J. Classif. **2**(1), 193–218 (1985). https://doi.org/10.1007/BF01908075

Short Papers

Development of the Test Suite
with Formally Verified FSM Coverage:
A Case Study

Iosif Itkin[1] and Rostislav Yavorskiy[1,2(✉)]

[1] Exactpro Systems,
Suite 3.02, St. Clements House, 27 Clements Lane, London EC4N 7AE, UK
iosif.itkin@exactprosystems.com
[2] Tomsk Polytechnic University, Lenin Ave, 30, 634050 Tomsk, Russia
ryavorsky@tpu.ru

Abstract. This short paper presents an experience report on using model-based testing approach for stock exchange software. A simplified model of an order book is used for test suite generation. Then Z3 prover is applied to prove the completeness of the created test suite in terms of transition coverage of finite state abstraction of the system. During the formal verification stage an error was found in the configuration of the random test generation procedure.

Keywords: Software testing · Test generation · Test selection · Formal verification · Case study

1 Introduction

The paper presents a case study on model-based testing of stock exchange software. Our goal is to create test suites with different coverage characteristics aimed at testing an order book. An order book is a list of buy and sell orders for a specific financial instrument organized by price level, see e.g. [6]. Our approach combines system modeling, random test generation from the model execution, and formal verification to ensure the completeness of the test suite with respect to the model coverage. See [7] for the description of the method and [1] for a similar approach.

The method of modeling with abstract state machines is described in [2]. The developed model falls into the well-known class of extended finite state machines, EFSM, see [5,8]. All the preconditions, postconditions and the state transition functions are formulated within the scope of linear arithmetic, so the reachability relation is decidable.

In Sect. 2 the simplified model of a single price order book is presented. Section 3 describes the configuration of the random test generation algorithm and the coverage characteristics of the created test suite. Section 4 gives an overview of Z3 prover being applied to the created test suite to prove its completeness

© Springer Nature Switzerland AG 2021
A. Kalenkova et al. (Eds.): TMPA 2019, CCIS 1288, pp. 197–202, 2021.
https://doi.org/10.1007/978-3-030-71472-7_16

in terms of of the coverage of finite state abstraction of the system, a graph of hyperstates. Section 5 provides the summary of the work done and lessons learned.

2   System Under Test and Its Model

2.1   The Modeling Restrictions

In order to illustrate our approach, we consider a simplified single price order book model. The motivation is the following:

- Avoiding unnecessary details. Test suite development workflow for more complex models would be exactly the same, so for the purpose of this paper a simple model is sufficient.
- Non-disclosure agreements. By opting for a simplified model we reduce the risk of disclosing sensitive information about our clients in financial software sector.
- Suitability for testers. One of our goals is to show that even simple models can produce quite meaningful test scenarios.

The modeling restrictions are the following.

First, we restrict the size of the order queue. Potentially, it could be arbitrarily large, but for the formal verification task it is preferable to impose an upper bound, which leads to a simpler underlying theory. Our model is specified in terms of a fixed number of state variables of the integer type and a transition function which describes simultaneous updates of these variables.

Second, we consider a single price order book model. That means that all buy and sell orders have the same `OrderPrice` parameter. Similarly to the previous restriction, it is important to have a fixed upper bound on the number of trading price levels so that the model is in the EFSM class. The actual value does not matter. We choose one level because of its more compact visualization in MS Excel, see Fig. 1. Each table row presents a current system state, a randomly generated input, precondition check results, and codes for current and next hyperstates correspondingly. Each random scenario consists of 10 steps, so the table presents a complete description of the system's trace.

Third, the order trading volume is restricted to 9. Interval $\{1, 2, \ldots, 9\}$ seems to be big enough to produce all reasonable scenarios. At the same time, small values are more convenient for manual inspection of the generated test scenarios. This restriction is used for random test generation only. For verification of the completeness of the generated test suite, we assume that order volume could be any positive integer.

2.2   Model State, Input and Transition Function

Under the restrictions specified above, the model state is characterized by four integer variables: `Bid2`, `Bid1`, `Ask1`, `Ask2`. In any reachable state, if the book is not empty, then one has either a queue of bids or a queue of asks. Since the length of the queue is less than 3, one has four options:

State#	Current state					Input (Trading order)			Precondition	Hyperstates	
	Price	Bid2	Bid1	Ask1	Ask2	Type	Price	Volume		Current	Next
0	103	0	0	0	0	Sell	103	8	TRUE	00|00	00|M0
1	103	0	0	8	0	Sell	103	2	TRUE	00|M0	00|Mm
2	103	0	0	8	2	Buy	103	4	TRUE	00|Mm	00|Mm
3	103	0	0	4	2	Buy	103	1	TRUE	00|Mm	00|3m
4	103	0	0	3	2	Buy	103	3	TRUE	00|3m	00|20
5	103	0	0	2	0	Buy	103	3	TRUE	00|20	01|00
6	103	0	1	0	0	Buy	103	7	TRUE	01|00	m1|00
7	103	7	1	0	0	Sell	103	5	TRUE	m1|00	03|00
8	103	0	3	0	0	Sell	103	9	TRUE	03|00	00|M0
9	103	0	0	6	0	Sell	103	1	TRUE	00|M0	00|M1
10	103	0	0	6	1	Buy	103	5	TRUE	00|M1	0

Fig. 1. Random scenario for a single price level order book model in MS Excel

- the bid queue has length 2: $Bid2 \neq 0, Bid1 \neq 0, Ask1 = 0, Ask2 = 0$;
- the bid queue has length 1: $Bid2 = 0$, $Bid1 \neq 0$, $Ask1 = 0$, $Ask2 = 0$;
- the ask queue has length 1: $Bid2 = 0$, $Bid1 = 0$, $Ask1 \neq 0$, $Ask2 = 0$;
- the ask queue has length 2: $Bid2 = 0$, $Bid1 = 0$, $Ask1 \neq 0$, $Ask2 \neq 0$.

That could be easily generalized for any limit of the queue size and the number of trading price levels.

The order book changes when a trade order arrives. The order has the following three parameters:

OrderType can be "Buy" or "Sell";
OrderPrice indicates the intended trading price (worst acceptable case);
OrderVol is the order volume, the number of securities to be traded.

The transition function updates the state variables according to the standard exchange trading rules, see e.g. [6]. VB code, which computes an update of the state variable Bid1 is provided on Fig. 2. The other update functions are similar to that one.

```
Function NextBid1(Bid2, Bid1, Ask1, Ask2, OrderType, OrderPrice, OrderVol)
    If (OrderType="Buy") And (Bid1=0) And (OrderVol>=Ask1+Ask2) Then
        NextBid1 = OrderVol-Ask1-Ask2
    ElseIf (OrderType="Sell") And (Bid1>0) And (OrderVol<Bid1) Then
        NextBid1 = Bid1-OrderVol
    ElseIf (OrderType="Sell") And (Bid1>0) And (OrderVol<Bid1+Bid2) Then
        NextBid1 = Bid1+Bid2-OrderVol
    ElseIf (OrderType="Sell") And (Bid1>0) And (OrderVol>=Bid1+Bid2) Then
        NextBid1 = 0
    Else:
        NextBid1 = Bid1
    End If
```

Fig. 2. VB code in MS Excel to compute the next value of the state variable Bid1

2.3 Equivalence Classes of the System States

The concept of finite state machine (FSM) abstraction of a system is widely used in testing [4]. It is defined in the following way. For a given set of finite range state properties $P_1, \ldots, P_n$, we assume the system states s_1 and s_2 to be equivalent if they satisfy the same subsets of the properties:

$$s_1 \approx s_2 \iff \forall i \leq n (P_i(s_1) = P_i(s_2)).$$

A hyperstate is an equivalence class of the system states with respect to this equivalence relation. The hyperstates are the nodes of the FSM graph. Given two hyperstates h_1 and h_2, the FSM has edge (h_1, h_2) if there exist two system states s_1, s_2 such that $s_1 \in h_1$, $s_2 \in h_2$, s_1 is reachable, and for some input the system makes a one-step transition from s_1 to s_2. In our case the properties are based on the intervals for the values of the state variables, namely:

$$P_1(\text{Bid2}, \text{Bid1}, \text{Ask1}, \text{Ask2}) = if \ \ \text{Bid2} \leq 1 \ then \ \text{Bid2} \ else \ \text{"m"}$$
$$P_2(\text{Bid2}, \text{Bid1}, \text{Ask1}, \text{Ask2}) = if \ \ \text{Bid1} \leq 3 \ then \ \text{Bid2} \ else \ \text{"M"}$$
$$P_3(\text{Bid2}, \text{Bid1}, \text{Ask1}, \text{Ask2}) = if \ \ \text{Ask1} \leq 3 \ then \ \text{Bid2} \ else \ \text{"M"}$$
$$P_4(\text{Bid2}, \text{Bid1}, \text{Ask1}, \text{Ask2}) = if \ \ \text{Ask2} \leq 1 \ then \ \text{Bid2} \ else \ \text{"m"}$$

One can see that values of P_1 and P_4 are in $\{0, 1, \mathtt{m}\}$, while values of P_2 and P_3 are in the range of $\{0, 1, 2, 3, \mathtt{M}\}$. Each hyperstate is naturally identified by a 5-symbols string, e.g. "00|M1" or "03|00", where the first symbol is the value of P_1, the second symbol is the value of P_2, etc., see the corresponding columns on Fig. 1. Potentially, this FSM may have 225 nodes ($= 3 \times 5 \times 5 \times 3$).

3 Random Test Generation

For the model described above, 10,000 random scenarios that satisfy the specified preconditions were generated. That resulted in the discovery of 25 reachable hyperstates and 224 links between them. This computational experiment has been performed several times in order to collect the statistics, see Fig. 3.

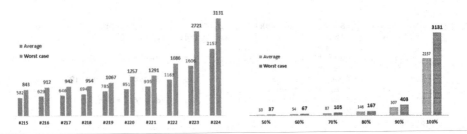

Fig. 3. Time to discover hypergraph links: last ten (left) and percentage (right)

The chart on the left in Fig. 3 shows average and worst-case numbers (in terms of the number of random scenarios) for the time to discover the last 10 links found. The chart on the right shows the time required to discover all found hypergraph links. One can see that the complexity grows exponentially, so the chances not to reach the 100% discovery rate are high.

Finally, we dismiss all the random scenarios except for those which are necessary to cover all the transitions between hyperstates. That resulted in a test suite consisting of 121 test scenarios with 10 steps each.

4   Verification of the Test Suite Completeness with Z3

The final step is to ensure that all the FSM hyperstates and links have been successfully discovered during the random execution phase. We use Z3 solver [3] to prove that there are no other possible transitions in the hypergraph besides the discovered ones.

First, all the preconditions, the transition function and hyperstate definitions have been translated into Z3, see Fig. 4.

```
Precondition_OrderType = Or(OrderType == 0, OrderType == 1)
Precondition_OrderVol = (OrderVol > 0)
Precondition_Bid = And(Bid1 >= 0, Bid2 >= 0, NextBid1 >= 0, NextBid2 >= 0)
Precondition_Ask = And(Ask1 >= 0, Ask2 >= 0, NextAsk1 >= 0, NextAsk2 >= 0)
Precondition_BidLimit = Implies(OrderType == 0, Bid2 == 0)
Precondition_AskLimit = Implies(OrderType == 1, Ask2 == 0)

Rule_NextBid2 = If(And(OrderType == 0, Bid1 > 0, Bid2 == 0),
    NextBid2 == OrderVol,
    If(And(OrderType==1, OrderVol>=Bid1), NextBid2==0, NextBid2==Bid2))
```

Fig. 4. A fragment of definitions of the preconditions and the transition function in Z3py

Then, for each hyperstate H_i, the following statement was formulated:

$$H_i(\mathsf{s}) \ \& \ \mathsf{Pre}(\mathsf{input}) \ \& \ \mathsf{Next}(\mathsf{s}, \mathsf{input}, \mathsf{s}') \ \& \ \neg H_{i_1}(\mathsf{s}')\& \cdots \&\neg H_{i_k}(\mathsf{s}'), \qquad (1)$$

where s and s' are the vectors of the state variables, input are input parameters, Pre is the conjunction of all preconditions, Next formalizes the transition function, and $H_{i_1}, \ldots, H_{i_k}$ are the hyperstates reachable from H_i with a direct link.

By default, we expect that the formula (1) is unsatisfiable. To our surprise, that was not always the case. Namely, for the hyperstate with the code 00|Mm the following model was found by Z3:

$$\mathsf{Ask2} = 2, \mathsf{Ask1} = 4, \mathsf{OrderType} = 0, \mathsf{OrderVol} = 10, \mathsf{Bid1}' = 4, \mathsf{Bid2}' = 0,$$

which discovers a new transition "00|Mm → 0M|00" in the FSM. This counter-example points to an error in the random test generation configuration: our decision to restrict the trading volume parameter to 9 turned out to be wrong.

5 Conclusion

Our experience confirmed that even very simple models could be useful for testing complex systems. An executable model allows one to generate test cases with known outputs. Besides, FSM abstraction of the model helps in selecting meaningfully different test scenarios from tons of randomly generated sequences.

There are at least two reasons why a test suite could be incomplete. First, the time to discover reachable transitions between hyperstates grows exponentially, so one is never sure when to stop. Second, the random test generation module could be faulty.

In our case, Z3 prover has been used to assess the completeness of the developed test suite. Application of formal methods helped to find a flaw in the configuration of the random test generation procedure.

References

1. Benjamin, M., Geist, D., Hartman, A., Wolfsthal, Y., Mas, G., Smeets, R.: A study in coverage-driven test generation. In: Proceedings 1999 Design Automation Conference (Cat. No. 99CH36361), pp. 970–975. IEEE (1999)
2. Börger, E.: The abstract state machines method for high-level system design and analysis. In: Formal Methods: State of the Art and New Directions, pp. 79–116. Springer (2010). https://doi.org/10.1007/978-1-84882-736-3_3
3. de Moura, L., Bjørner, N.: Z3: an efficient SMT solver. In: Ramakrishnan, C.R., Rehof, J. (eds.) TACAS 2008. LNCS, vol. 4963, pp. 337–340. Springer, Heidelberg (2008). https://doi.org/10.1007/978-3-540-78800-3_24
4. El-Far, I.K., Whittaker, J.A.: Model-based software testing. In: Encyclopedia of Software Engineering (2002)
5. Kalaji, A., Hierons, R.M., Swift, S.: A search-based approach for automatic test generation from extended finite state machine (EFSM). In: 2009 Testing: Academic and Industrial Conference-Practice and Research Techniques, pp. 131–132. IEEE (2009)
6. Preis, T., Golke, S., Paul, W., Schneider, J.J.: Multi-agent-based order book model of financial markets. EPL (Europhys. Lett.) **75**(3), 510 (2006)
7. Veanes, M., Yavorsky, R.: Combined algorithm for approximating a finite state abstraction of a large system. In: ICSE 2003/Scenarios Workshop, pp. 86–91 (2003)
8. Wang, C.J., Liu, M.T.: Generating test cases for EFSM with given fault models. In: IEEE INFOCOM 1993 The Conference on Computer Communications, Proceedings, pp. 774–781. IEEE (1993)

Generation of Test-Based Traces for Automated Partial Software Specifications Extraction

Inga Egorova and Vladimir Itsykson(⊠)

Peter the Great St. Petersburg Polytechnic University, Polytechnicheskaya str., 29,
195201 Saint Petersburg, Russia
isergegorova@gmail.com, vlad@icc.spbstu.ru

Abstract. Modern programmers' society suffers from lack of reusable software components specifications. Formal specifications can be restored in automated way by analysis of existing client projects, code of which can be obtained from publicly available software repositories such as GitHub. Such specifications can be used for documentation, code generation and bug finding. The most qualitative specifications can be restored with application of methods of dynamic analysis. Existing approaches doesn't support usage of client project tests for getting project traces, though methods of client projects should contain correct templates of components usage and some of them (unit and, partly, integration tests) also don't require user input. This paper reveals ways of getting possible application of provided and automatically created tests for software libraries formal specifications inference. Both search-based, as well as feedback-directed automated test generation techniques, are reviewed, and proper technique for suggested inference toolchain is chosen. Possible directions of further research are given.

Keywords: Formal specification inference · Software library · Test generation techniques · Search-based test techniques · Random testing

1 Introduction

Nowadays the most common practice of development of new software implies intensive usage of pre-developed third-party libraries and frameworks. As a rule, choice of a specific library is based on programmer's experience and on supplied documentation. Unfortunately, the documentation often suffers from incompleteness and ambiguity. One of the possible ways to withstand with such limitations is to apply formal library specifications captured with usage of specific formal languages. Usage of such descriptions isn't limited only to educational purposes, they also can be utilized for automated bug finding and code generation.

There exists a big quantity of both static and dynamic approaches to restore such formal specifications grounded in analysis of software components client projects [1, 2]. A great number of the target projects can be found in free online repositories, such as publicly available on GitHub. Dynamic approaches in general allow to get more complicated and more qualitative specifications, however, at the same time, they need in traces,

© Springer Nature Switzerland AG 2021
A. Kalenkova et al. (Eds.): TMPA 2019, CCIS 1288, pp. 203–208, 2021.
https://doi.org/10.1007/978-3-030-71472-7_17

containing calls of library methods, to get the work done. This requirement thoroughly narrows the number of client projects which can be used to obtain specifications, because usually full procedures of installation and run of mature projects require a lot of efforts and can't be realized in a fully automated way. Besides of it, most of the programs require interaction with users, that also leads to inability of usage of them for automated specification extraction. To overcome these restrictions, tests, either provided, or automatically created, can be employed. Most of test-based traces will not have the listed problems and so can be easily used for completion of the given task.

The objective of the research, presented in this paper, is to analyze existing ways to get executable test files for library client projects that can be used for software libraries specifications inference.

2   Strategies of Client Projects Tests Obtainment

Overall, there are 2 global strategies to get test-containing library client projects:

1. To download source code only for projects with sets of ready-to-use tests. Unit and, partially, integration tests will be appropriate for our purposes due to their nature. It's should be noticed that tests should contain calls to the library methods;
2. To download all target projects and to generate tests automatically. The preferable sources for tests creation still are not library's methods, but methods of the library client projects because they tend to encapsulate patterns of correct library's methods usage inside themselves;

2.1   Provided Tests

Despite of apparent simplicity of search tests-containing projects, there was found information about the only heuristic-based project [3]. To analyze whether a particular project contains tests, the authors suggest check if there are any files, which names contain "test" template, if they are located inside a folder, which name obeys the same rule, and additional analysis of whether the packages of popular test frameworks are included in the list of dependencies imported by the project classes is also held. After evaluating the project for all heuristic criteria, the final result is formed on the basis of a majority vote. The considered approach can be implemented, but it will not give any guarantees regarding the quality of the obtained results (both false positive and false negative responses are possible).

As one of the possible ways to improve quality of results can be seen usage of software lifecycle support systems, such as Maven. In most situations, presence of the tests in projects implemented on its basis can be easily analyzed by reading from their configuration files addresses of the folders that should contain tests source code and making attempts to access them. However, additional test source folders that can be added dynamically (for example, using Maven plugins) which couldn't be analyzed. At the moment, this approach has not been implemented and may become a further development of the work.

Analysis of sort of tests supplied is also an important task which should be accomplished in case of choice of this strategy of obtainment of test-containing projects.

2.2 Tests Generation

An alternative solution for getting the test-covered projects is an application one of test generation techniques. Each of them implements one of the following approaches:

1. Random testing. Functions of program components during the testing are called with random values of input variables. An important representative of this set of techniques is the controlled random testing in which additional information is used for input data generation. In particular, the driven by output random testing is a widely known successor of it. This technique is taking into account previously used historical data (to exclude incorrect and duplicate data) during the process of values generation. The most actively used and supported tool that implements this approach is Randoop [4];

2. Search-based testing. Process of test generation is recognized as a decision of optimization task. There are different objective functions (or their combination) can be chosen, e.g., code coverage metric functions. One of the most actively used approaches to find a decision of the given task is application of genetic algorithms. One of most mature tool, implementing such approach, is Evosuite [5]. Currently this tool is actively developed and supported and it won several SBST tool contests;

3. Symbolic testing. Program execution paths are represented as input value constraints. A constraint solver enumerates states characterized by "on/off" derived restrictions and generates various test input data. On top of this category of approaches only academic prototypes of instruments have been developed. Such instruments only allow generate test input data (tests themselves should be written manually). The criteria for comparing code generation tools may be code coverage and ability to detect errors.

Quality of tests, obtainable with application of listed approaches, can be estimated by code coverage and ability to detect errors with use of them. There is no information about systematic estimation of instruments according to the first criterion in papers. According to the second criterion, Evosuite tool, realizing search-based technique, allows to get far better results, than Randoop, which implementation is based on random testing: for the same industrial application they reveals 56.4% and 38% of errors respectively [6].

3 Application of Test Generation for Specification Inference

3.1 Evosuite Tool

According to the results of analysis, presented in Sect. 2, the preferable tool for tests generation is Evosuite.

Evosuite only needs binary files of the project and its dependencies as input. The approach implemented by the tool is based on application of genetic algorithms tools such as selection, crossbreeding, and mutation to the task of finding the optimal set of tests. Test suites that should take part in formation of a new generation are selected on the basis of values of the objective function. Several options for the objective function are supported. All of them are based on standard metric code coverage assessments. When crossing, the selected sets of tests exchange separate tests. The mutation can be carried out either by adding new, or by changing existing tests. To deal with unreliable tests (for example, the tests that modify resources of operating system), the JDK state is controlled and classes that implement interactions with the system resources are replaced.

Duration of the generation process is configurable (default value - 10 min).

As a result the tool under consideration produces test suites implemented with the JUnit 4 framework.

Seems to be a perfect candidate itself, Evosuite still should be integrated to a specific toolchain to get formal specifications restored. A fragment of chain, related to the test generation, proposed by the authors of this paper, is presented in the Fig. 1. Trace generation itself belongs to the phase "Execution trace production".

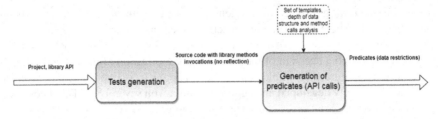

Fig. 1. Inference of predicates, describing data restrictions.

Since as input Evosuite only requires binary files of the target project and its dependencies and these data are available as a toolchain's input, there is no need in adaptation between actual and expected items. However, the phase of predicates generation requires that input files should not use reflection mechanisms. It's caused by the application of the widely used Daikon tool for predicates generation. Thus, here the task of adaptation the Evosuite output to the JUnit 3 form arises.

During experiments it was found that reflective calls are used, in particular, for test initialization, therefore the implementation of such an adaptation is not possible.

3.2 Randoop Tool

As input, Randoop, like Evosuite, accepts a set of project binaries and their dependencies.

During the test generation process different possible sequences of calls of all public methods of the classes-under-test are created, validated and classified. To get input data for method calls, both predefined set of primitives and values, obtained by executing earlier generated sequences, can be used. If the generated test is equivalent to the already existing one, it's discarded. In the process of further verification the generated test after each new method call is checked against the given contracts. Based on the results of these checks, the sequence may be classified as a regression or error-revealing test. If the sequence is correct, but the resulting object is null or can be obtained through a one of the previously generated call chains, as well as if it throws an exception, it will not be further expanded.

Working with unreliable tests can be carried out in the following modes:

1. Manual control. In case of generation of an unreliable test the tool should stop execution and display a diagnostic message for the user who needs to find and eliminate the cause of its occurrence;
2. Drop. Unreliable tests should not be displayed. This mode is inefficient, since a large number of tests will be generated and discarded;
3. Conclusion. Flaky tests are displayed in a commented form; also diagnostic message is issued about methods that might have caused the non-determinism.

The used lists of contracts and filters can be expanded. Generation duration is also customizable. Value by default is 2 min.

The result of the tool are test files generated with usage of a selected version of JUnit (in a such way absence of reflexive calls can be guaranteed). Therefore, the obtained tests can be directly used for deriving predicates using the Daikon tool discussed earlier.

4 Conclusions

To recapitulate, nowadays since the widely adopted practice of software reuse, the industry needs in qualitative software libraries specifications. Usage of formal specifications can fulfill this requirement. Such specifications can be obtained automatically from library client projects source code files and may be used for the generation of code and documentation and also for bug finding.

The most qualitative specifications can be obtained by dynamic analysis of client projects, but there is a bottleneck: only projects, containing entry point methods, are used as inputs by reviewed approaches. This limitation can be overcome with use of client project's test methods – either developed by project authors or generated on top of client project's methods since they encapsulate templates of correct usage of components. There exist several categories of test generation techniques. Tests of better quality can be obtained with the search-based tool Evosuite. However, because of complexity of the adaptation of instrument's output to the needs of the next tool, the more suitable feedback-directed tool Randoop was used to solve practical subtask of specification inference related to tests obtainment.

Further development can include support of identification and use of tests, provided with the client projects. To get over obstacles with test framework caused reflective calls special driver class may be implemented. But tackling with reflective calls by client code itself as well as tests classification, which is necessary for elimination of tests, requiring interaction with users, aren't such easy tasks and require additional exploration.

References

1. Egorova, I.S., Itsykson, V.M.: Survey of static methods for partial software library specifications extraction. Informatsionno-upravliaiushchie sistemy [Inf. Control Syst.] **6**, 66–75 (2017). (In Russian). https://doi.org/10.15217/issn1684-8853.2017.6.66

2. Egorova, I.S., Itsykson, V.M.: Review of dynamic methods for extraction of partial software library specification. Informatsionno-upravliaiushchie sistemy [Inf. Control Syst.] **2**, 67–75 (2018). (In Russian). https://doi.org/10.15217/issn1684-8853.2018.2.67
3. Gonzalez, D., Popovich, A., Mirakhorli, M.: TestEX: a search tool for finding and retrieving example unit tests from open source projects. In: 2016 IEEE International Symposium on Software Reliability Engineering Workshops (ISSREW), Ottawa, ON, pp. 153–159 (2016)
4. Pacheco, C., Lahiri, S.K., Ernst, M.D., Ball, T.: Feedback-directed random test generation. In: 29th International Conference on Software Engineering (ICSE 2007), Minneapolis, MN, pp. 75–84 (2007)
5. Fraser, G., Arcuri, A.: EvoSuite: automatic test suite generation for object-oriented software. In: SIGSOFT/FSE 2011 - Proceedings of the 19th ACM SIGSOFT Symposium on Foundations of Software Engineering, pp. 416–419 (2011)
6. Almasi, M.M., Hemmati, H., Fraser, G., Arcuri, A., Benefelds, J.: An industrial evaluation of unit test generation: finding real faults in a financial application. In: 2017 IEEE/ACM 39th International Conference on Software Engineering: Software Engineering in Practice Track (ICSE-SEIP), Buenos Aires, pp. 263–272 (2017)

Author Index

Printed in the United States
by Baker & Taylor Publisher Services